THE

ELEMENTS OF MORALITY,

INCLUDING

POLITY.

BY WILLIAM WHEWELL, D.D.,

AUTHOR OF THE HISTORY AND THE PHILOSOPHY OF THE INDUCTIVE SCIENCES.

IN TWO VOLUMES.

VOL. I.

Λαμπάδια ἔχοντες διαδώσουσιν ἀλλήλοις.

NEW YORK:

HARPER & BROTHERS, PUBLISHERS,

329 & 331 PEARL STREET,

FRANKLIN SQUARE.

1861.

TO

WILLIAM WORDSWORTH, ESQ.,

POET LAUREAT.

My dear Mr. Wordsworth,

I am desirous that, if the present book finds its way to the next generation, it should make known to them that I had the great privilege of your friendship. And there is no one to whom I could with more propriety dedicate such a work: since in your Poems, at the season of life when the mind and the heart are most wrought on by poetry, I, along with many others, found a spirit of pure and comprehensive morality, operating to raise your readers above the moral temper of those times. I shall rejoice if it appear from the following pages, that such influences have not been wasted upon me.

That you may long enjoy the reverence and affection with which England, on such grounds, regards you, is the wish and prayer of,

My dear Mr. Wordsworth,

Your cordial friend and admirer,

W. WHEWELL.

Trinity College, Cambridge,
April 14, 1845.

PREFACE.

The Reader will perceive that this Work is not described in the Title as having *Moral Philosophy* for its subject, but is entitled Elements of *Morality*. The distinction between the two subjects to which these two terms may be most appropriately applied, is important. Morality, and the Philosophy of Morality differ in the same manner and in the same degree as Geometry, and the Philosophy of Geometry. Of these two subjects, Geometry consists of a series of positive and definite Propositions, deduced one from another, in succession, by rigorous reasoning, and all resting upon certain Definitions and Self-evident Axioms. The Philosophy of Geometry is quite a different subject; it includes such Inquiries as these:—Whence is the Cogency of Geometrical proof? What is the Evidence of the Axioms and Definitions? What are the Faculties by which we become aware of their truth? and the like. The two kinds of speculation have been pursued, for the most part, by two different classes of persons;—the Geometers, and the Metaphysicians; for it has been far more the occupation of Metaphysicians than of Geometers, to discuss such questions as I have stated, the nature of Geometrical Proofs, Geometrical Axioms, the Geometrical Faculty, and the like. And if we construct a complete System of Geometry, it will be almost exactly the same, whatever be the views which we take on these Metaphysical questions. To construct such a System, requires labour and thought of quite a different kind from that which is requisite in the discussion of the questions, whether Geometry rest upon Axioms? whether man has a Geometrical Faculty? and the like. But though Geometry is a very different thing from such Philosophy of Geometry, the existence of a Scientific System of Geometry is very requisite for the progress of such philosophy. If we had had no Euclid, we should have had no dissertations on such philosophical questions as I have mentioned. It was the familiar possession of a body of Geometrical Truth, systematically arranged and solidly demonstrated, which led men to inquire, in virtue of what conditions, and what human faculties, such a body of truth was possible. Men would never have discussed whether and why Geometrical Truth was possible, if they had not had before them an undeniable collection of such Truth. Or if, without having any certainty or knowledge of Geometrical Propositions, men had speculated and disputed, as to whether they could have such knowledge and such certainty; we cannot suppose that they could have arrived at any distinct or stable result of such speculations. The construction of the Elements of Geometry, besides being the creation of a precious and imperishable body of Scientific Truth, was the first step in the Philosophy of Geometry.

It has long appeared to me that the relation which thus subsists between Geometry and the Philosophy of Geometry, must subsist also between Morality and the Philosophy of Morality. If we had a View of Morality, in which Moral Propositions were deduced from Axioms, by successive steps of reasoning, so far as to form a connected System of Moral Truth; we should then have before us definite Problems, if we proceeded to inquire, what is the nature and evidence of Moral Axioms; and what are the Faculties by which we know them to be true. On this account, it seemed to me that the Construction of Elements of Morality ought to precede any attempt to settle the disputed and doubtful questions which are regarded as belonging to the Philosophy of Morality.

Of course, as in the case of Geometry, the Construction of a Systematic Body of Truth in Morality, if it could be achieved, would have other, and perhaps far higher advantages, than the mere aid it would afford to the prosecution of the Philosophy of Morality. In Morality, indeed, this independent value of the Truth, could hardly fail to be more evident and more eminent than in any other Subject. A sure and connected knowledge of the Duties of man, of the Supreme Rules and Highest Objects of human action, would naturally throw most important light upon all the greatest concerns of man, both theoretical and practical.

It is true, that the difficulty of constructing a solid System of Morality may be expected to be, in some degree, great, in proportion to its great value and extensive bearings, when once constructed. But on the other hand, this acknowledged difficulty in the task will, it may be hoped, procure some indulgence to him who undertakes it, if he perform his labour patiently, and as far as he can, consistently. Even if he be not wholly successful, he may produce a result of which some part may have a permanent value, and which may be rendered more complete by his successors.

I do not know whether these general reflections will appear superfluous, to the Reader of the System of Morality now offered to his notice. I am desirous that he should understand that, though I do not speak of my work as a Philosophy of Morality, I have tried to make it a work of rigorous reasoning, and therefore, so far at least, philosophical.

I have, at the same time, used, as much as possible, the language in which moral opinions and moral arguments are expressed on common occasions; only attempting to give so much of precision to the meaning of the terms used, as may make the reasoning good. If the reasoning be really rigorous, it is, I conceive, a presumptive evidence of the truth of the System, that the arguments are expressed in language familiarly recognized as significant and convincing: just as the demonstrations of Geometry may, in many instances, be best expressed in the language of the practical land-measurer.

The Principles which are the foundation of the reasoning in this System of Morality are those which are given in Articles 269, 270, and 271, as the *Express Principles* of Humanity, Justice, Truth, Purity, Order, Earnestness, and Moral Ends. These Principles may be considered as, in some measure, analogous, in Morality, to the *Axioms* in Geometry. I have attempted to show how we are led to these Principles. But I hope I may once more refer to the analogy of Geometry; and remind the reader, that all the controversies which turn on matters *below* the Axioms do not affect the Superstructure which is built *upon* them. If any one believe that Humanity, Justice, Truth, Purity, Order, Earnestness, and Moral Purpose, are fundamental Principles of human action; in whatever manner he arrives at this conviction, he will be able to go along with me from this point; and to follow me into the Doctrines of the Morality of Reason, the Morality of Religion, Polity, and International Law.

I hope the Reader will find the convenience which I seem to myself to have found, in the Division of the general trunk of Morality into Five Branches: Jurisprudence; the Morality of Reason; the Morality of Religion; Polity; International Law. These five provinces, though intimately connected, appear to be distinct, and their boundaries well defined. The subjects belonging to each, and even the general style of treating them, are different. I hope, in particular, that the separation of the Morality of Religion from that of mere Reason, will be considered an improvement. It enables us to trace the guidance of human Reason, consistently and continuously, retaining a due sense of the superiority of Religion; and it shows that, in many places, this guidance of human Reason is insufficient without Religion, and points to Religion as a necessary higher guide.

By going through the subject in this shape, I have been unavoidably led to treat of subjects which are of a professional kind; and in which, therefore, an unprofessional writer is in great danger of error. This is especially the case with the first subject, Jurisprudence. I can scarcely hope that Jurists and Lawyers will not find, in what I have written, mistakes as to laws and legal expressions. These I hope they will pardon; seeing what

I trust I have made manifest, that some details on that subject were an essential part of my plan. This portion of my work has had the great advantage of being read and remarked on by my friend Mr. William Empson. I have taken the liberty of using some of his remarks, especially in the Notes on this Second Book. To him I am indebted also for a general reference to the Act of Crimes and Punishments, now under the consideration of the Legislature; of which I have made some use. Besides the common English law-books, I have referred to some American ones, especially Chancellor Kent's *Commentaries on American Law*, Judge Story's *Commentaries on Equity*, and his *Conflict of Laws*. In the Fifth Book, on Polity, I have made free use of many excellent works of my Contemporaries; especially Mr. Hallam's *Middle Ages*, and *English Constitution;* Mr. Allen's *Inquiry into the Royal Prerogative;* Sir Francis Palgrave's *History of the English Commonwealth;* Mr. Jones's work on *Rent*, and (particularly in the Chapter on the Representative System) Lord Brougham's *Political Philosophy*.

I have necessarily had to deliver opinions which bear, more or less closely, upon questions now agitated with a view to practical results. In doing this, I trust that I have said nothing but what belongs to a system of Morality, and that I shall be judged merely as a Moralist.

CONTENTS OF THE FIRST VOLUME.

BOOK I.

INTRODUCTION.

ELEMENTARY NOTIONS AND DEFINITIONS.

BOOK II.

JUS.

OF RIGHTS AND OBLIGATIONS.

BOOK III.

MORALITY.

OF VIRTUES AND DUTIES.

BOOK I.

INTRODUCTION.

ELEMENTARY NOTIONS AND DEFINITIONS.

CHAPTER I.

THE REASON.

1. In the present work I have to speak of the Actions of man, and of those Faculties by which he acts as man. These faculties belong to man in virtue of the Human Nature which is common to all men. They are Human Faculties, and give rise to Human Actions.

I and my readers share in this common Human Nature; and hence, instead of saying that *man* acts thus and thus, or has such and such faculties, I shall often say that *we* act thus, or that *we* have such faculties.

2. Man has faculties of Sensation, by which he perceives and observes *Things*, or objects without him; and faculties of Reflection, by which he is aware of *Thoughts*, or actions within him.

These faculties of Sensation and Reflection are inseparably combined in their operation. We cannot observe external things without some degree of Thought; nor can we reflect upon our Thoughts, without being influenced in the course of our reflection by the Things which we have observed.

3. Man, thus combining Observation and Reflection, is led to regard external things as grouped and classed, in his thoughts. He contemplates objects under *general* and *abstract* forms; and thus has Conceptions or Notions of them, and applies to them Names. Thus bread, fruit, flesh, are classed together and indicated by the general name of *food;* food, clothing, tools, arms, are all included in the general name *property*. Such terms are abstract, as well as general; in calling many different things *food,* we designate one certain use of the things, abstracting it from the things themselves, and neglecting their other qualities. In like manner, when we call many different things *property,* we abstract one special view of the things so described, from all various circumstances which may belong to them.

4. When we consider things under these general and abstract aspects, they can be denoted by Names, as we have said. Names indicate a class of things, or relations of things, which have all a single general and abstract aspect. The Conception is *that,* in our thoughts, which we express or signify by the Name.

Man not only contemplates things, or objects, and their relations; but he contemplates also Changes of things and of their relations, or Facts. Thus he observes that the stars move round the pole, or that Brutus stabs Cæsar. Or the absence of change may be a Fact; as, that the pole-star does not move.

Facts, as well as things, are described by general and abstract words. Things are described by Substantives; Facts, by Verbs, or words which assert.

5. When the relations or changes so asserted really exist or occur, the assertions are *true.* We can, by various processes, of observation and reflection, satisfy ourselves that some assertions are true and some false. We can be certain and sure of such truth and such falsehood. We may convince

ourselves and convince others of it; but we may also mistake in such conviction. Man has means of knowing Truth, but is also liable to Error.

Truth and Error are concerned about many General Relations of objects, which belong to them in the view in which we apprehend them. For example, we apprehend objects as existing in Space and Time; as being One or Many; Like or Unlike; as moving, and affecting each other's motions; and many other relations.

We can, in thought, separate these General Relations from the objects and facts. Such general relations are Space, Time, Number, Resemblance, Cause and Effect, and the like. These general relations thus separated may be termed *Ideas;* but the term Idea is often used more loosely, to designate all abstract objects of thought.

6. Objects and facts being regulated by these Ideas, we can, by the nature of our Ideas themselves, as for example the Ideas of Space, Time, Number, and the like, connect one fact with another by necessary consequence. Thus, we observe the fact that the stars move uniformly about the pole; we observe also their distances from each other. We can connect, with these facts, the times and places of their rising and setting, by a necessary process of thought. Such a process of thought is *reasoning.* We can reason, so that from the north polar distance of the star, and the latitude of the place of observation, we can deduce the interval of time between the star's rising and setting.

7. When we thus reason concerning things existing under these general relations of Space, Time, Number, and the like, we proceed upon, and necessarily assume, certain grounds, or Fundamental Principles, respecting these relations. And these Principles, the origin and basis of our reasoning, may

be separately asserted, as Axioms. Such Principles are the Axioms of Geometry.

8. By observation of the external world according to the general relations of Space, Time, Number, Resemblance, Cause and Effect, and the like, we become acquainted with it, so as to trace its course in some degree. We apprehend facts or objects, as conforming to a general Rule or *Law*. Thus, the Stars in general conform to the Law, that they revolve uniformly about the pole. The Planets conform to certain other Laws, which were discovered by the Chaldean and Greek astronomers. Such Laws are *Laws of Nature*.

When we discover such a constancy and sequence in events, we believe some to be the consequences of the others. We are then led forwards to future, as well as backwards to past events. We believe that some events will *certainly* happen, that others are *probable*. We believe it certain that the sun will rise to-morrow, and probable that he will shine.

9. We can, in our thoughts, separate Laws of Nature from the Facts which conform to them. When we do this, the Law is represented by the Ideas and Conceptions which it involves. Thus the Law of a Planet's motion round the Sun, as to space, is represented by the conception of an Ellipse, the Sun being in its Focus. Laws so abstracted from Facts are *Theories*.

10. The operations by which we frame and deal with Ideas and Conceptions, and all other acts of thought, are ascribed to the *mind*; they are *mental* operations and acts.

The mental operations which have been noticed; namely, to conceive objects in a general and abstract manner (3); to apply names to them (4); to reason (6); to apprehend first principles of reasoning (7); to conceive general rules (9); to apprehend facts as conformable to general Rules (8); are functions belonging to man, exclusively of all other animals. They are ascribed to a faculty specially human, the *Reason*.

The substantive *Reason*, thus used, has a wider sense than the verb *to reason*. The Reason is not only the faculty by which we reason from fundamental principles, when we have anyhow attained or assumed these; it is also the faculty by which we apprehend fundamental principles. By our Reason, we not only reason from the axioms of Geometry, but also see the truth of the axioms.

The special substantive, *a reason*, denotes a step in reasoning.

11. Of the processes which have been mentioned as belonging to the Reason, some are also ascribed to the *Understanding*, but not all. The Reason and the Understanding have not been steadily distinguished by English writers. The most simple way to use the substantive Understanding in a definite sense, is to make it correspond, in its extent, with the verb *understand*. To understand anything, is to apprehend it according to certain assumed ideas and rules; we do not include, in the meaning of the word, an examination of the ground of the ideas and rules, by reference to which we understand the thing. We understand a Language, when we apprehend what is said, according to the established vocabulary and grammar of the language; without inquiring how the words came to have their meaning, or what is the ground of the grammatical rules. We *understand* the sense, without *reasoning* about the etymology and syntax. Again, we understand a Machine when we perceive how its parts will work upon one another according to the known laws of mechanics, without inquiring what is the ground of these laws.

Reasoning may be requisite to understanding. We may have to reason about the syntax, in order to understand the sense: we may have to reason upon mechanical principles, in order to understand the machine. But understanding leaves still room for reasoning: we may understand the elliptical theory of Mars's motions, and may still require a reason for the theory. Also we may understand what is not conformable to Reason; as when we understand a man's arguments, and think them unfounded in Reason.

We understand a thing, as we have said, when we apprehend it according to certain assumed ideas and rules. We reason, in order to deduce such rules from first principles, or from one another. But the rules and principles which must be expressed when we reason, may be only implied when we understand. We may understand the sense of a speech, without thinking of rules of grammar. We may understand the working of a machine, without thinking of propositions in the sciences of geometry and mechanics.

The Reason is employed both in understanding and in reasoning; but the Principles which are explicity asserted in reasoning, are only implicitly applied in understanding. The Reason includes, as we have said, both the Faculty of seeing First Principles, and the Reasoning Faculty by which we obtain other Principles. The Understanding is the Faculty of applying Principles however obtained.

The Reason, of which we here speak, is the Speculative Reason. We shall hereafter have to speak of the Practical Reason also.

12. The term *Intellect* is derived from a verb (*intelligo*) which signifies *to understand:* but the term itself is usually so applied as to imply a Faculty which recognizes Principles explicitly as well as implicitly; and abstract as well as applied; and therefore agrees with the Reason rather than the Understanding; and the same extent of signification belongs to the adjective *intellectual.*

13. Man not only can contemplate external things; he can also *act* upon them and with them. He can gather the fruits of the earth, and make bread. He can take such things to himself, as his property, or give them to another man, as a reward.

The word *Action* may be applied, in the most general manner, to all exercise of the external or internal faculties of man. But we do not always so use the word. We often distinguish external *action* from internal *thought*, though thought is also a kind of activity. We also often distinguish *actions* from *words*, as when we say man's actions contradict his words. Yet in a more general sense, we include a man's words in his actions. We say that a man's actions correspond with his words, when he performs what he has promised; though the performance itself should be words; as when he has promised to plead a cause.

14. We direct our thoughts to an action which we are about to perform; we *intend* to do it: we make it our *aim:* we place it before us, and act with *purpose* (*propositum*): we *design* it, or make it out beforehand (*designo*).

15. Will, or Volition, is the last step of intention, the first step of action. It is the internal act which leads to external acts.

An action that proceeds from my will or volition is *my* act. But if it do not proceed from my will, it is not my act, though my limbs may be employed in it; as for instance, if my hand, moved by another man whose strength overmasters mine, strikes a blow. In such a case, I am not a Free Agent. Human Actions suppose the Freedom of the Agent. In order to act, a man must be so circumstanced that his volitions take effect on his limbs and organs, according to the usual constitution of man.

The Will is stimulated to action by certain Springs of Action, of which we shall afterwards speak.

16. Among the Springs of Action, are Rules or Laws. There are Laws of Human Action, as well as Laws of Nature (8). But while the Laws of Nature are assertions only, as; Mars *revolves* in an ellipse; a solar eclipse *will* take place at the new moon; the Laws of human action are *commands:* as, *Steal* not; or, Thou *shalt* not steal: We *must* be temperate. These imperative Laws of Human Action, we shall call *Rules*. Such Rules, when adjusted with due regard to the Springs of Action, direct the Will.

17. Actions may lead to events, as causes to effects: they may have consequences, immediate or remote. To steal, is an action which may have the gain of a shilling for its immediate, and whipping for its remote consequence.

An *End* is a consequence intended, aimed at, purposed, designed (14). When we act with purpose, we have an End, to which the action is a *Means*. To possess the fruit being my end, I purposely cultivate the plant as the means.

18. The Rules of Action (16) may command actions as means to an end: thus: Steal not, that thou be not whipt. Be temperate, in order to be healthy.

19. We have often a *Series* of Actions each of which is a means, towards the next, as an end. We dig the ground, that we may make the plant to grow; we make a spade, that we may dig the ground; we take a branch of a tree, to make a handle for the spade.

20. To discern the consequences of actions; to act with purpose; and to consider our actions as means to an end; are processes which are ascribed to the Reason, as well as the mental operations which have already been spoken of (10).

As possessing Reason, man is called *rational* or *reasonable*. But the latter term is often used in a more special sense; meaning, agreeable to such rules and measures as man, by the use of his reason, may discover.

21. The Reason, when employed in such processes as have been noticed already (10), is the *Speculative* Reason; we oppose to this the *Practical* Reason, which guides us in applying Rules to our actions, and discerning the consequences of actions (20). The Speculative Reason tends to speculative Truth; in which ideas, conceptions, and abstract propositions are contemplated: the Practical Reason guides us to truth, so far as it concerns our actions. By the Practical Reason, we apprehend objects and facts in a manner conformable to their true relations; and hence, we discern the true consequences of our actions, though the relations and the action are not explicitly contemplated. The true apprehension of the relations of things is only implied in the Act of the Will, by which we take such means as lead to our ends.

22. The ideas, relations, rules, conceptions of ends and means, and the like, which are implicitly involved in the exercise of the Practical Reason, may be *unfolded*, so as to be matter of contemplation. In this manner, the Practical Reason is developed into the Speculative Reason. Such a developement of the human mind is produced by the exercise of Thought.

23. Animals, as well as man, conform their actions to the true relations of objects (21), and perform actions which look like means to ends (17). Thus, bees build cells in hexagonal forms, so as to fill space; and birds build nests, so as to shelter themselves and their young. But in the case of animals, the tendency to action cannot be unfolded into ideas, and conceptions of ends. Bees have no conceptions of hexagons, separate from their cells. Birds do not contemplate an end, when they build a nest: for they build nests in a state of captivity, where there is no end to be answered. The ten-

dencies to such actions are implanted in the constitution of the animal, but are not capable of being unfolded into ideas, as in a rational nature they are (22). Hence such tendencies are called *Instincts,* and are distinguished from Practical Reason.

24. Instinct, as well as Reason, operates through the Will, to direct the actions. In both cases, the Will is stimulated into action by certain Appetites and Desires, which we shall term *Springs of Action.*

We use the term *Springs* of action, rather than *Principles* of action, because the term Principles is used equivocally, not only for Operative Principles, which produce action, but for Express Principles, which assert Propositions.

The Springs of Action of which we have to speak, are the Motive Powers of man's conscious nature, and might hence be called *Motives.* They first put man in motion; that is, in the state of internal motion which leads to intention and will. But in common language, the term *Motive* is rather used to designate the special object of the intention, than the general desire which impels us to intend. When a man labours hard for gain, his spring of action being the desire of having, his Motive is to get money. But he may do the same thing, his Motive being to support his family, and then his spring of action is his family affections.

CHAPTER II.

THE SPRINGS OF HUMAN ACTION.

25. THE Springs of Action in man may be enumerated as follows: The Appetites or Bodily Desires; the Affections: the Mental Desires; the

Moral Sentiments; and the Reflex Sentiments. We shall consider them in order.

1. *The Appetites.*

26. The Appetites or Bodily Desires are common to man and brutes. The strongest and most obvious of them are the Appetites for Food (Hunger and Thirst), by which the individual is sustained; and that by which the species is continued. These appetites are tendencies towards certain bodily things, and cravings for these things when they are withheld.

But besides these, there are many other bodily Desires which may be classed with the Appetites, and which are powerful springs of action. Such are the desire of rest after labour, the desire of sleep after long waking, the desire of warmth and shelter, the desire of air and exercise.

These Desires are *Natural Wants;* they are Needs of man's nature. Man cannot exist at all, except they are satisfied in some degree; and cannot exist in a healthy and stable condition, except they are satisfied in an adequate degree.

27. Moreover, by the constitution of man, certain Pleasures are conjoined with the satisfying of these wants; and the Springs of Action, of which we now speak, include the Desire of these Pleasures. Thus, man has not only an appetite for food, but a desire of delicious food, and a Sense of Taste, by which he relishes such food. He has, in like manner, a pleasure in sweet odours, and a desire of this pleasure; and similarly for the other senses.

Man uses various Arts, to satisfy his natural wants, and to gratify his desires for the pleasures of sense, of which we have spoken. As such gratifications, through means of art, become habitual, they also become Wants, and are termed *Artificial Wants.*

These Artificial Wants, no less than Natural Wants, are powerful Springs of Action among men.

2. *The Affections.*

28. The Affections are tendencies or cravings directed towards conscious individuals; not, like the Desires, tendencies and cravings for bodily objects. The Bodily Desires tend to things, Affections to Persons.

But the Affections are not mere tendencies or cravings, they are internal Emotions or Feelings: being directed to persons, not to things, they mould the thoughts in a way quite different from what the Appetites do.

29. The two principal affections are Love and Anger. The term Love, is sometimes used to describe the Bodily Desires, as when we talk of a Love of wine, or a Love of the pleasures of the table. But the more direct and proper sense of the word, is that in which it denotes an affection towards a person. A man's love of his wife and children is more properly Love, than his love of wine or of music.

30. The most important of the Affections which thus come under the name of Love are;—the Love of the mother and of the father towards the children, Maternal and Paternal Love;—the Love of children towards their parents, Filial Love;—the Love of brothers and sisters towards each other, Fraternal Love; the special and distinguishing affection of man towards woman, and woman towards man, which tends to the conjugal union; this is often expressed by the word *Love* without any epithet; its natural sequel is Conjugal Love. Also, among the kinds of Love we must enumerate Friendship, and our Love of our Companions; likewise the Affection, so far as it partakes of the nature of Love, with which we regard

our fellow-citizens, our fellow-countrymen, our fellow-men.

31. The Affection of Anger also appears in various forms. Anger comes into play against any one who assaults or threatens us, in man as in other animals; and this Affection, giving vehemence and rapidity to our actions, aids us in self-defence. Anger in this form is the natural repulsion and return to any harm which falls upon us or approaches us, and is called *Resentment*, as being the sentiment which is a natural re-action to the hostile sentiment of another person.

32. The Affections conspire with the Desires. We are angry with those who take from us, or prevent our obtaining, what we desire. We love those who aid us in gratifying our desires. These affections are modified according to the circumstances under which they thus arise, and receive special names. Men feel *Gratitude* towards those who have conferred benefits upon them. As they feel sudden *Resentment* against a sudden attack, they feel *Permanent Anger* against those who have inflicted or endeavour to inflict pain or harm upon them, or whose desires come in conflict with theirs. When this feeling is no longer a burst of emotion, but a settled and steady feeling, it is *Hatred, Malice*, or *Ill-will*. When malice prompts men to return pain and harm to those from whom they have received pain or harm, it is *Revenge*.

All these Affections belong to the *irascible* part of man's nature.

33. The Affections, as has been said, are directed towards persons. In speaking of them, we suppose him who feels them to live as a man among men. He is *in Society;* and his desires and affections are excited, determined, and modified by the circumstances of his social condition. These circumstances may be various, both for the individual, and

for the general body of the society. There are various Forms and Stages of Society. We may conceive, as the original form, a society in which there are no Affections except the Family Affection, and no Appetites except the Natural Wants. But as the Society becomes more numerous, and Artificial Wants increase, many other kinds of relation and dependence grow up among the individuals who compose the society, and the Affections are modified by these new conditions.

34. In speaking of other Desires and Affections which we still have to notice, we continue to suppose man existing in society: and we shall have to consider mainly, at first, those Desires and Affections which have reference to the intercourse of a man with other men.

3. *The Mental Desires.*

35. The Appetites are of the nature of Instincts, in that they tend to their objects, without their objects being present to the mind as abstract notions. But yet when we bring into view abstract notions, the bodily desires may be described as tendencies to such abstractions. Thus Hunger and Thirst may be described as the Desire of *Food;* which is, as we have seen (3), an abstract notion. All the Bodily Desires may be included in the Desire of *Pleasure,* which is a still more abstract notion.

As the developement of the human mind goes on by the exercise of thought (22), the objects of desire are all presented to the mind as abstract notions, more or less general. In this way, the Bodily Desires may be presented in a general and abstract form. But besides these general and abstract forms of Bodily Desires, there are other Desires which cannot be conceived in any other way than with reference to abstractions; as the Desire of Fame, the Desire of Knowledge. These we shall call *Mental Desires.*

36. We now speak of those Springs of Action which result from the operations of the mind. Among such operations, besides those which have been referred to, we must place *Memory,* by which past facts and objects are recalled to the mind, and subjected to its view, in the same manner as if they were present; and *Imagination,* by which the distant, the absent, and the future is represented to the mind, under combinations and aspects imposed by the mind itself. These faculties fill up the abstract outline of the objects of desire, with particulars and images, by means of which they obtain a far stronger hold upon the purpose and will, than the mere abstraction of itself could have. By their means, the desire of a general and abstract object impels us, not merely with the force residing in the ultimate generality, but with a power belonging to the whole of the successive steps of generalization, from objects of sense upwards.

37. Every object of desire as contemplated by the mind may be described by a general term as a *Good. Quicquid petitur petitur sub specie boni.* This is the most general aspect of the objects of desire. Opposed to the objects of desire, are objects which we shun, as Pain, Constraint, and the Want or Privation of objects of desire. These are *Evils.* The mind, furnished with the stores of Memory, and exercising the powers of Imagination, can contemplate remotely future, as well as immediate gratifications, arising from the attainment of objects of desire. Such objects, contemplated as future, are *wished for;* if the attainment of our wishes, is deemed probable, they are *hoped.* The infliction of future evils, if probable, is *feared.* Evil so contemplated is *Danger. Hope* and *Fear* are springs of action no less powerful than present Desire.

38. We must now consider the particular Mental Desires separately.

In order that we may distinguish and enumerate the more important and more elementary of the Mental Desires, we may remark, that Desires, operating merely as tendencies to action, and not unfolded by the exercise of thought, so as to become tendencies to Mental objects, (abstractions,) are like Instincts (23). Hence we may consider those Desires as distinct, which look like the developements of different Instincts. The Instincts of animals are a kind of image of the Desires of man; and we may consider those as so many distinct Elementary Desires, of which we find so many images in the Instincts of animals. And the Desires of which we shall speak, being also the most universal and most powerful of those by which man's actions are determined, are those which we have especially to notice among the Springs of Action.

The Mental Desires of which we shall first speak, are the Desire of Safety, the Desire of Having, the Desire of Society, the Desire of Superiority, the Desire of Knowledge.

39. *The Desire of Safety.* All the bodily desires may be included under one general expression, as the Desire of Personal Wellbeing, or the like. But in order to frame rules of action, we must refer to something more limited and definite than this. Moreover, in our view of the springs of human action, we are to suppose man to be in Society, and to have his desires determined by the circumstances of his social condition (34).

Now if the desires alone be taken into our account, a man living among men is liable to have his desires frustrated, and to suffer harm, pain, wounds, and even death, through the operation of the conflicting desires of other men. We can conceive a condition in which men are in a perpetual state of war and violence, like hostile beasts of prey. But the desires of man, when his irascible affections are not inflamed by conflict, tend towards a state of things the opposite of this. He desires peace and tranquillity. He hopes for these; he fears their opposites. These desires, hopes, and fears are so strong, that man's life is scarcely tolerable if they are not in some degree gratified. Man requires, as indispensable to his human condition, a removal of his fears of violence and harm to his body, arising from the conflicting desires of other men. This feeling we may call the Desire of Safety. It is one of the strongest, most universal and most constant of all the desires of men.

40. We find Instincts of animals which correspond to this Spring of action in man. Such an Instinct is variously described, as the Instinct of Self-defence, or of Self-preservation, the instinctive Love of Life, and the like. This Instinct stimulates all the faculties of animals in the most energetic manner; is able to master their strongest appetites and affections; and often calls into play an almost incredible sagacity and strength.

41. In man, the instinctive love of life, the instinctive desire to avoid privation, pain, and constraint, are expanded and unfolded by memory, reflection and foresight. Life, ease, comfort, peace, tranquillity, become objects to which man tends with conscious thought, as well as from blind impulse. Nor can he be at all satisfied, except he can look forwards to the future, as well as the present enjoyment, of these advantages. He must not only have present safety, but *Security* for the future. When, however, we speak of the Desire of Safety, as one of the principal elementary Mental Desires, we may understand Security to be included in the expression.

42. We have mentioned Constraint as one of the things which men desire to avoid. Even when unaccompanied with pain or danger, extraneous force,

compelling or restraining our motions, is felt as a grievous infliction. We cannot act so as to make our actions our own, without acting freely; and the Desire of Free Agency, which we naturally feel, is confirmed and made more urgent, by our perceiving that such freedom is necessary to all properly human action. Hence the Love of Liberty is one of the powerful Springs of human action; but so far as it is of an elementary nature, it is included in the Desire of Safety and Security from bodily harm of which we now speak.

43. The Safety, Security and Liberty of the body, which man thus requires, as conditions without which he cannot exist satisfactorily, are easily endangered by the angry affections of other men, stimulated by their desires, conflicting with his. By such conflicts Malice is produced (32); and malicious intention shows itself in deeds of force and violence, or in other kinds of attempts upon the safety and liberty of the man. Others become his Enemies, and he becomes theirs. And the natural Enmity, as well as the Society of mankind, modifies their other desires.

44. *The Desire of Having.* The Desire of Having, so far as it refers to the means of subsistence, is a developement of the instinct of self-preservation, which impels animals to seek food and other necessaries of life. But even in animals, we see a desire of having which goes beyond this; for some animals have an instinct of storing; and this instinct is very different from mere desire of food. It often controls present appetite, and leads the animal to hide what it cannot use as food, as well as what it can. In man the Desire of Having is apparent in all stages of Society (33). Food, clothing, weapons, tools, ornaments, houses, carriages, ships, are universally objects of his desire. In the first place, indeed, man desires these things as a means of gratifying his nat-

ural appetites, or his affections; of supporting and sheltering his family; of repelling and mastering his enemies. But the desire to possess such objects, as it exists in man, goes beyond the measure of their obvious use. He delights to consider them as connected with himself in a permanent and exclusive manner, and to look upon them as *his*, as his *own*. The things which he thus looks upon as his own, he is disturbed at the prospect of losing, and is angry at any one who attempts to take them from him. Nor can he be at ease in his thoughts, or act steadily and tranquilly, except he be allowed to possess in quiet and security what he thus has as his. He needs to hold it as his *Property*.

45. The objects to which the desire of possessing applies are called *Things*, as contrasted with *Persons*. In considering the rules of human action, Things are contemplated as morally passive, the objects of possession and use; capable only of being given, received, acted with or on: Persons are active, or capable of action; and are considered as conscious, intelligent, intentional agents.

Things, as objects of possession, are contemplated under various aspects of generality and abstraction. In a general way, they are termed Possessions, Wealth, Riches. There is one particular kind of Possession which is used in transferring all other kinds, and which hence measures and represents all other kinds. This is Money, which most commonly has the form of copper, silver, or gold, and which is especially called Riches.

46. Wealth or Property includes all objects which are subservient to the satisfaction of our wants; and thus the desire which regards property is strengthened by the progress of Artificial Wants (32). Again, most of the relations of society imply some intercourse with regard to property, some giving and receiving. The progress of society, with the exten-

sion and multiplication of these social relations, give additional operation to property, and increase its hold on men's minds. And thus, in a society in which artificial wants and social relations are extended and multiplied, still more than in more simple states of society, there can be no tranquillity, peace, or comfort, except man can possess in security and quiet that which he regards as his Property.

Without Property, and the recognition of Property in Society, even man's free agency cannot exist. If another may at any moment take from me my food, my clothing, my tools, I can no longer, with any confidence or steadiness labour, or travel, or reckon upon being able to live from day to day. In order to act, I must act on, or with things; and I must for that purpose have secure property in things.

47. The Desire of Society appears in man in two very conspicuous forms;—the *Desire of Family Society* and the Desire of Civil Society. These may be treated of as elementary desires; we have images of them in the instincts of animals;—of the former, in pairing animals, of the latter, in gregarious animals.

That man has a Desire of Family Society, in addition to his mere bodily desires, is plain. In the rudest tribes, the man and his wife are bound together by this desire. They wish for and seek habitual companionship and help, not merely occasional pleasure. The woman can hardly subsist through the time of child-bearing, or the child be supported, without the existence of the ties of family. When the family circle is completed by the addition of children, this desire of companionship is awakened and gratified in a wider sphere. The desires which first lead to the existence of the Family are refined, as well as extended, by the existence of the Family. A desire of a general sympathy among the members of the Family, purifies and elevates the operation of the mere bodily desires. There are added to the gratification of the desires, immeasureable new pleasures growing out of the offices of mutual love to which the family gives occasion.

These gratifications are so congenial to the nature of man, so universally and constantly sought, so uneasily and impatiently dispensed with, that no form of man's existence can be tolerable or stable in which men in general are not able to enjoy or to hope for them. There can be no peace, comfort, tranquillity, or order in a state of society in which there are not permanent conjugal unions.

The existence of permanent marriages is requisite, as has been said, for the sustentation of the mother and the child during its earliest age. It is requisite no less for the instruction of the child in the use of language, in the direction of its actions by rules, and in the other manifestations of a social and rational human nature. And thus the existence of marriage is requisite not only to continue the race of mankind, but also to transmit from generation to generation the social and rational character of man. And this necessity is perceived by man, when his reflection is called into play; and thus the Regard for Marriage which men feel is confirmed, and the Desire of Family Society strengthened in its general influence upon man.

48. *The Desire of Civil Society* also is an important spring of action in the nature of man. The other desires which we have mentioned, the desire of safety, and the desire of property, may be supposed to give rise to a desire of civil society, as of a means by which such objects may be secured. But there appears to exist in man a Desire of Society of a more unconscious and elementary kind; of which, as has been said, we have an image in the instincts of gregarious animals. Man also is a gregarious, or more properly, a social animal. He is nowhere found, nor

can he exist, in any other state than in Society, of some form or other. Indeed, the same conditions of his being which make him necessarily exist as a member of a family, make him also, after a few generations, necessarily exist as a member of a family in a larger sense; of a tribe, a clan, a nation. And though, in cases in which the free agency of the individual comes into play, these ties of family may be loosened or broken; man still only passes from one form of society to another, and his state is ever social. The existence of a language is, of itself, undeniable evidence of a recognized society among those who have this bond of union: for those who use the same language have common classifications of things and action, common generalizations and abstractions; which imply, in a great degree, common judgments and common rules of action. Society, bound together by such ties, is a Community.

Men, connected by this bond, have a pleasure in their mutual society. They are pleased with the companionship and intercourse which take place at the social board, in the street, the market, the council-room. Men desire to act, and are fitted to act, in common; declaring and enforcing rules by which the conduct of all shall be governed: they thus act as governors, legislators, judges, subjects, citizens. Without such community of action, and such common rules really enforced, there can be no tolerable comfort, peace, or order. Without civil society, man cannot act as man.

49. The Mental Desires which we have mentioned, include the Appetites and Affections, and may take the place of them in some of our future reasonings. The Desire of Personal Safety, and the Desire of Having, include the Desires of all bodily objects requisite for the support, ease and comfort of the individual. The Desire of Family Society includes the Love, of Wife, Parents, Children, Brothers, Sisters, and the like. The affection of Anger is an at-

tendant upon all our Desires; for we are angry with those who interfere with our Desires; angry with those who threaten our Safety, our Property, or our Family enjoyments.

50. There is another Spring of Action intimately connected with the existence of society, and in some measure implied in what has been said; but which we must also speak of separately: I mean, the Need of a *Mutual Understanding* among men. I speak of this as a Need, rather than a Desire; for Mutual Understanding is rather a necessity of man's condition, than an object of his conscious desire. We see this necessity even in animals, especially in those which are gregarious. In their associated condition, they derive help and advantage from one another: and many of them, especially those that live, travel or hunt in companies, are seen to reckon upon each other's actions with great precision and confidence. In societies of men, this mutual aid and mutual reliance are no less necessary than among beavers or bees. But in man, this aid and reliance are not the work of mere Instinct. There must be a Mutual Understanding by which men learn to anticipate and to depend upon the actions of each other. This mutual understanding presupposes that man has the power of determining his future actions; and that he has the power of making other men aware of his determination. It presupposes Purpose as its matter (14), and Language as its Instrument (4). The verb *to understand*, as has been said (11), has especial reference to the use of language.

When we have determined a future action by intention or settled purpose, we communicate the intention to another person who is concerned in the result, by a *Promise*. The person to whom my promise is made, (*the Promisee,*) understands my purpose, and is led to reckon in his actions upon my purposed action;

and I understand him to regulate his actions by this reckoning.

51. A large part of the actions which take place among men, are regulated by their mutual understanding established by promises, or in some other way. In most forms of society, each person depends for food, for clothing, for shelter, for safety, for comfort, for enjoyment, or for the greater part of these, upon a mutual understanding with other men. There is a mutual dependence, the result of a mutual understanding.

One of the ways in which this result is carried into effect is, by the establishment of different employments and occupations, businesses and offices, among different classes of men. One man employs himself solely in preparing food for men; others, in preparing clothing; and again; one, in preparing clothing for the feet; another, clothing for the body. Again, one man's business is to protect the other from foreign foes; he is a soldier: another's occupation is to decide disputes which occur within the society; he is a judge. Persons are placed in such situations by general understanding, express or implied; and each man, in his actions, reckons upon the others discharging their offices according to their respective trades and professions. This mutual understanding is a universal bond, which could not be removed without the community falling to pieces; it is force of cohesion, permeating the structure of society, so that if this force were to cease to act, the whole mass would crumble into dust. We therefore place this Need of a Mutual Understanding among the principal springs of human action.

52. *The Desire of Superiority* may be placed among the elementary Desires, since it is seen to exist as an instinct in many of the bolder animals, manifesting itself in the exertions which they make in their conflicts with one another. In such cases, this desire is often mixt up with the instinct of self-defence and the impulses of anger, as in the combats of pugnacious

animals; but in racing and hunting, we see, in dogs and horses, a desire of superiority, showing itself as a distinct spring of action; and the like may be observed in other similar cases.

In man, this desire of superiority appears on a wider scale, the subjects of comparison being vastly more numerous and complicated. A man desires to know himself more swift, more strong, more skilful than another; hence the contests of the palestra, and even wanton combats for life or death. A man desires to be more wealthy than his neighbours; and hence accumulates riches by labour, agriculture, trade or traffic. But man not only wishes to surpass, but to guide and control other men. He wishes that they should *obey* when he *commands*. He has a Desire of Power. To this object, strength and skill and riches may all be as means to ends. The desire of being superior as regards those circumstances, may be the desire of being more powerful than others, with whom we compare ourselves.

53. This desire of being superior to others in the advantages which we possess, and especially in power, is very general among men. Most men would wish to be strong, skilful, rich; but especially to be powerful, so that other men should conform to their will and do their bidding. But all cannot be superior to others. If each desire to be the strongest, there can be no repose or order, except these conflicting desires balance each other. All cannot be superior; but none need be inferior, for all may be equal. The universal desire of superiority cannot be gratified; but if it be transformed into a universal impatience of inferiority, it may become the regulating force of society.

When we say that none need be inferior, for all may be equal; it is not meant that all may have equal shares of the objects of human desires; but that each may equally have what is his, not holding it at the will or command of another man. The equality of which we speak, is the establishment of equal rules, not the establishment of a rule of equal division. Such a rule as the latter, would be inconsistent with the nature of property: for that which is a man's property, is his with its increase, and passes from him if he give or destroy it: so that the shares of different individuals, even if equal at first, cannot continue equal. But Equal Rules may be established; and the impatience of inferiority, which is natural to man, will not be satisfied with any rules which have not the aspect of equality. It is true, that this equality of rules may be modified by external circumstances; as we have just seen, that the equality of shares must be disturbed by passing changes: but still, the desires of men constantly point to equal rules, as those which alone are tolerable; and there can be no permanent tranquillity in a community, except under the sway of rules, which are equal for all; so far as the nature of man, and the previous condition of the society, allow of rules at the same time steady and equal. And thus, the Desire of Superiority, transformed into the Desire of Equal Rules, is one of the powerful springs of human action.

54. *The Desire of Knowledge* may also be enumerated among the elementary desires. Of this Desire, also, we see a sort of image, in the curiosity and prying propensities of many animals; but in them, these propensities are generally subservient to the actions by which sustenance is obtained or danger avoided.

In man, the Desire of Knowledge is identical with the desire or propensity of the mind to unfold itself (22); and with the desire which we have to contemplate our own conceptions, as distinctly and connectedly as is possible for us. Man, by his rational nature, is constantly impelled to think, to reason, to classify, to trace causes and consequences; to do this, is to know; and to continue to do it, is to go on from knowledge to knowledge.

55. Knowledge influences human actions, not so much by the exertions which it impels men to make for the purpose of acquiring knowledge, as by the different aspects which it gives to the other objects of desire. An ugly pebble may be a most desirable possession, if we know how to extract from it a cure for disease. The desire to possess a particular piece of ground, may become very vehement, by our knowing that it is the heritage left us by our ancestors. Our impatience of the constraint which a body of men impose upon us, may be much inflamed, by our knowing that such constraint is inconsistent with ancient maxims of law, or with rules of reason, or with the true destination of man. In such cases, our desires and actions are influenced by our knowledge, that is, by our *Reason*. Our knowledge, thus considered as a Spring of action, is identical with the Reason, by which we contemplate abstract and general conceptions, and thus determine for ourselves rules and ends of action. This is a task which it is our object to perform in the present work.

4. *The Moral Sentiments.*

56. That which is conformable to Rules of Action is *right*. What we mean by right, will be considered more particularly afterwards: but before we proceed to that question, we may observe, that our judgment of actions as right, or as *wrong*, the opposite of right, is accompanied with certain Affections, or Sentiments. That which is right we *approve;* that which is wrong we *disapprove*. What is wrong naturally excites a modification of Anger, which we term *Indignation*. Wrong done to ourselves excites instant resentment (31); but our anger against wrong as wrong, when we do not consider it as affecting our

selves, is Indignation. And in like manner, what is right is the natural object of a kind of love, namely, of *Esteem*. These Affections, Approbation and Disapprobation, Indignation and Esteem, are the *Moral Sentiments*.

Though the Moral Sentiments thus partake of the nature of the affections, they differ in this respect, that they have for their objects in the first instance, not Persons, but Actions. We love a friend ; we approve his acts of benevolence. We are angry with a man who picks our pocket, and disapprove of his act.

But the Sentiment is transferred from the action to the agent; and thus the Moral Sentiments combine with and modify our other affections, and are powerful Springs of Action. We befriend a man, or we choose him for our friend, and do him good offices, not because he is our brother, but because we approve his actions, and therefore love him, and would treat him as our brother. We help to inflict pain or even death upon a man, not because he has done us especially any harm, but because he has committed an act of which we strongly disapprove, and which excites a strong indignation against him.

There are Sentiments which partake of the nature of Esteem or Approval, but imply no settled Moral Rule, and include feelings of surprise and conscious inferiority in ourselves. Such are *Admiration* and *Awe*.

5. *Reflex Sentiments.*

57. Besides the Moral Sentiments which impel us to act in one way or another to other men, accordingly as we approve or disapprove their actions, there are also certain Sentiments which have a reference to their judgment of us and their affections towards us; and these Sentiments are also Springs of Action. These we shall term *Reflex Sentiments*, for they imply Reflex Thought. In order to regard another

man's Sentiments concerning me, I must form a conception of his Sentiments as the image of my own; and of myself as the object of those sentiments.

58. *The Desire of being loved* is one of these Reflex Sentiments. In minds so far unfolded by thought as to be capable of reflex processes, this Sentiment commonly accompanies love; but it belongs to a stage of mental developement higher than mere elementary love. Yet we see traces of it in the behaviour of those animals which seek to be fondled and caressed.

59. *The Desire of Esteem* is a powerful and extensive Spring of Action. We desire that other men should think that what we do is right. Hence, this desire assumes some generally established Rule of what is right. Without ourselves esteeming what is right, we cannot conceive Esteem, and thus truly cannot feel the Desire of Esteem. But in this case, we may still feel the *Desire of Admiration*, the *Desire of Honour*, the *Love of Fame*, the *Love of Glory*, and the like Reflex Sentiments; which do not imply our own approval of the Rule by which others judge. Yet these are very powerful Springs of action in many men.

60. Finally, there is a Reflex Sentiment which we may term the *Desire of our own Approval*. This implies that we have adopted a Rule according to which we judge Actions to be right, and that we desire to conform our own actions to this Rule. Such a Desire is a Spring of Action, which must balance all others, in order that the Rule may be really valid. What the nature of such a Rule must be, we shall have to consider: in the mean time, we may remark, that the Desire of our own Approval, of which we now speak, is included in the meaning of the term *Conscience*.

Among the Reflex Sentiments, we may place all those Springs of Action which are designated by some compound of the word *Self;* as *Self-Admiration Self-Love*. These, for the most part, are elementary Springs of Action, combined and modified by reflex habits of thought. Thus Self-Love may be understood to include the Desire of Property, of Bodily comfort, and the like, along with a distinct consideration of One's Self. In this view, Self-Love is rather a habit of regarding and providing for the elementary Desires, than a distinct Desire. It is sometimes spoken of as a General Regard for our own Good; and as we have said (37), the term *Good* is so used as to include the objects of all the elementary Desires.

6. *General Remarks.*

61. It appears by what has been said, that the different kinds of Springs of Action are distinguished by the nature of their objects. The Appetites have for their objects, Things; the Affections, Persons; the Mental Desires have Abstractions; the Moral Sentiments, Actions; and the Reflex Sentiments have for their objects the thoughts of other persons, or our own, about ourselves.

The Springs of Action which we have enumerated do not operate upon man as Forces operate upon inert Matter. They all operate through the Will. A man is moved by these Springs, when he *will* do that to which they impel him. Different springs of action may operate at the same time, and with opposite tendencies. The Desire of Safety would keep the sailor or soldier at home, but the Desire of Gain, or the Love of Glory, sends him to the sea or to the war. In either case, it is through his Will that the Desires act. He stays at home because he wills to do so; or he goes forth because he wills it.

62. In determining his actions, man is seldom impelled merely by the most elementary Springs of Action, bodily desire and affection. By the progress

of thought in every man, bodily desires are combined with mental desires, and elementary affections with moral sentiments.

The men who most seek the pleasures of eating, seek at the same time the pleasures of society. The most blind maternal love generally takes the form of approving, as well as loving, its darling. And thus, in man, the Desires and Affections are unfolded by thought, so as to involve abstract conceptions and the notion of a Rule. The Reason, to which such steps belong (10) is at work, in all the actions which the Springs of Action produce.

63. Reason is conceived as being in all persons the same in its nature. Different men desire different things, love different persons; but that which is seen to be true in virtue of the Reason, is true for all men alike. The influence of desire or affection may be mistaken for the result of Reason, for man is liable to error (5); and so far, the decisions of Reason may be different in different men. But such decisions are not all really reasonable. So far as men decide conformably to Reason, they decide alike. His Appetites, and Desires, and Affections are peculiar to each man; but his Reason is a common attribute of all mankind: and each man has his Reason in virtue of his participation of this common faculty of discerning truth and falsehood.

But though each man's Desires and Affections belong specially to himself, while Reason is a common faculty in all men; we consider our Reason as being *ourselves*, rather than our Desires and Affections. We speak of Desire, Love, Anger, as mastering *us*, or of *ourselves* as controlling them. If we decide to prefer some remote and abstract good to immediate pleasures; or to conform to a rule which brings us present pain; which decision implies the exercise of Reason; we more particularly consider such acts as our *own* acts. Such acts are deemed especially the result, not of the impulse of our desires, but of our own volition.

If we ask why we thus identify ourselves with our rational part, rather than with our desires and affections; we reply, that it is because the Reason alone is capable of that reflex act by which we become conscious of ourselves. To have so much thought as to distinguish between ourselves and our springs of action, is to be rational; and the Reason which can make this distinction, necessarily places herself on one side, and the Desires which make no such distinction, on the other. It is by the Reason that we are conscious; and hence we place the seat of our consciousness in the Reason.

64.. The habit of identifying ourselves with our Reason, and not with our Desires, is further indicated by the term *Passion*, which is applied to Desire and Affection when uncontrolled by Reason; as if man in such cases were passive, and merely acted on; and as if he were really active, only when he acts in conformity with his Reason. Thus, we speak, of a man being *in a Passion*, meaning an uncontrolled fit of anger; and *having a Passion* for an object, meaning an uncontrolled desire.

Still, it is to be recollected that man, under the influence of such Passions, is not really passive. When he acts under such influences, he adopts the suggestions of Desire or Affection, and rejects the control of Reason; but this is what he does in all violations of reasonable Rules. Passion does not prevent a man's knowing that there is a Rule, and that he is violating it. To say that Passion is irresistible, is to annihilate Reason, and to exclude the most essential condition of Human Action.

CHAPTER III.

MORAL RULES EXIST NECESSARILY.

65. In enumerating and describing, as we have done, certain Desires, as among the most powerful Springs of human action, we have stated (39) that man's life is scarcely tolerable if these Desires are not in some degree gratified: that man cannot be at all satisfied without some security in such gratification (41); that without property, which gratifies one of these Desires, man's free agency cannot exist (45); that without marriage, which gratifies another, there can be no peace, comfort, tranquillity, or order (47). And the same may be said of all those Springs of Action which we enumerated as Mental Desires. Without some provision for the tranquil gratification of these Desires, Society is disturbed, unbalanced, painful. The gratification of such Desires must be a part of the Order of the Society. There must be Rules which direct the course and limits of such gratification. Such Rules are necessary for the Peace of Society.

66. Man acts as man, when he acts under the influence of Reason, and Reason directs us to Rules. Rules of action are necessary, therefore, for the action of man as man. We cannot conceive man as man, without conceiving him as subject to Rules, and making part of an Order in which Rules prevail. He must act freely, therefore he must have Security. He must act by means of external things, therefore he must have Property. He must act with reference to other men's intentions, therefore there must be Contracts. He must act with reference to Parents, Wife and Children, therefore there must be Families. We cannot conceive man divested of free agency, of relation to external things, of communication with

other men, of the ties of blood and affection. We must therefore conceive him as existing in Security, with Property, Contracts and Family, subsisting about him; existing, therefore, under Rules by which these things are established; and thus, such Rules are necessary for the action of man as man.

Such Rules being established, that which is conformable to them is *right*, and the Rules are *moral* Rules. We must afterwards endeavour to establish such Rules in detail; but in the mean time, we have shown in general that the establishment of Moral Rules is necessary for the peace of society and for the action of man as man.

67. That Rules, determined by the Reason to be reasonable, are the necessary guides of Desire and Affection, is also apparent from a consideration of the nature of Reason. We cannot help recognizing, in the Reason, an authority to repress and resist Appetite and Desire, when the two come in conflict. The Reason is the light of man's constitution, which reveals to him himself, and enables him to choose between different objects. And this light, by being light, is fit to guide us; as in the world without, so in the world within us, the light, by guiding us, proves that it is its office to guide us.

68. It has been said by some that the Rules of human action, by which men in Society are governed, are the results of mutual Fear, by which the conflicting Desires of different persons are balanced. But this is not a true view of the subject. Mutual fear and conflicting desires prevail among wild animals; but yet animals have not among them Moral Rules of action. Brute beasts cannot properly be said to steal from one another, to wrong one another, to be morally guilty. They cannot transgress a Moral Rule; because they have not Reason by which they may conceive a Moral Rule. Mutual fear and conflicting desire cannot give rise to a Rule, when there

does not exist the Reason; which, presenting the objects of desire and fear under the general and abstract forms of conceptions, must supply the materials for a Rule. It is therefore not Fear and Desire, but Reason, which is the source of Moral Rules.

69. Moral Rules balance the repulsive tendencies of the Desires. The Desires, so far as they are desires of external objects in each person, tend to disunite men; for they make each person the sole centre of his own springs of action. Further, they tend to bring men into conflict and opposition; for two men desire the same field, the same house, the same wife. But there are also faculties which draw men together, as the Affections of Family and of Civil Society. The mutual understanding of men, expressed in Language, enables them and leads them to act in union, and to help each other. The objects of desire being assigned by general Rules, the repulsive influences are controlled, the attractive are confirmed in their effect. General Rules being established, the Desires are sources, not of opposition, but of agreement. All men sympathise with my Desire to keep my own; all men approve of General Rules, and of those who conform to them. The Reflex Sentiments strengthen this mutual attraction. The Desire to be approved, and the Desire to be esteemed, draw men together. These Sentiments, resulting from settled Moral Rules, remove discord, and establish concord. They tend to make men unanimous.

And, on the other hand, such Rules as tend to produce this effect, agree with that character of Moral Rules, which we have shown to belong to them. Such Rules, with regard to the Affections and Desires, as tend to control the repulsive, and confirm the attractive forces which operate in human Society; such as tend to unite men, to establish concord, unanimity, sympathy; agree with that which is the general character of Moral Rules. And as there is a

Universal Human Reason, common to all men, so far as it is unfolded, and to which each man's reason must conform; so is there a Universal Moral Sympathy, common to all men, so far as it is unfolded; a Conscience of mankind, to which each man's Conscience must conform.

But in order to arrive at such Moral Rules as we have spoken of, we must proceed by a series of several steps, and upon this course we now enter.

CHAPTER IV.

RIGHT, ADJECTIVE, AND *RIGHT*, SUBSTANTIVE

70. In order to establish Rules of human action we must consider more exactly the import of the terms *right* and *wrong*, which we have already used (56).

It has been said (18) that Rules of Action may direct actions to be performed as means to an end. Examples of such Rules are these: Be temperate, in order to be healthy: Labour, that you may gain money.

The adjective *right* signifies *conformable to Rule;* and is used with reference to the object of the Rule. To be temperate, is the *right* way to be healthy. To labour, is the *right* way to gain money.

In these cases the adjective right is used *relatively*; that is, relatively to the object of the Rule.

71. It has been said also (19) that we may have a Series of actions, each of which is a means to the next as an end. A man labours, that he may gain money: he wishes to gain money, that he may educate his children: he would educate his children, in order that they may prosper in the world.

In these cases, the inferior ends lead to higher ones, and derive their value from these. Each subordinate action aims at the end next above it, as a good (37). In the series of actions just mentioned, a man's gain is regarded as a good, because it tends to the education of his children. Education is considered as valuable, because it tends to prosperity.

And the Rules which prescribe such actions, derive their imperative force and validity, each from the Rule above it. The Superior Rule supplies a reason for the inferior. The Rule, *to labour*, derives its force from the Rule, *to seek gain:* this Rule receives its force (in the case we are considering) from the Rule, *to educate our children:* this again has for its reason, *to forward the prosperity of our children.*

72. But besides such Subordinate Rules, there must be a *Supreme Rule of Human Action.* For the succession of Means and Ends, with the corresponding series of subordinate and superior Rules, must somewhere terminate. And the inferior ends would have no value, as leading to the highest, except the highest end had a value of its own. The superior Rules could give no validity to the subordinate ones, except there were a Supreme Rule from which the validity of all of these were ultimately derived. Therefore there is a supreme rule of Human Action. That which is conformable to the Supreme Rule, is *absolutely right;* and is called *right,* simply, without relation to a special end. The opposite to right is *wrong.*

73. The Supreme Rule of Human Action may also be described by its Object.

The Object of the Supreme Rule of human action is spoken of as the *True End of human action, the Ultimate or Supreme Good,* the *Summum Bonum.*

74. There are various other ways of expressing the opposition of right and wrong, and the Supreme Rule of Human Action; namely, the Rule to

do what is right and to abstain from doing what is wrong. We say, we *ought* to do what is right; we *ought not* to do what is wrong. To do what is right is our ***Duty;*** to do what is wrong is a transgression, an offence; a violation of our Duty.

75. The question *Why?* respecting human actions, demands a reason, which may be given by a reference from a lower Rule to a higher. *Why* ought I to be frugal or industrious? In order that I may not want a maintenance. *Why* must I avoid want? Because I must seek to act independently. *Why* should I act independently? that I may act rightly.

Hence, with regard to the Supreme Rule, the question *Why?* admits of no further answer. Why must I do what is right? Because it *is* right. Why should I do what I ought? Because I ought. The Supreme Rule supplies a reason for that which it commands, by *being* the Supreme Rule.

76. Rightness and Wrongness are, as we have already said, the *Moral* qualities of actions. The rules which, in subordination to the Supreme Rule, determine what is right and what is wrong, are *Moral Rules*. The doctrine which treats of actions as right and wrong, is *Morality*.

77. Since, as we have seen (58), Moral Rules are necessary, according to the constitution of human nature; Man is necessarily a Moral Being.

78. We have now to establish Moral Rules; and for that purpose, we must consider in what kind of Terms they must be expressed. Among those Terms must be ***Rights;*** and Rights must exist, as we proceed to show.

Rules of human action must be expressed by means of words denoting those abstract and general Conceptions which include the principal objects of human desire and affection. And, in order that these Conceptions may regulate men's actions, they must be Conceptions of something which really exists among men. If they are not this, they cannot, by their operation, balance, moderate, check and direct the desires and affections which tend to really existing objects. For instance, my desire to possess what another has, may be checked and controlled by the Conception of *Property;* by my looking upon it as his Property. But this could not happen, if there were no such thing as Property. If Property had not been a reality among men, the Conception of it could never have had the power, which in human Society it constantly has had, to suppress or moderate the greater part of the acts to which the bodily desires, and the desire of having, would naturally impel men. In like manner, the Conceptions of Promises, of Contract, of Marriage, and the like, restrain or limit most of the acts to which the uncontrolled desires and affections would give rise. This must necessarily be, in order that Rules of action may operate upon men; but this could not be, if the things thus conceived did not really exist among men.

Further: the conceptions on which Rules of action depend must not only be realized among men, but their results must also be assigned and appropriated to particular men. The realities which are conceived as Property, as Personal Security, as Contract, as Marriage, must be attached to persons, and vested in them, as attributes or possessions. We must be able to conceive such things, as being one man's or another man's: as *my* property, *your* debt, *his* wife. Without this condition, the Rules of which we speak could not produce their effect of counteracting and balancing the Desires and Affections. For the Desires and Affections are tendencies to action residing in Persons. Each Person's Desires have a tendency to himself: the Affections have Persons for their objects; the Desires of things also give rise to Affections towards Persons. Since all these tendencies to action are thus directed to and from Persons, the

Rules of action, which balance these tendencies, must also point to Persons. My desire to take away what another man has, and my anger against him for withholding it from me, must be balanced by the thought that it is *his* Property. To use a mathematical image, the centres of the forces, attractive and repulsive, which we have termed Spings of Action, are in Persons; and therefore the Conceptions by which these forces are kept in equilibrium must also point to Persons.

The Rules of Action, being Moral Rules, must necessarily be subordinate to the Supreme Rule of human action: and combining this condition with the two others of which we have spoken, we are led to this conclusion: That in order that Moral Rules may exist, there must be abstract Conceptions, including the principal objects of human desire and affection; which abstract Conceptions must be Realities, vested in particular Persons as attributes or possessions, according to Rules subordinate to the Supreme Rule of Human Action.

But Abstractions vested in particular Persons, as possessions, by Rules subordinate to the Supreme Rule, are *Rights;* and our conclusion may be expressed by saying, That in order that Moral Rules may exist, Men must have Rights.

We have already given examples of Rights; such as a man's Right to his Personal Safety, to his Property, to his Debts, to his Wife. Without supposing the existence of such Rights, no Moral Rules can be given.

79. What has been said in general (65 and 78), to prove the necessary existence of Moral Rules, and therefore, of Rights, among men; may be further illustrated by considering, separately, the principal Springs of Action of which we have spoken; and especially the Mental Desires; for these include the Appetites and the Affections (49). It is evident that

the Desire of Personal Safety (39) requires that there should exist a Right of Personal Safety. Without such a Right, the Desire would give rise to a constant tempest of Anger and Fear, arising from the assaults, actual or apprehended, of other men. But a Right of Personal Safety, when actually established, holds in check the impulses which give rise to such assaults, and reduces the tempest to a calm. In this calm, man, free from extreme agitations of Fear and Anger, can act with a reference to Rules founded on other men's Rights; and can thus, and no otherwise, exercise his rational and moral nature. And in like manner, the Desire of Having requires that there should exist a Right of Property: for without the establishment of such a Right, the possession of any objects of desire would, in like manner, give rise to Fear and Anger; and to an agitation of men's minds, in which rational and moral action could not take place. But a Right of Property once established, there may be a state of repose, in which the Reason and the Moral Sentiments can act. Again, the Need of Mutual Understanding requires that a Right of Contract should exist. If no man could depend upon the actions of other men, every man's actions must be performed in a tumult of vague conjectures, hopes and fears, like the actions of a man when surrounding objects are whirled about him by shifting winds. Each man having no certainty as to what another man would do, Society must be dissolved by the repulsion of conflicting Desires and mutual Fears. But if the Right of Contract be established, so that one man can depend upon what another has contracted to do, as something certain; the mutual Fears are removed; the objects included in the Contracts, and the intentions of the Contractors, become stable things; and man can act with reference to fixed moral Rules, as his moral nature requires. Again, the Desire of Family Society requires the establishment of Family Rights; that is, of those peculiar Rights, respecting the Members of the Family, to which the Desires point. The Husband must have an exclusive Right to the Society of the Wife, as a Wife. The Father must have Rights over his Children, which other men have not. Without these ties, which bind Families together in a manner in some respects exclusive, ungoverned bodily Desire and irregular Affection would tend to transient and capricious unions of man and woman; and these would lead to storms of angry rivalry, and the pains of deserted affection. Moreover, on this supposition, the suffering mother and the starving child have no one to depend on: the child has no one to educate him; to introduce him into Human Society; to bring him acquainted with the Rules of Action of mankind; and thus to evoke his rational and moral nature. In the bosom of the Family, when its inclosure is protected by Family Rights, the woman and the child are sustained through seasons of helplessness, the desires of Family Society are gratified, and the moral nature of man is unfolded; and thus Family Rights necessarily exist.

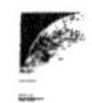

In the same manner, the Desire of Civil Society requires a peculiar Class of Rights, which we shall call the Rights of Government. For the actual establishment of Rights is the actual enforcement of Rules; and this requires that the office of enforcing Rules should be committed to some special body of men, as the guardians of the Rules. In order that Rights may really exist in a society, the Governors of the Society must have the Right of enforcing the Rules by which such Rights are defined. If such a Right be not vested in the Governors, other Rights, however they may be nominally acknowledged, do not really exist in the Society. If Personal Security and Property, and Contract, and Marriage be spoken of as actual realities; but if, notwithstanding this, the Right of Government to enforce the consequences of these realities be not upheld; there are, in fact, no real Rights in such a Society; and in proportion as the unreality of the Rights of Government becomes manifest, the Society loses its social character; and the moral character of man cannot find its sphere of action in such a condition.

80. There are other Rights, required by other Desires: but none of so primary and universal a character as those which I have now mentioned. The Desire of Knowledge requires Rights which, under the names of the right of Self Culture, the Right of Education, the Right of Freedom of Opinion, and the like, may come to be of importance, in the Stages of Society in which men's habits of thought are much developed; but which may be omitted in our primary system of Rights. The Desire of Superiority, as we have said (53), requires that men, in a Society, shall have their Rights assigned by equal Rules; and thus strengthens such Rights when they exist. The Reflex Sentiments have also, in some Stages of Society, their corresponding Rights. Thus, men have a Right to their Reputation allowed them in the Laws of many Societies.

But the primary and universal Rights of men are those five which we first enumerated: the Right of Personal Security; the Right of Property; the Right of Contract; Family Rights; and the Rights of Government.

81. The opposite of Rights are *Wrongs*. A man's Rights may be infringed, transgressed, violated, by the actions of other men. Thus, a man infringes my Right to Personal Safety by striking me; my Right to my Property, by stealing it; my Right to a Contracted Debt, by not paying me. He who thus violates a man's Rights, does him a *Wrong*.

The word *Injury* is also especially used to designate the infraction of a Right. This is sometimes used merely to express harm; but in correct language *harm* is distinguished from *wrong*, *damnum* from *injuria*.

82. It has been said that Rights must be Realities in human Society. Rights are made Realities in human Society by its conduct as a Society. The conceptions of personal security, property, contract, marriage, and the like, are realized among men by their actions. Men, existing in the condition of a Society, regulate their conduct by these conceptions: they appropriate to each his Rights: for the most part they respect each other's Rights; and they constrain, expel, or otherwise punish, those who by their actions contradict these realities, or disturb the appropriation of them. The appropriation of Rights is established and declared by *the Law;* or by Custom, which is Law expressed in actions instead of words; and the Law also gives Rights validity or reality, by assigning *Punishment* to those who violate them.

83. Punishment is itself a Reality, and thus gives reality to the Rights which Laws establish. The various forms of Punishment, constraint, bodily pain, loss of possessions, exile, death, are among the most common and palpable of the real things from which the human affections and desires recoil. And by the existence of Law, supported, when necessary, by Punishment, Personal Safety, Property, Contracts, Marriage, become things no less real than the most palpable objects of bodily desire. Through the reality of such things, human Society, instead of being a mere struggle of appetites, desires and affections, tending to and from different quarters, is a balanced system, governed by a coherent body of Rules. And all these Rules spring, not from Desire or Affection, which know nothing of Rules, or of the terms in which they are expressed: but from Reason, which, apprehending Rules, directs us to right actions, as those which are conformable to the Supreme Rules; and to Rights,

as the Terms in which subordinate Rules must be expressed.

84. From what has been said, it will be seen that the adjective *right* has a much wider signification than the substantive *Right*. Every thing is *right* which is conformable to the Supreme Rule of human action; but that only is *a Right* which, being conformable to the Supreme Rule, is realized in Society, and vested in a particular person. Hence the two words may often be properly opposed. We may say that a poor man has no Right to relief, but it is right he should have it. A rich man has a Right to destroy the harvest of his fields, but to do so would not be right.

85. To a Right, on one side, corresponds *an Obligation* on the other. If a man has a Right to my horse, I have an Obligation to let him have it. If a man has a Right to the fruit of a certain tree, all other persons are under an Obligation to abstain from appropriating it. Men are obliged to respect each other's Rights.

86. My Obligation is to give another man his Right; my Duty is to do what is right (74). Hence *Duty* is a wider term than *Obligation;* just as *right*, the adjective, is wider than *Right*, the substantive.

We have here fixed the term Obligation to a narrower sense than is sometimes given to it; but it will be found most convenient to use the word in the way just defined, according to which it is a correlative to *Right*. We shall also use the participle *obliged*, with the same limitation.

87. Hence there is a difference between *obliged* and *ought*. I *ought* to do my Duty; I am *obliged* to give a man his right. I am not *obliged* to relieve a distressed man, but I *ought* to do so. There are other phrases which are employed on such subjects. We speak of a man being *bound* in conscience to tell the truth, and *bound* in law to pay his debts. But

when the word *bound* is used simply, it more generally refers to Duty than to Obligation.

88. Duty has no correlative, as Obligation has the correlative Right. What it is our Duty to do, we must do because it is right, not because any one can demand it of us. We may, however, speak of those who are particularly benefited by our discharge of our Duties, as having a *Moral Claim* upon us. A distressed man has a Moral Claim to be relieved, in cases in which it is our Duty to relieve him.

89. The distinctions just explained are sometimes expressed by using the terms *Perfect Obligation* and *Imperfect Obligation* for *Obligation* and *Duty* respectively: and the terms *Perfect Right* and *Imperfect Right*, for *Right* and *Moral Claim* respectively. But these phrases have the inconvenience of making it seem as if our Duties arose from the Rights of others; and as if Duties were only legal Obligations, with an inferior degree of binding force.

We must treat of Rights before we treat of Duties; for as we have said (78), the terms which express Rights are necessarily employed in laying down Moral Rules. We must establish the Rights, and the Laws of Property, before we can lay down the Moral Rules, Do not steal, or Do not covet another man's property.

90. Hence before we treat of the Doctrine of Duties, which is Morality, we must treat of the Doctrine of Rights and Obligations.

There is no term in the English language which denotes the Doctrine of Rights and Obligations. In Latin, French and German, the same term which denotes a Right denotes also the Doctrine of Rights. Thus we say *Jus meum*, and *Studium Juris: mon Droit* and *l'étude du Droit: mein Recht*, and *die Kentniss des Rechts*. In English, we say *my Right, their Rights*, but we do not use the term in the other sense. Instead of this, we employ various phrases: thus *Jus*

Naturæ has sometimes been translated *The Law of Nature ;* sometimes, *The Rights of Nature, Natural Rights, Natural Justice.* But no one of these phrases fully expresses the Doctrine of Rights: for Rights are not Law only, nor Justice only; (meaning by Law the Law of Society, and by Justice, that which is right) they are both Law and Justice; Law because Justice; Justice expressed in Law.

Hence, when we have occasion to speak of the Doctrine of Rights and Obligations in a single word, we shall borrow the Latin term *Jus :* and by the adjective *jural,* we shall denote that which has reference to the Doctrine of Rights and Obligations; as by the adjective *moral* we denote that which has reference to the Doctrince of Duties. We have already in the English language several derivatives from the term *Jus* in the technical sense which we adopt: as *Jurist, Jurisprudence, Jurisdiction ;* so that the word need not sound strange in our ears. Jus is the study of the Jurist. The term *Jurisprudence* has sometimes been applied by English writers to describe the Doctrine of Rights and Obligations in general: but the corresponding Latin term is often written in separate words *Juris Prudentia,* a knowledge of Jus. It seems unreasonable and inconvenient to make the English name of this Doctrine so much more complex than its names in other languages. The word *Jus* is also implied in the word *Injury.* The words *just* and *Justice* are connected with the same root; but by these, we express moral, not merely jural, notions.

91. Rights, and the difference of right and wrong, being once brought into view, there are many terms both moral and jural, which can be explained by reference to those fundamental notions. *Duties,* are Actions, or Courses of Action, considered as being right. *Virtues* are the Habits of Mind by which we perform Duties. And *Virtue,* used generally,

includes all special Virtues; as *Duty* includes all special Duties. Virtue and Duty are the objects of our Moral Sentiments (55). We *approve* Duty, but we esteem and admire and *love* Virtue. Virtue is the natural object of Love, and is in this view called *Goodness.*

Actions which are opposite to right are *Violations* of Duties, *Transgressions, Offences.* As transgressions of Law, they are *Crimes.* They are of various degrees of *Guilt.* Some are *atrocious* or *heinous* Crimes: others are slighter Offences, more *excusable* and *pardonable.*

The transgression of a Duty, considered as a Habit, is a *Vice:* and *Vice* in general includes all special Vices.

The sentiment of disapproval of Offences or Vices admits of various modifications. Some vices are *hateful,* some, *despicable:* some render the perpetrator *odious,* some make him *contemptible.* Some things we more lightly *blame,* others we more strongly *condemn,* or look upon with *detestation* and *horror.*

92. The sentiments with which we regard Virtue and Vice, Virtues and Vices, Acts of Duty and Violations of Duty, are applied to the internal acts which determine the external action. Thus we speak of a *good intention,* a *laudable purpose,* a *vicious thought.*

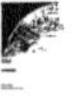

These Sentiments are extended also to the persons who perform the acts, external or internal. Men, as well as actions, are called on the one hand *good, virtuous, praiseworthy, admirable, excellent;* on the other hand *bad, vicious, blameable, abominable, wicked.* When men's actions are right, both they and their actions are *moral;* if the contrary, *immoral.*

Virtues and Vices have been spoken of as Habits: but they may also be considered as the results of the *Dispositions* and *Characters* of men. Considered as a Disposition, Vice is Depravity, or *Wickedness.*

93. The consideration of Virtue and Vice, with reference to Religion, will come before us in a succeeding part of this work. But we may here remark, that Virtue, which is conformable to the Supreme Law of our Nature, is the *Will of God*, the Author of our Nature. Hence, the Law of Duty is the Command of God.

Transgressions of Duty, considered as Offences against God, are *Sins*. God upholds the Law of Duty by Rewards and Punishments, which are assigned to the Souls of men.

94. Rights, as we have said (71), are established in Society by the Law; that is, in such Society by the Law of that Society. When this Law is not merely a Rule, tacitly understood and naturally growing into being, but expressly declared and really enforced, it is termed *Positive Law*, in distinction from *Natural Law*, or *the Law of Nature**. Society when it thus declares and enforces Laws, acts as a *State;* not merely as an assemblage of individuals, but as a Collective Agent. A State has an organization by which it acts. It has a Government, Tribunals, stated modes of action. It has Governors, Magistrates, Judges, Executive Officers, and all requisite provisions for the Administration of the Law. When need arises in consequence of men's actions, and transactions one with another, a man charged with a crime is apprehended; or of two persons who allege conflicting Rights, one institutes a Suit against the other. The case is brought before a Court or Tribunal, in which the Judge takes cognizance of such matters; and is tried. Evidence is adduced. Witnesses are heard. The accused man is found guilty; or is acquitted, if it do not appear that he is guilty. Between the two contending parties Judgment is

* It will afterwards appear that no Body of Definite Laws can be proved to be the Laws of Nature.

given. The Sentence of the Court is carried into effect. And thus, Rights are realized, and Remedies are provided for Wrongs.

CHAPTER V.

IMMUTABLE MORALITY AND MUTABLE LAW.

95. It has been stated (78) that Moral Rules must be expressed by reference to Men's Rights; and thus they necessarily depend upon Rights actually existing. Further, it has been stated (94) that Men's Actual Rights are determined by Positive Law; Men's Rights in each Community are determined by the Positive Law of that Community. But the Laws of different Communities are different; and the determination of Men's Rights by various States are various. Personal Security, Property, Contract, Marriage, are regulated by very different Rules in one State and in another. Private War, Slavery, Polygamy, Concubinage, have been permitted by the Laws of some States; and many other practices which are forbidden by our Laws. And it seems to follow from this, that Morality, which depends on the Laws, must prescribe different Rules, in the States in which such practices are permitted, and in those in which they are forbidden.

But on the other hand, we have shown (66) that Moral Rules exist necessarily; that they are necessary to the action of man as man; and that they result necessarily from the possession of Reason. From this it seems to follow, that Moral Rules must be necessary truths, flowing from the moral nature of man; and that therefore, like other necessary truths, they must be universal and unchangeable.

And accordingly, Moralists have constantly spoken of Morality as a body of fixed, immutable, universal Truths.

How are these two opposite doctrines to be reconciled?

96. They are thus reconciled. The *Conceptions* of the fundamental Rights of Men are universal, and flow necessarily from the Moral Nature of Man: the *Definitions* of these Rights are diverse, and are determined by the Laws of each State. The Conceptions of Personal Security, Security, Property, Contract, Family, exist everywhere; and man cannot be conceived to exist as a moral being, in a social condition, without them. The Rules by which Personal Safety, Property, Contract, Families are maintained and protected, are different in different Communities, and will differ according to the needs and purposes of each Community. The Rules of Morality are universal and immutable, so far as they are expressed in terms of these Conceptions in their general form: it is always our Duty to respect the Personal Safety, the Property, the Contracts, the Family Ties, of others. But if we go into those details of Law by which these conceptions are in different Communities differently defined, the Rules of Morality may differ. In one country the wayfarer may morally pluck the fruits of the earth as he passes, and in another he may not; because when so plucked, in one place they are, and in another they are not, the Property of him on whose field they grew. The Precept, *Do not steal*, is universal; the Law, *To pluck is to steal*, is partial.

97. All Truths include an Idea and a Fact. The Idea is derived from the mind within, the Fact from the world without. In the instance of Rights, of which we are now speaking, the Idea, or Conception of the Right, is supplied by our consciousness of our Moral Nature and its Conditions; the Fact, or

Definition of the Right, is supplied by the Law of the Society in which we live, and the train of events which have made that law what it is. The Moral Nature of Man is moulded into shape by the History of each Nation; and thus, though we have, in different places, different Laws, we have everywhere the same Morality.

98. The existence of Rights gives rise to a *Sentiment of Rights* and a *Sentiment of Wrongs*, which may be arranged with the Moral Sentiments among our Springs of Action. Rights, as we have seen, procure and secure to us the gratification of certain Desires and Affections. These gratifications become more important in our eyes, by being permanent and stable possessions; which we hold, not only without fear of interruption, but with the consent and sympathy of all mankind. And with this affection for our own Right, grows up an affection for Rights in general. We see with complacency and sympathy the manifestations of this regard for Rights in others. We recognize it as a sentiment which binds us to all men, and all men to us.

99. Also, Rights being established, Wrongs, the violations of these Rights, excite a stronger feeling than the mere privation or interruption of our gratifications. Rights, being assigned to each person by Rules to which the common Reason of mankind assents, we resent the violation of these Rights, not only as an assault upon an individual, but as an aggression upon all mankind. When we receive a Wrong, we know that we have with us the resentment of all our fellow-men, at the infraction of a Rule which all acknowledge. We entertain our resentful emotions with complacency; they become strengthened and rooted, by this conviction of general sympathy. The anger which we feel, is no longer the impulse of our own individual feelings: it is an affection of the common heart of mankind. We not only

entertain our wrath, we cling to it as something good, and admire it as something laudable. We deem our indignation to be virtuous.

100. This Sentiment of Wrongs, along with the Sentiment of Rights, operate powerfully in supporting Rights when they are once established, and in maintaining that peace and order of Society, which are the proper atmosphere of man's moral nature. For these sentiments give force and energy to the exertions with which men resist any violation of established Rules; and they fill with fear and shame those who know themselves to be violators of such Rules. The man who has Rights on his side, is bold and vigorous; the conscious wrong-doer is, by that very circumstance, deprived of courage and energy. Men will not willingly expose themselves to the indignation, as well as resistance and punishment, with which the perpetrators of Wrongs are received; and thus Rights are, for the most part, observed, and treated with respect.

101. These, which may be called *Jural Sentiments*, are the germs of Moral Sentiments, of a larger and deeper import. The sentiment of Indignation against Wrongs, when expanded and unfolded by habitual thought, leads us to the condemnation of all dispositions which tend to produce Wrongs. All such dispositions are disapproved of, as immoral. In like manner, the Sentiment of Rights, when extended and unfolded by the thoughts of what is due to others, as well as to ourselves, produces a Sentiment of Obligation, and hence a Sentiment of Duty, or, as it is often termed, a *Sense of Duty*. And this Sense of Duty, and Condemnation of immoral Dispositions, are important parts of our Moral Sentiments.

102. Man, recognizing Moral Rules as the necessary conditions of his being (66), and recognizing Punishment as a necessary means of giving reality to such Rules, (83), recognizes himself as liable to

Punishment for transgression of Moral Rules. Even before he learns what the consequences to himself of transgression will be, he knows that he is exposed to those consequences, whatever they may be. He must *answer* for his actions, when the demand is made by real authority; he is *responsible*. If his actions are condemned, the results of the condemnation fall upon him. On the other hand, if his actions are approved, the results of the approval belong to him. He *deserves* these results whatever they may be. And thus he has a *Sense of Responsibility* and a Sentiment of the *Merit* and *Demerit* of Actions.

103. When man has distinguished actions in general, according to their Moral Character, as good or bad; and has assigned to them Merit or Demerit; he must, in order to apply these distinctions, judge of particular actions, and determine to which moral class they belong. His judgments, both in the adoption of Moral Rules, and in the application of them to particular actions, must be formed by the use of his Reason. By the use of his Reason, dealing with all the elements of the human constitution within him, and the world without him, he is led to *Convictions*, both as to Rules and as to Facts; both as to what has been done, and by whom, and what is its Merit or Demerit.

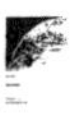

104. The Moral Sentiments are further unfolded and expanded by action, habit and thought. And this process is the *Moral Cultivation* or *Moral Education* of Man. This Cultivation and Education depend upon various conditions, and are promoted or extended by various causes. Among these, we may notice the influence of one man upon another, in affecting his Moral Sentiments, or the application of them to actions. We have already spoken of the influence exercised by the parents upon the child, in educing his moral nature (47). But in many other ways, as well as in this, men exercise an influence in

modifying each other's Moral Sentiments and Convictions. Men may, by speaking, by writing, by all the modes of the intercourse of life, direct the course of other men's thoughts; and thus affect their judgment of what is right and what is wrong, and their feelings with regard to actions and persons. And the exercise of such influence, by one man upon another, is an important kind of Action; and one for which the Agent is responsible, as well as for any actions which directly affect his primary Rights.

Rights are, as we have said, in every particular case, determined by actual Law and History. Before proceeding with Morality, we shall take some examples of such actual determinations.

BOOK II.

JUS.

OF RIGHTS AND OBLIGATIONS.

CHAPTER I.

RIGHTS IN GENERAL.

105. WE have seen (94) that Rights are defined by Positive Laws; but we have seen also, that according to the Conception of Rights (78), they are to be conformable to the Supreme Rule of human action. The Law assigns to each person his Rights; but the Law also aims at giving to each person what it is right he should have. That which is legally fixed, is also intended to be morally right. *Jus* has for its object to conform to the idea of Justice.

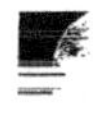

Hence it appears as if Law must depend upon Morality; whereas we have previously stated (90) that we must treat of Rights before we treat of Duties. We must explain this apparent inconsistency.

Law must be considered, in the first place, as positively and peremptorily fixed; it judges everything according to its own legal Rules and Definitions. But these Rules and Definitions may change from time to time; and in the course of the moral cultivation and education of man, of which we have spoken (104), do change. Men change their Rules, with the view of making them more nearly conformable to the

Supreme Rule of human action. They endeavour to determine Rights more rightly; to make Laws more just. And thus, for the moment, at any time, Morality depends upon Law; but in the long run, Law must be regulated by Morality. The Morality of the individual depends on his not violating the Law of his nation; but the National law must be framed according to the National view of Morality. The moral offence of coveting my neighbour's goods, as well as the crime of stealing, extends to everything which the Law determines to be his goods. But the Law which gives him everything, and leaves me to starve, may be an unjust Law; and if so, may be altered by the progress of time, and by the improved Morality of the legislative body.

106. Hence, in the first place, we must consider the Law as fixed and given; and this we shall do in the present Book. But even in presenting the Law under this aspect, we shall find indications of that moral aim, which, as we have said, the Law has. We shall often find expressions of the Legislator, or of the Jurists who comment upon the Law, which imply that they could not conceive a Law which did not aspire to be just. We shall find Reasons given for Laws, all of which depend upon the Supreme Reason for a Law, that it is right.

107. Of the Systems of Law actually established in the world, two especially deserve our notice, and may throw light upon our subject, if we follow them into some detail; namely, the System finally established in the ancient world, and the System actually established in our own country. The former Body of Law was that which prevailed when the whole civilized world was one single State; the latter is that which prevails in the State in which we live. I speak of the Roman Law, and the English Law. These two Systems of Law are those in which we are most interested, as past and present re-

alities. They are the Laws of two nations, both of them eminent for the clearness of their jural perceptions, and their vigorous habits of jural action. We may also take some examples of Laws from the Laws of the Jews; for these are of importance, in consequence of their antiquity, their authority, and their influence upon Christians. And for the reason just mentioned, we shall take into our review some of the Comments of Jurists, as well as the Decrees of Legislators.

108. In order conveniently to survey the legal Definitions of Rights, we must divide Rights into their kinds, and arrange them in order. The Division and Arrangement of Rights in different Codes, and different Jurists, have been various. We shall have before us the Division and Arrangement which are most suited to our purpose, if we take those Classes of Rights to which we have been led by our survey of the Springs of Human Action. Of these Classes, the principal are, as we have said (80), *the Rights of Personal Security, the Rights of Property, the Rights of Contract, the Rights of Marriage*, and *the Rights of Government*. To these we might add, as has been said, other Rights, arising from less simple and universal springs of action, as the Right of Freedom of Opinion, and the Right to Reputation. But these are less important; and we shall for the most part confine our attention to the *Five Principal Classes* of Rights which we have mentioned.

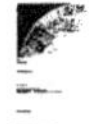

In the Roman and in the English Law, all the five Classes of Rights are, for the most part, clearly and fully established; and the same is the case in all communities, in which Law has made any considerable advance. In rude and turbulent conditions of Society, it may happen that some of these Rights are very imperfectly defined, and very precariously held; or it may be, that from a portion of the community some of them are withheld altogether. Thus, in countries where Slavery exists, the Slave has not the Rights of Personal Security. The constraint which Slavery implies, is of itself an entire violation of the Rights of Security. And the Slave is further liable to blows and wounds at the will of his master. He has no legal remedy for such inflictions, which would be Wrongs, if any Rights of the Person existed for him. And with the loss of this class of Rights he loses all. He can have no Property; for he can have nothing which his master may not take from him, using violence if other courses fail. He cannot Contract to do anything; for what he is to do, must depend on the Will of his master. He cannot even have the Rights of Marriage; for his master may at any time separate him from the sharer of his bed.

109. Thus, in such cases, we have an absence of all the Classes of Rights. Such cases are recognized in the Roman Law, for Slavery was one of the elements of Roman Society. One of the distinctions laid down as the basis of the Roman Code is, that all men are *Freemen* or *Slaves*. "Summa divisio de jure personarum hæc est, quod omnes homines aut liberi sunt aut servi*." But this state of things was afterwards altered, by the improved condition of the national morality. The steps of transition in the abolition of slavery are gradual. In many countries, there exist classes which, without being Slaves destitute of Rights, have Rights inferior in kind to the Classes above them. In many cases these inferior Classes are the successors of a vanquished race: for in ancient times, by the custom of nations, the conquered in war became the slaves or servants of the conquerors. The stages by which, from this condition, men pass to an equality of Rights, are generally connected with the Right of Property, and especially with the tenure of property in land. Thus, in many

* Inst. I. 3.

countries, in which the land is cultivated by *Serfs*, who are allowed to raise their own subsistence from the soil, but compelled also to labour for the Master to whom the land belongs, men are often *ascripti glebæ;* bought, sold, and inherited with the land: yet they are not slaves. They have a right to their own share of the produce; and, under favourable circumstances, pass by various gradations into the condition of Freemen; a change which is taking place extensively at present, in the state of the cultivators of Europe. Property in Land is a Right which exists in all States; yet in some States the Right of Property of individuals has been much limited. In some of the ancient Republics, as for instance Sparta, the land belonged in common to all the citizens. And in another form of Society, which prevailed in India, the Ryots or Cultivators generally occupied the land in common, and were collected in villages under officers who distributed to the cultivators and tradesmen their respective shares of the produce*. Out of the earlier forms of tenure of land, emerged the more complete Rights of Property of modern times; bearing traces however, in many respects, of their historical origin.

The Rights of Marriage are justly considered as essential to settled Society: and those who look back to the origins of things, speak of those men as the founders of Society, whose office it was to establish this institution: *concubitu prohibere vago*. Yet the female slave has been at the mercy of her master, wherever slavery has existed: polygamy has been a practice extensively prevalent, and has only gradually given way to more perfect forms of the Rights of Marriage.

110. It may be asked whether the Five Principal Classes of Rights, which we have mentioned, are entirely distinct; whether one Class does not run into

* Jones *On Rent*, p. 116.

another. Especially, it may be asked whether Contracts do not necessarily imply Property; for we contract to buy and sell our property; and whether Property be not merely a general tacit Contract that each shall have his share. To this we reply, that Contract is really distinct from Property: We contract for services, for bodily labour, for mental labour, for knowledge and intelligence, as in hiring a teacher, or combining in a literary work. It may perhaps be said, that a man's limbs, his knowledge, his intelligence, his mind, are his property: so that, in these cases also, Contract implies Property. But to speak thus, is to introduce a lax and fanciful use of words, which renders all exact expression and rigorous reasoning impossible. Such a use of words annihilates the fundamental distinction of Persons and Things; and is inconsistent with our previous reasonings, in which we established the existence of Rights. For the right of Property was shown to be necessary, by considering that man cannot act without some command of the external world, the world of material objects. By the nature of our arguments, we spoke of Property as something external, visible, tangible; or at furthest we included, (as we shall see,) only the inseparable appendages of such material Property. We cannot consider *knowledge* and *mind* as Property, without making *Property* cease to have any definite meaning at all. Hence Contract may exist where Property does not; the two Conceptions, and the corresponding Classes of Rights, are independent of each other.

Again: we reply, that Property cannot be said to depend upon tacit Contract, if we are to classify Rights at all. For Contract, as we now consider it, is the result of a Special Act; or at least of an Understanding founded on some distinct analogy. A Contract implies Language, or something equivalent to Language: Property does not imply the use of

Language, or any substitute for it. A tacit Contract, not understood from any special act, but, without any special ground, assumed as a universal fact among men, is not a Contract, in the sense in which we have used the term in our previous reasonings. Moreover, if we suppose the prevalent respect for the Right of Property to be founded upon a tacit general Contract, we must, for the like reasons, suppose the prevalent respect for the Rights of the Person, and for the Rights of Marriage, to be founded upon tacit general Contracts: and thus, all Rights would be identified with Rights of Contract. But such a use of terms would make all classification of Rights impossible. We must, therefore, make Contract a special and definite kind of Right: and if we do this, Property will be independent of Contract, and the corresponding Classes of Rights will be distinct from each other.

The Five Classes of Rights of which we have spoken do not occur, in that form, in the Roman Law. But we see in that Law indications which readily direct us to those Rights. The leading distinction of heads, in the Institutes of the Roman Law, is of Persons, Things, and Actions. *Omne jus quo utimur vel ad Personas pertinet, vel ad Res, vel ad Actiones**. Here *Actiones* means legal proceedings; but we may take the term as representing peculiarly the Class of Rights of Contract; for these derive their reality especially from the support of the judicial authority. The Second Book of Justinian's Institutes is mainly concerning Property, *De Rebus;* and the Third, concerning Contracts. Family Rights also are distinguished in the Institutes from the other Rights of Persons. Thus, in the First Book, the ninth and tenth Titles are, *De Patria Potestate* and *De Nuptiis*.

111. In both the Roman Law and the English

* Inst. I. 2.

Law, there is a distinction of Wrongs, as Private and Public Wrongs. For the Social order being established, in which respect for the Rights of all is commanded, those who transgress this respect, offend, not only against the particular persons whom they injure, but also against the State, the general protector of Rights. If one man violently beats or wounds another, he not only wrongs him, but violates the general order of Society. On the other hand, if one man claims another's field or house, he may do him wrong, but he puts forward his claim under the show of law and justice. The former is a Crime; a Public Wrong; and a Crime belongs to *Criminal Law*, and must be tried by Criminal Courts. The latter is a question of Private Rights, belonging to *Civil Law*, and to be decided by an Action or Suit, *Actio*. In England, the Office of the State as the guardian of Order, and of the Rights of all, is embodied in the person of the Sovereign. A person who commits violence, breaks *the King's Peace*.

Taking the Classes of Rights as we have stated them, we shall now notice some of the jural expressions and distinctions by which these Rights, and the corresponding Classes of Wrongs, have been practically carried into effect in particular circumstances.

CHAPTER II.

THE RIGHTS OF THE PERSON.

112. THE Rights of the Person are the Rights to Safety, Security, and Free Agency, which, as we have said (67), are requisite for the peace of Society, and the human and moral character of man's actions. These Rights are protected by the Laws, which pro-

hibit deeds of force and violence in general. But from the extreme of violence, the infliction of death, there is a gradation to slighter acts, which also are Wrongs or Injuries. The division of these *Wrongs against the Person* is very similar in the laws of most countries.

In the Laws given to the Jewish people, the primary Law upon this subject was the Command, *Thou shalt not kill:* and this Law was followed out by various Rules concerning *Smiting:* which are given in the Book of Exodus, chap. xxi. verse 12, and the following verses.

In the English Law, proceeding from *Homicide,* which is the highest crime against the Safety of the person, the following offences are treated of: *Maim;* (anciently *Mayhem,*) which is an injury depriving a man of the use of some bodily member: *Wounding;* which consists in giving a man some hurt with a weapon which breaks the skin: *Battery;* which is any, the least, Hurt or Violence unlawfully and wilfully done: *Assault;* which is an attempt to do such violence. *Threats* and Menaces, by which a man is put in bodily fear, are not punishable; but they may be the ground of compelling the person who uses them to give sureties that he will keep the peace.

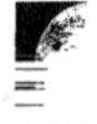

The least touching of another person wilfully or in anger is Battery: for the Law, as the Commentators upon it remark, cannot draw the lines between different lower degrees of violence, and therefore totally prohibits the lowest degree. In like manner among the Romans, the Cornelian Law, *De Injuriis,* prohibited *Pulsatio,* as well as *Verberatio:* distinguishing Verberation, which was accompanied with pain, from Pulsation which was not.

113. Besides the above, there are other Wrongs against the person, consisting in Violations of the Right of Personal Liberty. These come under the head of *False Imprisonment;* so called in opposition to *true*

Imprisonment, which is constraint put upon the person by the authority of the law.

To these offences may be added *Kidnapping*, the forcible abduction or stealing away of a man, woman, or child from their own country, and sending them into another. This offence was noticed also in the Jewish Law*: "He that stealeth a man and selleth him, or if he be found in his hand, he shall surely be put to death." So likewise in the Roman Law, *Plagium*, the offence of buying, selling, taking or keeping as a slave, a freeman, was severely punished. The *Plagiarius* was generally condemned to the mines.

114. The English Law also takes cognizance of injuries affecting a man's health, arising, not from Malice, but from neglect. Thus a remedy is given when a person is injured by selling him unwholesome provisions or wine; or by a neighbour's exercise of a noisome trade which infects the air. There is also a legal remedy given to a man for the neglect or unskilful management of his physician, surgeon, or apothecary, which is called *mala praxis*. The same is the course of the Roman Law†: *Imperitia culpæ adnumeratur: veluti si medicus curationem deliquerit, male quampiam secuerit, aut perperam ei medicamentum dederit.* The Injuries which are under our consideration, in this part of our work, are, for the most part, accompanied with Malice; but the physician's Indifference to his patient's health, and Disregard of the Trust reposed in him, are held by the Legislator to give to such damage, so inflicted, the character of Wrong, as well as Damage.

Malicious Intention is requisite to the notion of the Wrongs or Crimes here spoken of. But in the cases

* Exodus xxi. 16.

† *Inst.* IV. 3. Want of skill is accounted an offence; as in a case in which the physician leaves off his attendance on the patient while the cure is incomplete, or performs a surgical operation wrongly, or gives pernicious medicines.

which have just been mentioned, the Malicious Intention is inferred from the act itself. In all cases of personal damage inflicted, the law infers malicious intention, except there be some circumstances to excuse, mitigate, or justify the act.

115. Homicide is *excusable* when it is committed without intention; in the Law phrase, *by Misadventure, per infortunium;* as in the case mentioned in the Jewish Law*: *When a man goeth into the wood with his neighbour to hew wood, and his hand fetcheth a stroke with the axe to cut down the tree, and the head slippeth from the helve, and lighteth upon his neighbour that he die.* But though this is termed excusable Homicide, the Jewish Law did not protect the slayer till he had reached one of the Cities of Refuge; and the English Law levied a fine upon the delinquent, and made him forfeit the thing which was the instrument of death, under the name of a *Deodand.* The fine has been remitted at the suit of the person concerned as far back as our legal records reach; but the law of Deodand is still in force. These enactments seem to be intended to express the high value which the law sets upon human life; so that it always supposes some degree of blame in the conduct of him who takes away life, except by express permission of the Law itself.

116. In the same spirit, the Law does not generally allow Games, which may end in blood, to be received in justifications of homicide; as Tilting, Sword-playing, Boxing. And in general, if death ensue in consequence of idle, dangerous, and unlawful acts, as shooting, or casting stones in a town, the slayer is guilty of Manslaughter, and not of Misadventure only. But to show how much such distinctions depend upon the actual law, we may observe, that by the English Law, if the king command or

* Deut. xix. 5.

permit such diversions, and death ensue, it is only Misadventure. In like manner, by the Laws both of Athens and Rome, he who killed another in the Pancratium or Public games, authorized or permitted by the State, was not held guilty of Homicide*. *Si quis colluctatione, vel in pancratio, vel pugilis, dum inter se exercentur, alius alium occiderit, cessat Aquileia* (*Lex*), *quia gloriæ causâ et virtutis, non injuriæ gratia, videtur damnum datum.*

117. Homicide in Self-defence, *se defendendo,* upon a sudden affray, is excusable rather than justifiable by the English Law. When a man protects himself from assault in an unpremeditated quarrel, and kills him who assaults him, it is termed by the Law *chance-medley;* (or, as some choose to write it, *chaud medley;*) which signifies a *casual affray,* (or else an affray in the heat of blood, *chaude meslée*). This term is rightly applied, when the slayer engages in no struggle, except what is necessary for self-defence.

118. When Homicide results from sudden heat of passion, arising naturally from provocation, without an intention previously formed, it is in English Law termed *Manslaughter;* as when one person kills another in a sudden quarrel. For the Law pays, say the Commentators†, such regard to human frailty, as not to put hasty acts, and deliberate acts, on the same footing with regard to guilt. But in cases where homicide is committed upon provocation, if there be a sufficient cooling time, for passion to subside, and reason to interpose; and if the person so provoked afterwards kill the other, this is deliberate revenge, and not heat of blood, and amounts to murder.

119. *Murder* is Homicide committed with previous intention, which is termed *Malice prepense,* or *Malice aforethought.* This is the most atrocious of Crimes.

* Plato *Leg.* Lib. VII. *Dig.* ix. 2. 7. † Blackstone, IV. 191.

120. Homicide is *justifiable* by the Law of England when it is committed for the prevention of any forcible and atrocious crime. If a person attempts robbery or murder, or endeavours to break open a house in the night-time, and is killed in such attempt, the slayer is acquitted*. The Jewish Law had the like rules†: *If a thief be found breaking up, and be smitten that he die, there shall no blood be shed for him.* So also in the Roman Law: the Law of the Twelve Tables was, *Si nox (noctu) furtum faxit, sim (si eum) aliquis occisit (occiderit) juræ cæsus esto.* But there was, in this case, to be no attempt at secrecy on the part of the slayer; but, on the contrary, a loud appeal to any one within hearing ‡; *Lex* XII. *Tabularem furem noctu deprehensum occidere permittit, ut tamen id ipsum clamore testificatur.* In the day-time, the person attacked by a robber is allowed to put him to death if he cannot otherwise defend himself: but we are not, by the English law, allowed to kill any one in order to prevent a crime, if the crime be unaccompanied by violence. In this case, the law requires us to cause the offender to be legally apprehended and tried. So also the Jewish law, in the place already quoted§: *If the sun be risen upon him, there shall be blood shed for him, for he should make full restitution.* And the Roman Law is similar||: *Interdiu deprehen-*

* By the more modern decisions of law, the distinction of night and day is no longer noticed. The owner is now understood to be entitled to defend his own to the last extremity; subject to the condition of showing that *that* extremity was requisite for the defence.

† Exod. xxii. 2.

‡ *Dig.* ix. 2. 4. The Law of the Twelve Tables makes slaying a thief detected in the night to be allowable, provided the slayer call aloud on the occasion of the act.

§ Exodus xxii. 3.

|| *Dig.* ix. 2, 3. A thief detected by day may be slain if he defend himself with a weapon, and if, as before, the slayer call aloud. And if a man slay him who assaults him with a weapon

sum ita (lex) permittit occidere, si is se telo defendat, ut tamen æque cum clamore testificetur. And again: *Sed et si quemcunque alium ferro se petentem quis occiderit, non videbitur injuriâ occidisse; et si metu quis mortis furem occiderit. Sin autem cum possit adprehendere maluit occidere, magis est ut injuriâ fecisse videatur.*

121. The Laws of Solon*, and the proposed Laws of Plato†, agree with those already mentioned, in making a wide distinction between the modes of resistance permitted against the nocturnal and the diurnal thief. It has been discussed among Jurists‡, what is the ground of this difference. The reason which they assign is this: that the Law does not allow a man to be put to death by a private hand, on account of an expected loss for which the law can give redress; but only on account of danger to the person, which may be beyond redress; that therefore by day, when the person attacked can see the extent of his danger, he is justified only to the extent of his danger, and so far as the wrongs are of an irremediable kind: but that by night, when the unknown extent of the danger may lead him to believe it extreme, and when aid and testimony are difficult to obtain, he is justified to the extent of his fear. The Law is willing to accept such justification, because it cannot afford him redress any other way.

122. When a person commits acts of violence against another, having received extreme *Provocation*, but not being in danger, by the Law of England, the provocation *mitigates*, but does not justify the offence. The Mitigation is not available, if there have intervened time sufficient for the passions to cool: for if

it is justifiable; and if a man slay a robber, being in fear of his life. But if he was able to apprehend him, and chose rather to slay him, it is not justifiable.

* Demosth. adv. Timocrat. † *Legg.* Lib. ix.

‡ Grot. B. et P. II. i. 12

that be the case, the Law itself is ready to redress the injury. Hence, when two persons in cold blood meet and fight, any mischief done by one to the other cannot be excused by alleging previous Provocation. And thus, in the case of a Duel, in which the combatants take measures tending to destroy each other's lives, the Law has fixed the crime of Murder on them.

123. A person committing an act of violence may have others who assist or *abet* him, without their taking the same share in the act which he does himself. He is the *Principal*, they are the *Accessories*. And these are distinguished into Accessories before the Fact, as those who urge a man to commit murder, and provide him with arms; and Accessories after the Fact, as those who harbour the murderer, knowing the crime to have been committed. Some distinctions are made in the assignment of punishment to Principals and Accessories: but absence when the crime is committed is requisite to make a man an Accessory. Thus the seconds in a Duel are guilty of murder as Principals in the Second degree.

124. As we have said, the English Law does not allow Provocation to excuse acts of violence, except when there has been no time for passion to cool; and therefore does not acquit either of the combatants in a Duel on the ground of any provocation which he may have received. Yet the administration of the Law has often been so conducted, that it has seemed to recognize the Challenge as an excuse for the attempted Homicide. This inconsistency, between the letter and the practice of the Law, has, perhaps, in some measure, arisen out of the customs which prevailed in Europe some centuries ago, when Duels were permitted openly by Christian States; and the person who did not seek redress, by such means, against any expression of contempt or menace

utterred against him, incurred general blame and contempt as a coward.

125. Among the justifiable acts of violence, we may notice those which the Law not only permits, but authorizes and commands; as the Imprisonment of criminals, and their Punishment by stripes, wounds, maiming, exile, or death. But in such cases, nothing is allowable which the Law does not require. To kill the greatest of malefactors extra-judicially, that is, not according to the prescribed course of the administration of the Law, is Murder. Hence, if the judge who condemns, be not lawfully authorized to do so, he is guilty of murder. And the judgment must be executed by the proper Officer, for no one else is authorized by law to do it. The Judge may condemn, but must leave it to the Sheriff or his Deputy to execute the sentence. Even if the Officer alters the manner of execution, as if he beheads one adjudged to be hanged, it is murder.

126. Other cases in which Homicide is justifiable, because committed for the furtherance of the law, are these: when an officer, in the execution of his office, kills a person who resists him:—when prisoners assault the gaoler or officer, trying to escape, and he kills them:—when an assembly of persons (that is twelve, or more) has become riotous, and being required to disperse by the proper magistrates, refuse to do so. But it is added by the expositors of these laws, that there must be in such cases an apparent necessity on the officer's side in order to justify him. It must appear that the culprit could not be apprehended, the prisoner could not be kept in hold, the riot could not be suppressed in any other way.

127. There is another class of actions which may assume the aspect of infringements of the Rights of the Person, but which are justified in virtue of the Authority which the Law recognizes as residing in

the persons who commit the acts. According to the English Law, the Father has an authority over his Children which entitles him to strike or constrain them, under certain conditions. A Master has a like authority over his Apprentice, and a Schoolmaster over his Scholar. In these cases, it is justifiable to beat or confine the pupil in a moderate degree, in the way of *Chastisement* or *Correction*. In cases of voluntary service, the Employer is allowed to exercise constraint over the hired Servant or hired Labourer, in whose services he for the time obtains a Right. Thus, I prohibit my Servants from going out of my house except at stated times, and when I do not require their services. I have a Right to continued and active labour from the workmen whom I have hired.

128. In some countries, the Master has a legal Right to inflict stripes or other violence upon his Servant, the Landlord upon his Tenant, or one Class of the inhabitants upon another. In these cases the Class thus subjected possess in an imperfect degree the Rights of the Person. Such classes have been called by various names, in various ages and countries, according to their history and circumstances: as *Helots*, *Vassals*, *Serfs*; and when entirely divested of Rights, *Slaves*. We do not here inquire how far it is really consistent with justice and humanity that men should be thus partially or entirely deprived of Rights. But even when such classes legally exist, the Law limits the power of the Master over the Dependent. Some such Dependents can be sold with the land, but cannot de separated from it: they are *prædial* Slaves, *Serfs*, *Ascripti Glebæ*. Other Slaves may be sold off the land, and disposed of at the will of the Master. These may be kept in the house for menial services, as *domestic* Slaves; or employed in various labours for the Master's benefit and at his pleasure. Thus the ancient Greeks and Romans employed slaves as their Artisans.

The relations between Master and Servant, are thus connected with the relations between Landlord and Tenant; and thus point out to us a close connection between the Rights of the Person and the Rights of Property.

CHAPTER III.

THE RIGHTS OF PROPERTY.

129. As we have already said, the existence of the Right of Property is requisite as a condition of the Free Agency of man, and the Peace and Order of Society (79). Accordingly, in all Countries such Rights do exist. In every form of Society, there are circumstances under which the necessaries and comforts of life,—food, clothing, tools, arms—are held to belong to a man, so as to be *his Property*. The Rights of Property being established, the Sentiment of Rights and the Sentiment of Wrongs (98, 99) give great force and stability to the institution. We cling with strong and tenacious affection to what is our *own*. We earnestly approve the rule which makes it ours, and which consequently makes yours what is yours. A regard for the distinction of *meum* and *tuum* prevails. A reverence for Property is felt. The necessity of its existence, as a condition of human society, is generally perceived, and this perception gives force to the Rules by which Property is defined.

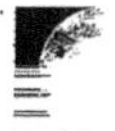

These Rules are, in each particular case, supplied by the Law of the Land. The Law determines what shall belong to one man, and what to another.

130. With regard to some Kinds of Property, when they are thus assigned, the Right of the *Pro-*

prietor or *Owner* shares itself in a distinct, visible form. The objects are taken hold of, carried about, used, consumed; as for instance, clothing, food, tools, arms. Things of this kind are *moveable Property.* Moreover, such Property may be retained by the Proprietor, or given by him to another person, at his pleasure. It may be given either absolutely, or on condition of receiving a return; that is, given in Barter or Exchange. Thus, Property leads to Exchange; and Exchange again leads to the establishment of some general Instrument and Measure of Exchangeable Value; that is, to the use of *Money.* The natural Measure of the Exchangeable Value of any objects is the labour of producing, or the difficulty of procuring the objects. Gold and Silver have been most commonly used as Money, because they are procured with a tolerable uniform degree of labour; because they perish very slowly when kept; and because they are easily divisible into definite portions.

131. When mankind have settled employments, and settled habits of intercourse, the natural Value in Exchange, either of these, or of any other objects, can never long differ from the Standard, or Measure, of which we have spoken; the labour of producing and difficulty of procuring them. For if the Exchangeable Value of any class of things were less, proportionally, than the Labour of producing them, men would turn themselves from this kind of Labour, to other employments, in which an equal Exchangeable Value might be obtained with less labour; and thus, the number of persons employed in producing this class of things being diminished, the difficulty of other persons procuring them from the producers would be increased, and the Exchangeable Value would rise. And in like manner, if the Exchangeable Value of any class of things were greater, proportionally, than the Labour of producing them, other

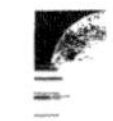

persons would turn themselves to this kind of Labour, and the value of the class of things would fall. Thus if the exchangeable value of gold and silver were greater than that of other objects, obtained with equal labour, men would turn their exertions to the collecting gold and silver, as the easiest way of obtaining the other objects of their desires. And though the intercourse of men, and their power of changing their employments, may not be so unfettered as to produce this result immediately; yet, in the long run, the Measure of Value in Exchange will be the amount of Labour employed in producing the objects.

132. But, besides Moveable Property, consisting of objects which the Proprietor can hold, remove, consume, or transfer in a manifest manner; there is Property of another kind, which cannot be removed or destroyed, or possessed in a visible manner; and which yet must be, and by the Laws of every Country is, vested in Proprietors. We speak now of *Property in Land*. It is requisite that such Property should be established; for in every Country, man subsists on the fruits of the Earth, or on animals which are supported by the Earth; and in order to live, he must have, on the face of the earth, his dwelling-place, and the source of his food and clothing; he must have his house and his field. In most countries, the earth does not supply man with what he needs, except by cultivation; and the *Cultivator* must be stimulated to perform his task, by having his portion of the fruits of his labour assigned to him as his Property. But whatever amount of Cultivation be necessary, the produce of the earth, and the soil itself, are, in every country, assigned to some class of *Landlords* as Property, or are assumed as Property by the State itself.

133. The assignation of Landed Property to its owners, as of all other Property, is defined and determined by the Law of the Land. But in Landed

Property, tne acts of Ownership are less obvious, natural and effective, than they are in other kinds of property; and therefore Property in Land is more peculiarly and manifestly determined and directed by the Law, than Property in Moveables.

The ancient Law of England treats Land as that *Thing* which is eminently and peculiarly the subject of Laws concerning Property, while all other Things are considered as only appendages to *Persons*. Hence, Land is termed *Real* Property; everything else is *Personal Property*.

134. In most countries, the Cultivators are a different class from the Proprietor of the Land; whether the Proprietor be another Class, or the State itself. The Rights of the Cultivator and of the Proprietor are determined by Law, or by Custom equivalent to Law, and are various in various countries. The share given by the Cultivator to the Proprietor is *Rent*. He who *holds* the land is the *Tenant*, in contradistinction to the Landlord, who owns it.

135. In the greater part of Asia*, the Sovereign is the sole Proprietor; and as such, receives a fixed portion (commonly one-fifth) of the produce from the Cultivator; who is, in India, called a *Ryot*. In Russia, and a great part of Germany, the Cultivator supports himself on a part of the Land; and pays a *Rent* to the Landlord in his *Labour*; being obliged, during a fixed portion of his time, (as for instance, during three days in the week,) to work in the cultivation of the Landlord's exclusive share: such Cultivators are *Serfs*. But these Labour-Rents sometimes became unlimited, and the Serf approached in condition to a Slave. In other parts of Europe, as in Greece, Italy, and France, in ancient and in modern times, the Cultivator has been supplied by the Landlord with the means of cultivation, and has paid to

* Jones *On Rent*.

him a fixed portion of the produce; generally one half. Hence such Cultivators are called *Coloni Partiarii, Coloni Medietarii, Metayers.* In a few spots on the Earth, of which England is an example, there are, between the Landlord and the labouring Cultivator, an intermediate class, the *Farmers;* who pay a *Money-Rent* to the Landlord, *Wages* to the Labourer, and have for themselves the whole produce obtained from the Land. The Farmer must be able to subsist the Labourer, while he is toiling so as to raise a future crop of produce: therefore he must possess a *Stock* or *Capital,* already accumulated. The amount of the produce which the Farmer has, after paying Rent, Wages, and other expenses, is the *Profits* of his Stock.

136. These various forms of the distribution of the wealth produced by the soil of each Country affect very greatly other Rights, as well as the Rights of Property (129). The Serf generally possesses in a very imperfect degree the Rights of the Person against his Lord; but against other persons, his Lord is supposed to afford him protection. In modern Europe, there prevailed, for several centuries, a system of Tenure of Land with such mutual Rights and obligations; namely, *the Feudal System.* According to this system, Land was held on the conditions of Protection from the Superior, and Service from the Inferior; and according to these conditions, a series of Persons, each subordinate to the one above him, had a modified Property in the Land. Each such person was the *Vassal* of the one above him, his *Superior Lord* or *Seignior.* Each Lord had a Right to certain Payments or Dues from his Vassals; and the Vassal, being marshalled as a Soldier under his Lord, was enabled to protect himself and others. The Land thus granted by a superior to an inferior was called a *Feud* or *Fee.* None of these Feuds or Fees was an absolute Property; all were held of the Sovereign,

at least in England. He was the only *Landlord*, and the highest Title of Ownership under the Feudal System was *Tenant in Fee Simple*. Besides Tenants of various kinds, there were mere Labourers who held no Fees, and were called *Villeins*. At first, this cultivator in England was precisely in the situation of the Russian Serf*. In the three centuries beginning from about A.D. 1300, the unlimited Labour-Rents paid by the English Villeins for the lands allotted them were gradually commuted for definite services, still payable to the Lord. Out of this grew a legal Right of some of the cultivators to the occupation of their Lands, which were registered in a list kept by the Lord. Hence these were called *Copyhold Tenures*, in distinction to the usual possession of the Soil by a freeman, which was a *Freehold Tenure*.

137. The relations which the Tenure of Landed Property establishes among different classes continue to influence the Laws, and still more the Forms of Law, in each country, long after their original force has been lost. Two hundred years have barely elapsed since the personal bondage of the Villein ceased to exist among us. Copyhold Tenures are still familiar. The Lord of the Manor, the representative of the Feudal Seignior, has still various Rights, due to him from Copyhold Tenants: as Heriots, payable on the death of the Tenant; Fines, payable when the Land is alienated by the Tenant to another person; the Rights of pursuing Game, which are reserved to the Lord of the Manor, even in Freeholds. And the phrases used in transferring Landed property still have many traces of the Feudal System.

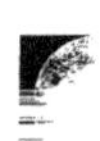

138. In like manner, in the Roman Law the conditions of Property and the modes of transferring it retained to a late period traces of the earlier modes of Tenure. In the earliest known stage of the Ro-

* Jones *On Rent*, p. 40.

man Law, Lands, with the Slaves and Cattle requisite for their cultivation, were transferred by a ceremonious form called *Mancipatio;* and the Quirites, or original Roman citizens, could not transfer ownership in any other way. Hence arose a division of *Res Mancipi,* things which could be thus transferred, and *Res nec Mancipi,* things which could not. But though a man could not acquire Quiritarian ownership or *Dominium,* without this process, he might have *possession* and *use* of a thing without such ownership; and the later jurists recognized this kind of Right. They say*, There is among foreigners only one kind of ownership (*dominium*), so that a man is either the owner of a thing, or he is not. And this was formerly the case among the Roman people; for a man was either the owner *ex jure Quiritium,* or he was not. But afterwards the ownership was split; so that now one man may be the Owner of a thing *ex jure Quiritium,* and yet another person may have it in his possession (*in bonis*). For instance, if in the case of a thing which is *res mancipi,* I do not transfer it to you by mancipatio, but merely deliver it to you, the thing indeed becomes your thing (*in bonis tuis*), but it will remain mine *ex jure Quiritium,* until by continued possession you have acquired a Right (*donec tu eam possidendo usucapias*). When that is complete, it is yours absolutely (*pleno jure*).

139. Upon the conditions of tenure of land, depend the *Title* or evidence of ownership; the modes of *Conveyance* or Transfer by Contract; the modes of *Succession* on the death of the Proprietor, whether by his *Testament,* or *ab intestato:* the judicial *Remedies* for Wrongs: and the like. A person's landed property so much determines his condition, that we commonly speak of his land as his *Estate.* The posses-

* Gaius II. 40, who lived in the time of the Antonines.

sion of a house, or habitation, is important to man in his social condition, not only as a means of shelter and bodily comfort, but also as giving him a fixed local position in the Community. By such possession, he is a *Householder;* and for many important purposes the State or City is considered as consisting of Householders. The place, neighbourhood, city, or country in which a person has his habitation, is his *Domicile* (*Domicilium*). A person's Domicile, for the most part, places him under the Laws of the State in which it is situated.

140. As Property in Land, and in the fruits produced by the cultivation of the Land, is established and realized by the Laws and Customs of each country; in like manner is established Property in other objects, which can be distributed and assigned to special persons; for instance, in flocks and herds, and their produce; in the produce of the interior of the earth, as mines; in all that we fabricate by fashioning into a new form the materials thus produced, —wood, stone, metal, and the parts of plants and of animals. With regard to all these, and other forms of material or corporeal Property, the Law in every Country recognizes certain modes of acquiring, possessing, and transferring them, as conferring Rights.

141. The Wrongs, or Injuries by which the Rights of Property are violated, are distinguished and classed by the Law according to their circumstances. The Command, *Thou shalt not steal,* is the basis of all Laws on this subject. The definition of *Stealing,* or *Larceny* (*Latrocinium*), in the English Law*, is "the felonious taking and carrying away the goods

* Blackstone, IV. 229. The more exact definition, by modern lawyers, of Theft is, a taking or removing of some Thing; being the Property of some other Person and of some value; without due Consent (to be separately defined); with intent to despoil the owner, and fraudulently appropriate the thing

of another." The definition of the Roman Law* was nearly the same. "Furtum est contrectatio fraudulosa, lucri faciendi causâ, vel ipsius rei, vel etiam ejus usus possessionisve." The English Law further distinguishes *privately Stealing*†, as for instance, picking the pocket; and open and violent Larceny, which is *Robbery;* this the Romam Law‡ calls *Bona vi rapta.* Another crime against property is *Burglary* (*Burgi Latrocinium*), or nocturnal Housebreaking; for the Law considers the crime if committed by night as much more heinous than the like act committed by day; as we have already seen that it makes a difference in the Right of self-defence in the two cases.

142. The crime of Theft, as above defined, includes only the cases in which the Thief touches and takes the material object: but besides these, a person may be despoiled of his property by *Fraud;* as for instance, when an Order to deliver goods is fabricated or forged by some one who has no Right to give such Order. This is *Forgery.* In the Roman Law§ it was *Crimen Falsi.* "Lex Cornelia *de falsis* pœnam irrogat ei qui testamentum aliudve instrumentum fal

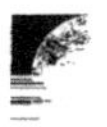

* *Instit.* IV.

† The distinction of privately stealing is now done away as an aggravation.

‡ *Dig.* XLVII. 8.

§ *Inst.* IV. 18. 7. "The Law of Forgery appoints a punishment for a man, if knowingly, and with fraudulent intent, he has written, sealed, recited, or substituted a testament or other instrument: or if he has, with like knowledge and intent, forged the signet of another person, by marking, or other way of expressing." The English Law is, "Whosoever by means of any false Seal, Signature, Stamp, Impression, or Mark, deceptively used to obtain undue credit, &c. or by means of any Machine, Instrument, or Thing, artfully contrived and fraudulently used for the purpose of Deception, or by the false and deceptive Use of any other Instrument or Thing by Sleight of Hand or other Device, or by any false Personation, shall cheat or defraud any other Person of any Property, shall incur Penalties," &c.

sum scripserit, signaverit, recitaverit, subjecerit; vel signum adulterinum fecerit, sculpserit, expresserit, sciens, dolo malo." We need not here attempt to enumerate the various forms of fraud and deception by which a person may be deprived of his property. They are all included in the term *Cheating*.

143. According to the English Law, Larceny applies only to moveable Property; for landed Property, by its nature, cannot be taken and carried away. And even of things that adhere to the Land, as Corn, Grass, Trees, and the like, no Larceny can be committed by the Common Law of England. The Severance of these from their roots is an Injury against the real Estate, which is termed a *Trespass*. But this state of the English Law has in several instances been altered in modern times*.

144. There are some further distinctions with regard to Property, which it may be useful to notice. According to the Roman Lawyers, the power of individuals over their property, which they termed *Dominium Vulgare*, was subject to the power which the State, or the Sovereign had, to prescribe the conditions on which they were to hold and enjoy their possessions: this power was *Dominium Eminens*. The State, which defines and establishes the Rights of the Owner, always limits those Rights; either by national maxims, as in Asiatic Empires, where the Sovereign is the Proprietor of the Soil; and in Feudal Kingdoms, where the King is the Sovereign Lord of every Fee; or by cases of public necessity and convenience; as when a man is compelled by the State to part with his house, that the street may be improved.

145. Again: besides Private Property, *Res*

* The ultimate conclusion at which English Lawyers have arrived on this subjest is, that it would be desirable to abolish the distinctions of the Law of Theft with regard to things severed and not severed from the reality. See *Act of Crimes and Punishments*, Chap. XVIII. Sect. 1. Art. 6.

Singulornm, the Roman Lawyers reckoned various kinds of Public Property; thus, among *Res Publicæ* are highways, streets, bridges, the walls and gates of a city; public gardens, grounds, fields and estates; markets, courts of justice; prisons; docks and harbours; fleets and their furniture, and the artillery, arms, and carriages of public armies; also the wealth of the public Treasury; and many other kinds of property, according to the various institutions and modes of administration of different states.

146. There are other things, which are common in their use, hence called *Res Communes;* but incapable of being appropriated, hence also called *Res Nullius;* as air, running water, the sea, the shore. These can be used by each person without any hurt or loss to other persons, and are hence said to be things *quorum innoxia est utilitas.* Yet these are not, in all cases, reckoned *Res Nullius.* States claim a property in their navigable rivers, and even in the sea near their shores. And by the English Law, although a person can have no property in running water, he may possess as property a lake or river, under the designation of "so many acres of ground covered with water." He may also have a property in the *use* of running water; but this belongs to property of another kind, which we must now notice.

147. Private property is *corporeal* or *incorporeal.* Corporeal property is such as we have mentioned, both moveable and immoveable: the immoveable being lands, houses, mines, and the like. But besides these kinds of property, a man may have a property in the *Use* of land or its adjuncts. This is the case, for instance, when a man has a Right of way over another's land; or has a water-mill, of which the water flows through another's estate: for he has a Right to the flow of the water; and the owner of the other estate is not allowed to stop or turn aside

the stream which drives the mill. Such Limitations of the Propritor's Right, by the Right of another to some use of the property, arising from neighbourhood (*vicinage*), or other relations, are called in the Roman Law, *Servitutes*, Servitudes or Services; and are treated with great detail and distinctness by the Roman Lawyers. Such Property is termed by English Lawyers *incorporeal* Property. Servitudes of a Property for the convenience of a neighbouring property are called in English Law, *Easements*.

148. The Feudal System in England gave to the Tenant an ownership charged with several *Services*, as homage, ward, marriage, relief, and (in the principal Tenures) with the Service of following the Lord to the wars. As wars became of less consequence in the internal condition of the nation, and property of more, this kind of Tenure became very burdensome: and at length, at the Restoration of Charles the Second, all these *Military Tenures*, as they were called, were abolished; and were reduced by Act of Parliament to the Tenures which were called *Free Socage*, and *Freehold*. This implies a Tenure by certain and determinate services of no degrading kind. Yet even freehold Proprietors still owe certain Services to the *Lord of the Manor*, who now stands in the place of the Feudal Lord. Services, due from land, and other kinds of Incorporeal Property, are capable of being inherited, and are termed in English Law, *Incorporeal Hereditaments*. Such incorporeal property must necessarily be an adjunct to corporeal property: it must have a corporeal subject, land, or something else, in which it inheres. For Property is of the nature of a Thing (45).

149. There are some things, with regard to which the Definition of Law, as to whether they are private property or common things, are very various. Tame animals, *animalia domitæ naturæ*, as horses,

cattle, and sheep, are the subjects of direct Property. But wild animals, *animalia feræ naturæ*, as fish, and several kinds of birds which are not housed or domesticated, do, by the Roman Law, cease to be our property as soon as they go away from us. Wild birds and wild beasts, when they quit my land, cease to be my property; and even while they continue there, are mine only by the Right which I have of pursuing them. The Roman Law gives a Right of taking such creatures, even in another man's land. "Occupanti conceditur: nec interest, quod ad feras bestias et volucres attinet, utrum in suo fundo aliquis capiat an in alieno." The Jurists appear to have given such Rules, from a wish to exemplify their doctrine, that there are things which become property by the act of taking them. Such a Rule would be very inconvenient in a well cultivated country. Accordingly, later commentators (as Heineccius) add "modo non prohibeamur ingressu fundi a domino." By the ancient law of England the Game, so long as it is on the land, belongs to the owner of the land *rationi sole.* But this state of the Right was interfered with by royal and other privileges. A *license* from the State was required to kill game; and at one period, none were allowed to do so without the *qualification* of possessing certain property. The Right of taking the game still remains, in many instances, not a Property commonly transferred with the land, but a service under the control of the Lord of the Manor; and in our Game Laws, we have a laborious system of Enactments for the purpose of protecting this Right.

150. The property of things which have no apparent owner, ἀδέσποτα, has been variously assigned by the Laws of various Countries: such things, for instance, as Treasure found by accident, which is called in the English Law *Treasure Trove*, and is given to the King, or the Person to whom he grants it. Another instance is, land left dry by some alteration in

the course of a river. The Roman lawyers laid down various Rules according to which they assigned this land to the Proprietors of the adjacent banks. More modern writers give it to the State*.

151. In like manner, the Law determines what length of time of undisturbed possession or enjoyment of things is to be considered as conferring the Right of Property. In the early Roman Law this mode of acquiring the Right of Property is termed *Usucapio*. Gaius† says, "Usucapio mobilium quidem rerum anno completur; fundi vero et ædium biennio; et ita Cap. XII. tabularum cautum est." And he gives the reason for this‡: "Quod ideo receptum videtur ne rerum dominia diutius in incerto essent: cum sufficerit domino ad inquirendam rem suam anni aut biennii spatium." But this refers to the formalities of the Roman Law in its early stages. The more general term for this mode of acquiring a Right by lapse of time was *Præscriptio*, or *Temporis Præscriptio*. This is regulated by various laws; for instance§: "Præscriptione bona fide possidentes adversus præsentes annorum decem, absentes autem viginti muniuntur." In the English Law, Prescription is made a valid source of Right by the Statutes of Limitation, that is, Acts of Parliament which limit the time within which actions for Wrongs may be brought. The period of unquestioned possession which establishes a Right is in different cases, sixty, fifty, thirty and twenty years||: And the Commentators state that the reason of these

* Grot. B. et P. II. 8. 8. † Gaius, II. 42.

‡ Id. II. 44. Prescription in moveables is established by a year's possession; in land and house by two years. Which seems to have been made the rule in order that the ownership of property might not be longer uncertain. For one or two years was time sufficient for the owner to ascertain his property.

§ Cod. VIII. 35. 7.

|| Blackstone, III. 307. The last Statute of Limitations assigns twenty years as the period for land; and various periods from six years downwards are fixed as to personal actions.

Statutes of Limitations is to preserve the peace of the kingdom, and to prevent the frauds which might ensue, if a man were allowed to bring an action for any injury committed at any distance of time. To this effect, they quote the maxim of the jurists*: "Interest reipublicæ ut sit finis litium."

152. Besides the ownership of a thing, by which a person is entitled to use it, there are cases in which a person is recognized as the owner by law, and yet bound to give to another the advantage of the use of a property. Property so committed to a person is called in Latin, *fidei commissum*, in English, a *Trust:* the person to whom it is committed is *fidei commissarius*, a *Trustee*. A Trustee possesses and administers property for the benefit of others; generally, on certain conditions and according to certain rules.

153. The Right of Moveables generally implies a *Right of Alienation;* that is, of transferring them to another, by Gift, Sale, or Barter. The Right to Immoveables does not so universally imply a Right of Alienation; for the *Dominium Eminens* (144) of the State or the Sovereign may come in, and may prohibit or limit such a transfer. Thus a Feudal Tenant could not alienate his Fee to another Person. The Fee must be granted by the Lord only.

154. Again; the State regulates, by special Laws and Customs, the *Succession of Property;* that is, the disposal of a man's property after his death, whether moveable or immoveable. It determines whether he shall have the power of disposing of the whole, or of part, by his *Will* and *Testament*. And if the man die *intestate*, the Law determines in what manner his property shall be assigned to the members of his family, or to other persons. In some States, as in ancient Rome, the property was equally divided

* It is for the public good that there be an end to lawsuits.

among the children; in others, as in England, there is a *Law of Primogeniture*, by which a larger portion, or the whole (so far as landed property is concerned), is given to the eldest son. Such differences depend upon the different views of the relations of Families, and their Property, to the State, which prevail in different times and Countries.

155. To give, or alienate Property, some external act is requisite; for we are now speaking of Laws which deal with external acts. The Law must define what *Act*, (including words in the term *Acts*) shall constitute giving or alienating. It must determine, for instance, whether *Words of Transfer* be sufficient for this purpose; and if so, with what publicity they must be uttered, in order to be valid; or whether some *Act of Delivery* be also requisite. The latter was the case in the Roman and in the English Law; at least in the most formal kinds of transfer.

Also an *Act of Acceptance* on the other part is requisite; for it would be intolerable that a person should, without my consent, have the power of giving me what might be in the highest degree burdensome or troublesome; as if he were to give me a wild beast. And the act of acceptance must also be defined by Law.

156. Questions have been discussed among Jurists as to the Rule which is to be followed when the Right of Property comes in conflict with the Needs of Personal Safety. For instance; When, in a ship, the common stock of provisions fails, is it allowable for the Passengers to use that which belongs to one of them in spite of his will? When a fire is raging in a town, is it allowable, in order to stop it, to pull down a house without consent of the owner? When a ship runs foul of the cables of other ships, is it allowable for the captain to cut these cables if his ship cannot otherwise be extricated?

In such cases, it has been decided by the Roman

Law, and its Commentators, that the Right of Property must give way. Necessity, they say*, overrules all Laws. But this is to be required only in extreme cases, and when all other courses fail. To which is added, by most Jurists, that when it is possible, restitution is to be made for the damage committed. A like Rule is recognized in the English Law†.

It has been held by some English Lawyers, that a starving man may justifiably take food; but others deny that such necessity gives a Right; inasmuch as the poor are otherwise provided for by Law‡.

CHAPTER IV.

THE RIGHTS OF CONTRACT.

157. We have already (50) spoken of the necessity of mutual understanding and mutual dependence among men; and the consequent necessity of the fulfilment of Promises, as one of the principal bonds of Society. The necessity of depending upon assurances made by other men, gives birth to a Right in the person to whom the assurances are made. A person has, under due conditions, a Right to the fulfilment of a promise. The Law realizes this Right, and must therefore define the conditions. The mutual assurances, which the Law undertakes to enforce, are called *Contracts*. In the language of the Roman Law, the Judge is made to say§, "Pacta Conventa quæ

* Grot. II. 2. 6. 4. † Kent's *Commentaries*, II. 338.
‡ Bl. IV. 32.

§ *Dig.* II. 14, 17. I will enforce Pacts and Contracts which are made in conformity with the Laws, the Decrees of the People and of the Senate, the edicts of the Emperor, in good faith, and with no fraudulent design.

neque dolo malo, neque adversus leges, plebiscita, Senatus consulta, edicta Principum, neque quo fraus cui rerum fiat, facta erunt, servabo.

158. The Law, which enforces Contracts, must determine what Promises are valid Contracts. To show the necessity of recurring to actual Law on this subject, we may remark how vague, arbitrary, and inconvenient are the maxims on this point, which Jurists have attempted to draw from the nature of the case. Thus it has been asserted*, that of the three ways of speaking of the future: *I intend to give you: I shall give you: I promise you:* the two former do not give a Right to the person addressed; but the third does. It is evident that this distinction is as arbitrary as any merely legal one can be: and if such rules are arbitrary, they must be established as a matter of fact, not of reasoning: that is, they must be established by actual Laws.

159. But according to the Roman Law, even the last formula, *I promise you,* did not convey a Right. It was called a bare Promise, *Nudum Pactum;* as not being clothed with the circumstances of mutual advantage and formal act, which are requisite to a valid engagement.

In thus refusing to recognize a bare Promise as creating a Right, the Law proceeds with a due regard to the gravity of Rights. Relations so important must be brought into being only by acts of a calm and deliberate kind. If a verbal promise, however hasty, informal, and destitute of reasonable motive, were to be sanctioned as creating a Right, the Law must carry into effect the most extravagant proposals of gamesters; as for instance, when a man stakes the whole of his fortune on the turn of a die: for the meaning of such an act is, "I promise to give you so much, if the cast is so." But the Law, whose pur-

* Grot. B. et P. II. 11. 2.

pose is to produce and maintain a moral and social condition of man, in which human actions are deliberate, rational and coherent, refuses its sanction and aid to such rash, irrational, and incoherent proceedings.

Hence the Roman Law rejects Contracts in which there is no *Cause* or *Consideration**: "Cum nulla subest causa propter conventionem, hic constat constitere non posse obligationem. Igitur nuda pactio obligationem non facit." And the same is the case in the English Law: in which a Contract is defined†, "An agreement of two or more persons, upon sufficient *Consideration*, to do or not to do a particular thing:" and the consideration is necessary to the validity of the Contract.

160. The Law, though it requires a Consideration on each side as a Contract, does not undertake to provide an equality of advantage to both; but is contented with any degree of reciprocity, leaving the force of the Consideration to be weighed by the contracting parties. Thus money paid is a valuable consideration: but a good consideration also is that of blood, or of natural love and affection, when a man grants an estate to a poor relation on motives of generosity, prudence, and natural duty‡. And as a Consideration is made necessary by the Law, in order to avoid the inconvenience of giving legal force to mere verbal promises, the Contract may be made in so solemn a manner that the Law will suppose a Consideration, though it be not expressed. This is the case in the English Law, when a man executes a bond under his seal.

On the other hand, the Law will not recognize a Contract for which the Consideration is an illegal

* *Dig.* II. 14. 7. When there is no reason for the contract, there can be no obligation. Hence a nude pact does not establish an obligation.

† Bl. II. 445.

‡ Bl. II. 297

act. Thus the Roman Law*: "Pacta quæ causam turpem habent non sunt servanda." And the English Law† recognizes a number of cases of this kind, as annulling Contracts.

161. *Contracts* are *void* also when made under violence and constraint. In such cases the person so constrained and compelled is, in the language of the Law, in *Duress* (*Durities*). The Law also recognizes *Durities per minas*, *Fear* arising from threats, as a circumstance which invalidates a contract made under its influence. But this fear must be of a serious kind; fear of loss of life, or of limb; and this upon sufficient reason; or, as an ancient English Law-writer expresses it‡, "Non suspicio cujuslibet vani et meticulosi hominis, sed talis quæ possit cadere in hominem constantem." A fear of being beaten, though ever so well grounded, is no duress; neither is the fear of having one's house burned, or one's goods taken away or destroyed; because, in these cases, a man may obtain redress; but no sufficient compensation can be made for loss of life or limb.

162. Contracts are also void, from the want of that free agency which the law requires, when the deficiency arises, not from violence or threats, but from the condition of the party as to age or understanding. Persons under the legal full age, called *Minors* or *Infants* by the Law, cannot make a valid Contract. By the English Law the *Wife* also is incapable of binding herself by Contract; her interests being supposed to be so inseparably bound up with those of her Husband, that she cannot act indepen-

* *Dig.* II. 14, 17. Pacts for a shameful consideration are not to be enforced.

† Kent's *Com.* II. 466.

‡ Bracton. quoted Blackst. II. 131. Not the suspicion of a light-minded and timorous person, but such as may fall upon a man of firm mind.

dently of him. A Contract made by a person not having the use of Reason, *non compos mentis*, is void. The Contracts of *Lunatics* are void from the time when the Lunacy commences. It has also been settled by the English Law*, that a contract made by a man in a state of intoxication, if his state be such that he do not know the Consequences of his conduct, is void. Imbecility of Mind is not sufficient to set aside a Contract, when there is not an essential privation of Reason, or an incapacity of understanding and acting in the common affairs of life.

163. Contracts may be rendered void by *Deception* or *Fraud* practised on one side; but it is a matter of no small difficulty to lay down consistent Rules on this subject. The Roman Law, as we have seen (157), does not enforce Contracts which are made *dolo malo*. And this is further explained in the same place†: "Dolus malus fit calliditate et fallaciâ. Dolo malo pactum fit quoties circumscribendi alterius causâ aliud agitur et aliud agi simulatur." But it is easier to lay down Rules on this subject when Contracts have been distinguished into different kinds.

164. The Roman Jurists have divided Contracts, according to the Consideration, into four Kinds, expressed by the four Formulæ: *Do ut des; Facio ut facias; Facio ut des; Do ut Facias.* The First includes Contracts of *Buying and Selling*, of Barter or Exchange, and Loans of Money: the Second includes Contracts of *Commission*, Partnership, and the like: the Third includes Contracts of *Hiring and Service*, as when a Servant or Workman engages to work for certain wages: the Fourth is the Counterpart of the Third, when one person Contracts to pay the other who serves or works.

* Kent, II. 151.

† *Dig.* II. 14, 17. Fraud is the use of trick and deception. A pact is fraudulent when, for the purpose of circumventing some person, one thing is done and another simulated to be done.

165. The most common of these Contracts, in which there are familiar names for the correlative acts; *Buying* and *Selling;* a *Commission given* and *taken;* *Letting* and *Hiring;—Venditio et Emptio, Mandatum, Locatio et Conductio;* the Roman Jurists termed Contractus *Nominati*; all others, as Barter, were Contractus *Innominati;* and they laid down different Rules for the two Classes.

Thus a *Sale* was valid, as soon as the price was agreed upon; *re integrâ,* that is, before payment or delivery. But in the innominate Contracts, *re integrâ,* the parties were allowed to retract. This difference was founded in the greater frequency and familiarity of the nominate Contracts, which made deliberation less necessary, and delay more inconvenient. But in Sales, in order to remove any doubt which might arise, as to whether the Sale was completed, the practice was sometimes adopted of giving *Arrha, Earnest,* a portion of the price; which, however small, made the Contract binding. Among the Northern Nations, shaking the parties' hands together had this efficacy; and a sale thus made was called *handsale;* whence *handsel* was also used for the earnest of the price*. In the same manner a *symbolical delivery* of the goods was introduced: as for instance, the delivery of the key of the warehouse in which they were contained.

166. Borrowing and Lending is a Contract, in which the Romans distinguished two different cases, which we confound under one term. *Mutuum* was applied to the lending of those things which are reckoned by number, weight, and measure; as wine, oil, corn, coined money, of which the borrower receives a stated quantity which he may use, consume, or part with. *Commodatum* was that which was lent, to be restored identically the same; as a book, a harp, a

* Blackstone, II. 448.

horse. And the Law made a distinction in the responsibility of the borrower in these two cases. The person who had received a thing as *commodatum*, was bound indeed to keep it with as much care as if it were his own, or with more, if more were possible: yet if it were lost or destroyed by no fault of his, he was not bound to make compensation. But if he had received a thing as *mutuum*, it was to be repaid at any rate, in whatever way it had been consumed or lost*. Paley† calls *commodatum, inconsumable property*. The other kind, *consumable property*, is also termed *Res fungibiles* by the Roman Law; for one portion can discharge the office of another. "Res ejus generis functionem recipere dicuntur; id est, restitui posse per quod genere idem est‡."

167. Besides the Hiring of Labour, *Locatio Operis faciendi*, there is *Locatio Rei*, the Letting of a Thing to hire, as letting a house. In this case, also, the Hirer is bound to ordinary care and diligence, and is answerable for neglect: but the extent of his Obligations, as to Repairs and Expenses, must be settled by Express Rules of Law or Custom§.

168. When the Obligation of one party to pay Money to the other is established, and not yet performed, the money to be paid is a *Debt*, due from the Debtor to the *Creditor*. Hence Debt may arise out of any of the above kinds of Contract, as Sale, Hiring, and the like.

169. Among many forms of Debt, we may no-

* *Inst.* III. 15. The principle of the distinction by which *mutuum* and *commodatum* are opposed, as to liability of risk in the case of loss, is the principle of ownership: *Res perit domino*, in case of innocent loss, is a universal rule. In *mutuum* the property is transferred to the Borrower: in *commodatum* it remains with the Lender. Therefore the loss in the first case falls on the Borrower, in the second on the Lender.

† *Moral Phil.* B. III. c. 3.

‡ Grot. B. et P. II. 10. 13.

§ Sir W. Jones, *On Bailment*, classes the scale of liabilities.

tice those recorded in writing: thus, when I write, *I promise to pay to A. B. one pound,* I acknowledge myself indebted to A. B. to the amount of one pound. When I write to M. N., *Pay to A. B. one pound,* and M. N. does this, I make myself indebted to M. N. one pound, which is to be afterwards reckoned between M. N. and me. Documents of the former kind are *Promissory Notes;* those of the latter kind are *Bills of Exchange.* These Documents may be transferred from hand to hand, and may, with them, transfer the Debt. This may be done by making them payable to A. B. *or Bearer;* or by their being *indorsed* by A. B. when he transfers them to C; by C when he transfers them to another; and so on. Bills and Notes thus transferable, and still unpaid, may answer the purpose of Money; they may constitute a *Paper-Money.*

170. Other kinds of *Deposits,* on express or implied Contract, are enumerated in the Roman Law: as *Pignus,* a *Pledge,* or *Pawn* for a Debt; *Depositum,* a Deposit without Reward. Delivery of Goods from one person to another on trust is called by the English Lawyers *Bailment**, and the Goods are said to be *bailed* to him who receives them.

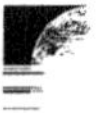

171. With regard to Contracts of Sale, Questions occur, How far the Seller is obliged to make good the *Title* (135) to the thing sold: How far he is responsible for its quality: How far, in making the bargain, he is bound to disclose all circumstances which may affect the price.

With regard to the Title, by the Roman Law† the Seller was responsible, "Sive tota res evincatur sive pars, habet regressum emptor in venditorem‡." The same is the case in the English Law: a fair price implies warranty of Title§.

* See note §, p. 121. † *Dig.* XXI. 2. 1.

‡ If it be proved that the Title is bad, either for the whole or part, the Buyer has his remedy against the Seller.

§ Kent, *Com.* II. 478.

As to the Quality of the goods sold, the Seller is not responsible, when they can be judged by the Purchaser's own discretion. The rule then is *Caveat emptor*. If goods ordered, be found not to correspond with the order, the Purchaser is required immediately to return them to the Vendor, or give him notice to take them back: otherwise he is presumed to acquiesce in the result.

172. The Obligation of disclosing the circumstances which affect the price of a thing sold, has been a matter of great discussion among Jurists and Moralists. Cicero* states such a case. A merchant of Alexandria brings a supply of corn to Rhodes in a time of great scarcity and dearth. He knows that many other merchant-vessels laden with corn are also on their way to Rhodes, which the Rhodians do not know. Is he bound to disclose this circumstance? As a matter of legal obligation, which is the point now under consideration, it is agreed that the seller is forbidden to misrepresent the intrinsic qualities of his wares. But it is pronounced that he is not obliged to disclose all extraneous circumstances which may affect their value†. "Venditorem, quatenus jure civile constitutum est, dicere vitia oportere; cætera sine insidiis agere; at, quoniam vendat, velle quam optimé vendere. Adduxi, exposui, vendo meum; non pluris quam cæteri; fortasse etiam minoris, cum major est copia. Cui fit injuria?" In the same manner it has been decided by an English court‡, that the Purchaser of an estate was not obliged to

* *Off.* III. 12.

† So far the rules of Civil Law go, the Seller must disclose the defects of his wares: as to the rest, he must act without deceit: but, being a seller, he must wish to get the best price. "I bring my wares to market: I offer them for sale; I sell what is my own; not dearer than others; perhaps cheaper, as I have a larger stock. Whom do I wrong?"

‡ Kent, II. 489.

disclose to the Seller his knowledge of the existence of a mine on the Estate.

But it is further stated to be law*, that the Seller is liable, if he fraudulently misrepresent the quality of the thing sold, in some particulars in which the Buyer had not equal means of knowledge: or if he do so, in such a manner as to induce the Buyer to forbear making the enquiries, which, for his own security and advantage, he would otherwise have made.

173. It has been attempted† to express all Rules on this subject by saying that the Rule of Contract is *Equality:* "Ut ex inæqualitate jus oriatur minus habenti‡." But this maxim must not be carried so far as to destroy the nature of a Contract: for by that, we do not agree, generally, to give and receive equal things; but we determine *what* we are to give and receive. The Rule is rather to be sought in the intentions and expectations of the parties contracting. Each is obliged to do that which he gives the other reason to expect, and knows that he does expect. This is expressed by saying that the transaction is *bonâ fide, in good faith.*

174. Yet in many cases, the estimate of the intentions and expectations of the parties must be vague and obscure; and instead of attempting to regulate the course of law by these, it may be more proper to apply strict rules of interpretation to the language of Contracts. Hence the Roman Law makes a distinction of actions *bonæ fidei,* and actions *stricti juris.*

Rules of *Interpretation* of the Language of Contracts have been laid down by Jurists; and are an important part of the doctrine of Contracts, in its applications. These Rules, for the most part, have for

* Kent. II. 487. † Grot. B. et P. II. 12.

‡ So that he who receives the less has a claim arising from the inequality.

their object to combine good faith with exact Law. Such are these, for instance; that common words are to be understood in a common sense; Terms of Art in their technical sense: that when it is necessary, words are to be interpreted by the matter, effect, and accompaniments: and the like*.

175. The wrongs which violate the Rights of Contract are *Fraud*, of which some causes have been considered; and *Breach of Contract*, against which the Law provides Remedies, by actions of various kinds; but on these we need not further dwell.

CHAPTER V.

THE RIGHTS OF MARRIAGE.

176. We have already pointed out (47) that one of the most powerful Springs of action in man is the Desire of Family Society, which grows out of his Appetites and Affections. The needs of man's condition so operate, that he cannot exist in a social and moral state, except there be, established in Society, Rights which sanction and protect the gratification of this Desire. Such Rights, with the corresponding mutual obligations, are given to the Husband and Wife, united in a legitimate Marriage; and the Rights thus vested in the Husband, and in the Wife, are the *Rights of Marriage*.

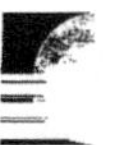

Marriage and Property are termed *Institutions;* inasmuch as they imply the establishment of General Rules, by which, not only the special parties are bound, (as in Contracts); but by which the whole Society also is governed. These two Institutions are

* Grot. P. et B. II. 16.

the basis of Society. The Right of Personal Security is requisite, in order to preserve a man from hour to hour, and from day to day; the Institution of Property is requisite, in order that man may subsist on the fruits of the earth from year to year; the Institution of Marriage is indispensable, in order to the continuance of the community from generation to generation.

177. The Desires and Affections, growing out of the Institution of Marriage, tend to balance the action of the elementary Desires and Affections, and to maintain man in a moral and social condition. The Elementary Desires and Affections, which lead to the Union of the Sexes, are refined and tranquillized by the marriage tie. The Mutual Confidence, and the identification of habits and interests between husband and wife, which marriage, in its most complete form, tends to generate, give a new charm and a new value to life. When such a conception of a happy married life is formed, it is universally approved of; and thus the Moral Sentiments confirm the Conjugal Affections. Each successive generation of young persons, catching the like sentiments, and susceptible of the like affections, looks with hope and desire to this image of a happy marriage, as an important part of the business and object of life. Thus there is produced a National Sentiment respecting Marriage, which makes the Institution still more efficacious in its influence upon the moral and social condition of those among whom it prevails.

178. The Children which Marriage produces give rise to Affections which still further tend to bind together the Community by Moral and Social links. In the first period of their existence, Children are a common object of Affection to the parents, and draw closer the ties of their mutual Affection. Then comes the Education of the child; in which the parents have a common care, which further identifies

their sympathies and objects. The Brothers and Sisters of the child, when they come, bring with them new bonds of affection, new sympathies, new common objects. The habits of a Family take the place of the wishes of an Individual, in determining the habitation, the mode of living, the meals, and the like; and thus, these circumstances are determined by influences, more social and more refined than mere bodily desire. *The Family* is one of the most important elements of the social life of every Community.

Familia is the word by which the Romans denoted the persons thus collected in the house, along with their parents: and also along with the servants of the House. (*Famuli*) The head of the family was called *Paterfamilias;* his wife was *Materfamilias.*

179. The nature and extent of the Rights, which Marriage gives, have been different in different ages and countries; and the national conception of the conjugal bond has often fallen short, in various degrees, of that complete and permanent union of one man with one woman, which we have pointed at. Polygamy, Concubinage, and arbitrary Divorce, have been tolerated in many States; but still, the notion of a complete Marriage appears always to have been, the union of one Husband and one Wife for life.

Although Polygamy existed in the earlier periods of the Jewish nation, we find, in the Scriptures, that, beginning with man, at his creation, a single woman was given to him as his helpmate. And though Solomon is related to have had many wives, as the custom of Asiatic Sovereigns has generally been; in the description of a good wife which is inserted in his Book of Proverbs*, she is represented as sole mistress of the household, and as the object of an entire trust and respect, inconsistent with her being one of several

* Prov. xxxi.

wives. And though Moses permitted to the Jews more than one wife, he prohibited many*; which "many" is believed by the Commentators to be more than four. This permission was rather a concession to an existing practice, than a law consistent with the general scheme of the Laws of Moses. The practice of polygamy is said† to have ceased entirely among the Jews after the return from the Babylonish Captivity.

180. Polygamy was not a Grecian practice. The Heroes of Homer appear never to have had more than one ἄλοχος; though they are sometimes represented as living in concubinage with παλλακάι. According to the views of Greek Legislators and Philosophers, Marriage was to be considered as having for its object the maintenance of the State, by the continuation of the race of citizens: and we see, in the Republic of Plato, and elsewhere, indications that they could tolerate extravagant deviations from the more complete domestic conception of marriage, if the political object was provided for.

181. The Roman Law, however, approached closely to the conception of a complete marriage, which has been noticed. The Definition given in the Institutes is this‡: "Nuptiæ, sive Matrimonium, est viri et mulieris conjunctio, individuam vitæ consuetudinem constituens." In another place§ it is described as "Consortium omnis vitæ: divini et humani juris communicatio."

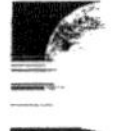

182. The English Law goes further, and considers the Husband and Wife as one Person. As the Lawyers state it‖: the very being or legal existence

* Deut. xvii. 17. † Mich. *Law of Moses*, II. 12.

‡ *Inst.* I. 9. Marriage or Matrimony is the union of a man and a woman so as to constitute an inseparable habitual course of life.

§ *Dig.* XIII. 21. A partnership for life, with a joint participation in all Rights human and divine.

‖ Blackst. I. 442. But perhaps it would be more just to say

of the woman is suspended during the marriage, or at least is incorporated and consolidated in that of her husband: under whose wing, protection, and cover, she performs everything; and is therefore in our Law French a *feme-covert, fœmina viro co-operta;* and her condition during marriage is called her *coverture.* Hence a man cannot grant anything to his wife by a legal act, or enter into covenant with her; for this would be to covenant with himself. The husband is bound by law to provide his wife with the necessaries of life; if she incur debts for such things, he is obliged to pay them. Even if the debts of the wife have been incurred before marriage, the husband is bound to discharge them: for he has espoused her and her circumstances together. If she suffers an injury, she applies for redress in her husband's name as well as her own. If any one has a claim upon her, the suit must be directed against her husband also. In criminal prosecutions, indeed, the wife may be indicted and prosecuted separately; for the union is only a civil union. But even in such cases, husband and wife are not allowed to be Evidence for or against each other: partly, say the Lawyers, because it is impossible their testimony should be impartial; but principally, because of the union of Person. For being thus one Person, if they were admitted witnesses *for* each other, they would contradict one maxim of Law*; *Nemo in propriâ causâ testis esse debet:* and if *against* each other, they would contradict another

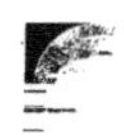

that the principle which limits the rules of Law, as between Husband and Wife, is not that of the union of the two, but of the conjugal supremacy of the Husband.

* *No one can be a witness in his own case. No one is bound to accuse himself.* But perhaps it would be more just to say, that the principal reason is not that of the identity of person; but that community of *interest,* which prevents their being evidence *for* each other; while the public policy of preventing domestic quarrels, prohibits their being evidence *against* each other

Maxim: *Nemo tenetur se ipsum accusare.* In the Roman Law, on the contrary, the Husband and Wife are considered as two distinct Persons, and may have separate Estates, Debts, Contracts, and Injuries. And hence, in the Ecclesiastical Courts of England, which derive their views and maxims from the Roman Law, a woman may sue and be sued, without her husband.

183. According to the System of Law which we have been describing, the husband is the Head of the Family, and the Wife is subordinate to him. He represents the Family in its legal relations; and in such matters she has no Rights against him. He has a Right to act for her; and even, in some cases, to coerce her. The Roman Law allowed the husband, for some misdemeanours*, "Flagellis et fustibus acriter verberare uxorem;" for others, only† "Modicam castigationem adhibere." Something of the same kind was allowed by the old Law of England; for, say the Lawyers, since the husband is to answer for her misbehaviour, the Law thought it reasonable to entrust him with the power of restraining her. And the Right to obedience, from the Wife, is vested in the Husband, for the sake of preserving Order in the Family, and of protecting and benefiting all the Members of it.

184. The inequality between Men and Women, which thus appears in the ancient conceptions of Marriage, is shown also in the established notions of the Wrongs, by which the Rights of Marriage are violated. *Thou shalt not commit adultery*, is the fundamental Law on this subject; but this was commonly applied only to the offence committed by or with the wife. By the Jewish Law‡ the adulterer and the adulteress were to be put to death. By the Old Roman Law, the adulterer was at the mercy of the in-

* To beat his wife severely with whip or stick

† To apply moderate correction

‡ Levit. xx. 10

jured husband, and might be prosecuted by any person; but under the emperors, the Right of prosecution was limited to the husband, or the near relatives of the adulteress. The adulteress was to be repudiated and otherwise punished. In England, adultery, as a public crime, is under the jurisdiction of the Ecclesiastical Courts; but the Common Law also gives, to the Husband, Damages from the person who was guilty of Criminal Conversation with his wife.

185. The Right of the Parent to the obedience of the Child is a fundemental Rule in all the ancient Forms of Society. The Law of Moses, *Honour and obey thy Father and thy Mother;* is recognized in all nations. The ancient Roman notions carried this so far, that they gave the Father a Right over the life of the Son. Even in the latest times, the Son is contemplated as entirely *in the power* of the Father; and this expression implied that the Father was invested with the Right to act for the Children upon all legal occasions. The Institute says*: "Qui ex te et uxore tuâ nascitur, in tuâ potestate est: Item qui ex filio tuo et uxore ejus nascitur, id est nepos tuus et neptis, æque in tuâ sunt potestate; et pronepos et proneptis, et deinceps cæteri. Qui autem ex filiâ tuâ nascuntur, in potestate tuâ non sunt, sed in patris eorum." And this went so far that the Son could have no Rights against his Father. All that he acquired became, not his, but his Father's. Some Jurists refer this to a legal fiction of the unity of the Father and the Son; others, to a maxim that the condition of the Master of the Family might be made better by the

* *Inst.* I. 9. He who is born of you and your wife is in your power: also he who is born of your son and his wife, that is, your grandson and grand-daughter, are likewise in your power; and so your great-grandson and great-grand-daughter; and in the same way, for the succeeding steps. But they who are born of your daughter are not in your power, but in their father's.

acts of the other members of the Family, but could not legally be made worse.

186. The English Law does not go so far as the Roman in this respect; but still invests the Father with considerable Rights over his Son. He may correct him in a reasonable manner. He may delegate part of this parental authority to a Tutor or Schoolmaster, who is *in loco parentis**. He has the benefit of his children's labour so long as they live with him. He has, however, no power over any property which the son has acquired, except as Trustee or Guardian; but on the other hand, the Son, while under age, is not capable of acquiring any property, by Contract made independently of his father.

The Rights with which the head of the Family was thus invested carried with them corresponding obligations. As we have already stated (182), the husband is bound to provide his wife with the necessaries of life, and also to pay her debts. Also, the Father is, by the English Law, bound to provide maintenance for his own offspring. By the Roman Law† this obligation was reciprocal. "Si quis a liberis ali desideret, vel si liberi ut a parente exhibeantur, judex de eâ re cognoscet." The Head of the Family was the Supporter, Protector, and Director of all the other members. The Education of Children, so that they may, in their turn, become good members of new Families, and good Citizens, is contemplated as an important object by most legislators; but is, in a great mersure, left to the unforced care of parents.

* Perhaps it would be more correct to say, that the Schoolmaster's authority is not delegated from the parent, but analogous to the parent's. It depends on some of the same reasons; and exists where there is not a parent to delegate, as well as where there is.

† *Dig.* xxv. 3. 5. If any one requires to be supported by his children, or if children require to be maintained by the parent, the judge shall take cognizance of the matter.

To neglect this office, is rather the omission of a Moral Duty, than the violation of a Legal Obligation.

187. The Family Affections, and the Moral Sentiments connected with them, make both men and women look with grief and indignation upon the violation of female chastity, in those who are under their care and protection. The woman who gives up her person to any other man than her husband, is conceived to be destitute of the proper affections and sentiments of a wife; and therefore, unfit for the proper destination of a woman. To seduce her to this condition, is to bring her to disgrace, and to make her marriage with another man almost hopeless. To force her person, brings upon her some portion of this disgrace and calamity, in addition to the injury which is involved in all violence. The laws of most countries recognize these Wrongs against Female Chastity, *Rape* and *Seduction*. Thus by the Jewish Law*, the Man who forced a betrothed woman was to be put to death. If she was not betrothed, he was to make her his wife, without being allowed afterwards to put her away. The Roman Law justified homicide, when committed by the woman in defence of her chastity; or by a man, in defence of his relatives, when force of this kind was offered. The English law, likewise, excuses a woman killing a man who attempts to ravish her; and the husband or father is justified in killing a man who attempts a Rape upon his wife or daughter. The Roman Law, in the time of Justinian, refused to make any distinction in the guilt of the violator of chastity, whether the woman consented or not†: "Si enim ipsi raptores, metu vel

* Deut. xxii. 25, &c.

† Cod. ix. 13. If through fear, and in virtue of the severity of the punishment, seducers abstain from such offenses, no woman, willing or unwilling, will have an opportunity of transgressing. The will of woman is itself forced by the arts of the ravisher.

atrocitate pœnæ, ab hujusmodi facinore se temperaverint, nulli mulieri, sive volenti sive non volenti, peccandi locus relinquetur: quia hoc ipsum *velle* mulierum ab insidiis nequissimi hominis qui meditatur rapinam, inducitur."

188. The English Law punishes Rape with death, but makes it a necessary ingredient in the crime that it be committed against the will of the woman. It is sometimes assigned as a reason for the capital punishment, that the offence is a destruction of the woman's moral being. But the English Law has no direct punishment for the moral offence of Seduction, as we have seen that it has none for Adultery. These crimes are punished indirectly, as Loss inflicted, on the Father and the Husband. In the latter case, the Husband may receive Damages from the Adulterer, for the Injury done him: in the case of Seduction, the Father may recover Damages for the loss of his daughter's Services during her pregnancy, by the act of the Seducer, *per quod servitium amisit.* The necessity of taking this course for the remedy of these wrongs, is explained, by considering that the Common Law of England has, for its main objects, the security of person and property; and therefore, does not undertake to treat offences according to their moral depravity, or the grief and indignation which they produce.

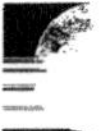

189. According to the ancient legal views of the Family, in most nations, as we have seen in the cases of the Roman and the English Law, the possession of property in land is an attribute of the Family, rather than of the individual; the right of the wife and children being merged in, or derived from, that of the Head of the Family. Following the same view, the Law directs that, on the death of the Father, the Land shall descend to the children: for they then, in their turn, one or more of them, become Heads of Families, and take the place of the Father,

as members of the State. Accordingly, in the Roman Law, when the Father died, those of his children who were then under his power (*in patriâ potestate*), were his proper heirs (*hæredes sui*), and divided his possessions among them; all other heirs were *hæredes extranei*. In England, on the establishment of the Feudal Constitution, by William the Conqueror, the law of primogeniture was established, by which Lands descended to the eldest son alone. In this view, the Property was considered as a Fief to be held by military Service; and the whole property was assumed to be a proper means of supporting the dignity of the holder. The younger sons were supposed to be provided for by the eldest, and by their own exertions in the various professions which were open to them, military, civil, ecclesiastical, and mercantile. It is consistent with the view which this Rule assumes, that the Rule was not extended to personal Property; for such property was not held as a Fief. In this, no primogeniture is allowed, all males and females of equal degree sharing equally.

If direct and proper heirs failed, the same view, of the transmission of Property in the Family, led to Rules of Law which determined the persons to whom it was to be given; but upon these Rules, and their differences in different states, we need not now dwell.

190. In most Systems of Law, though the Law assigned a Rule for the disposal of a man's property after his death, the proprietor has been allowed to vary this disposal, partly or entirely, on declaring his intention before proper Witnesses. Hence, the Declaration so witnessed is called *Testamentum* in Latin, *Will* in English. The ground of this Right of the Testator is, that a man, previous to his death, may dispose of his property, and may exercise an authority over his children; and that the continuity and order of the Family were supposed to be preserved, by allowing this Right to operate through the time of his

death, and therefore after that moment. Yet the Right of the Testator, like the other Rights of Property, is limited by Rules of Law. The Roman Law says*: "Testamenti factio non privati sed publici juris est." In the early times of Rome, the citizens made their Wills at the Public Assemblies (*Calata Comitia*), although afterwards, other modes of procedure were introduced.

191. The Right of disposing of property by Testament, was not unlimited. If a man had a Son *under his power*, he was obliged either to make him an heir, or to *exhæredate* him, expressly assigning a reason: and even if other near relations, who would without a Testament have inherited, were passed over in silence, they could claim a portion of the property: the Testament in such a case was called *inofficiosum Testamentum*, as being made *non ex officio pietatis*.

192. In England, the power of disposing by Will of a portion of a man's moveable property was recognized by Magna Charta†: but until modern times, a man could leave only one-third of his moveable property away from his wife and children. No Will of lands was permitted till the time of Henry the Eighth; and then, only of a certain portion‡: nor was it till after the Restoration of Charles the Second, that the power of devising became so universal as it is at present. By the English Law, a man's Heirs were contemplated as interested in his property, as well as the man himself. Property, from this attribute of being inherited, was called *Hereditaments*. Hence it was held, by the Lawyers, that no freehold interest in land could be conveyed, without the use of the word *Heirs*. If Land be given to a man for ever, or to him and his Assigns for ever, this vests in him

* *Dig.* XXVIII. 1. 3. The Right of making a Testament is a Right by Law.

† Bl. IV. 423. ‡ Ib. II. 12

but an estate for life. This limitation was founded upon a view borrowed from the Feudal System, according to which the estate was given in consideration of the Tenant's personal qualities, to be held by personal service. The limitation was upheld by a maxim of the Roman Jurists: "Donationes sunt stricti juris, ne quis plus donasse præsumatur quam expresserit."

193. Although at present the proprietor in England has, in general, the Right of disposing of the Estate by Will, there is an exception to this, in the case of *entailed* Estates. This power of entailing was established by the Statute of Westminster, the Second, (in the thirteenth year of Edward I.), which is commonly called the Statute *De Donis Conditionalibus*. This law gave the Proprietor a power of transmitting to his Heirs the enjoyment of the Property, without their having the Right of transmitting it to any one, except the Heirs who should come after them. Property, thus limited, was termed *Feudum talliatum*, a curtailed fief, *feetail;* from which expression the word *entailed* comes.

194. Besides the power of disposing of the whole Estate, both the Roman and the English Law allow the Proprietor the power of giving *Legacies* (*Legata*) to special persons. But all such Bequests are limited by the condition, that the Testator's Debts must first be paid.

195. There are other distributions of property, which, according to the laws of various countries, arise out of Marriage; as the *Dowry*, or *Dower* of the Bride, (*Dotarium*, *Douaire*), in the Roman Law, *Dos*: and the *Jointure* of the widow; (*Junctura*, a joint possession). On these it is not necessary here to dwell.

196. As the Law, in the general case, directs that the heir should receive the benefit of his Father's property (*Patrimonium*) after his death, so it also directed that he should, if it were necessary, receive the benefit of his Father's guidance. In the Roman

Law, the Father had power to appoint, by Testament, a person to exercise parental care and responsibility for his son or daughter after his death, so long as the child was of unripe age (*impubes*). This Guardian was called *Tutor*, or *Curator;* the child was his *Pupillus*. The Tutor had the care of the person, the Curator of the estate. Without the sanction of the Curator, the Pupillus could do no act by which he diminished his property. But the care of the person of the child belonged, in a great degree, to the Mother, as the care of the property did to the Curator When the Father did not appoint a Tutor by his Will, the Law of the Twelve Tables gave the *Tutela* to the nearest relatives*; "Legitimæ Tutelæ lege XII Tabularum agnatis delatæ sunt, et consanguineis; item patruis: id est, his qui ad legitimam hæreditatem admitti possunt: hoc, summâ providentiâ, ut qui sperarent hanc successionem, iidem tuerentur bona, ne dilapidentur." The view of the ancient English Law was quite different. It also gave a Guardian to a Minor; but the Guardianship devolved upon the next of kin who could *not* inherit the Estate. The Law, it is said†, judges it improper to trust the person of an infant (*Minor*) to a person who may by possibility become heir to him; that there may be no temptation, nor even suspicion of temptation, for him to abuse his trust.

197. An English Law of more modern times, (the 12th year of Charles II.) allows the Father to appoint a Guardian to his Son, by Deed or Will, so long as he is a Minor, that is, under the full legal

* *Dig.* XXVI. 4, 1. Guardianship according to Law is by the Twelve Tables given to the father's relations and to relations by blood, that is to those who may have a legal claim to the inheritance. And this was prudently done, that those who are allowed to look for the succession may see that the estate is not dilapidated.

† Bl. I. 461.

age. This age is in England twenty-one: Scotland agrees with England, both probably copying the old Saxon Rules which prevailed on the Continent. By the Roman Law, a youth could perform certain legal acts at the age of fourteen; but up to the age of twenty-five, he could not dispose of property without being supported by the Authority of a *Curator*.*

198. All that has been said of the Rights and Obligations of a Man with regard to his Wife and Children, apply only to such wife and children as the law recognizes: to his *lawful* wife, and his *legitimate* children, born of a lawful marriage. What a Lawful Marriage is, the Law must define.

Marriage is a Contract; and though it is, in most countries, a Contract of a special character, solemnized with peculiar ceremonies, it must be, in many respects, governed by the general Rules of Contracts. Thus, the persons marrying must be of sound mind; of the age which the Law considers as mature; and free from other legal impediments, such as an inconsistent previous Contract. They must also understand each other to intend that perpetual union which Marriage implies.

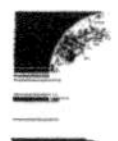

199. By the Roman Law, the essence of Marriage was Consent; the Consent "both of those who come together, and of those under whose power they are." This Consent was to be manifested by some public act; for instance, Declaration before friends, and afterwards continued Cohabitation for a year. This mode of marriage was *Usus*. But ancient custom had handed down and sanctioned other forms of marriage, *confarreatio* and *coemptio*, by which the woman became part of the man's household. She was then said *in manum viri convenire*.

200. By the old Law of England†, a Contract made *per verba de præsenti*, by words in the present

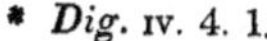

* *Dig.* IV. 4. 1. † Bl. I. 439.

tense, was a valid marriage: thus, *I take thee M. for my husband: I take thee N. for my wife.* The same is still the case by the Law of Scotland. Also, a promise of marriage *per verba de futuro;—I will marry thee;*—became a valid marriage by cohabitation; in the same way in which a contract concerning goods became valid by the delivery of the goods By later English Statutes, marriages in England were, for many purposes, not allowed to be valid, except such as were celebrated after due notice (*Banns* or *License*) in some parish-church or public chapel; and by a person in Sacred Orders. But this restriction has since been enlarged, so that the religious part of the ceremony is no longer necessary.

201. With reference to the grounds on which Marriage has very generally been accompanied with a religious sanction, we may remark, that the Conjugal Union is contemplated, not as a mere Contract for Cohabitation, but as an engagement binding the parties to mutual affection, and to a community of the scheme and ends of life. Hence a mere legal Contract, which must regard actions alone, cannot express its full import. The Sentiment of Duty must be brought into operation, and the appeal to this sentiment belongs to the province of Religion (84).

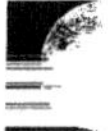

202. *Divorce* is the Separation of the Marriage Union. According to the Roman Law, as the Consent and Conjugal Affection of the parties was an essential part of a marriage, their acquiescence was necessary to its continuance. Either party might declare his or her intention to dissolve the connexion; and no judicial decree, or interference of public authority, was requisite in order tc carry this purpose into effect. Yet such separations were generally made with some form. As there was Marriage by *confarreatio* and *coemptio*, there was Divorce by *diffarreatio* and *emancipatio*. *Repudium* was the rejection of a Marriage promised by *Sponsalia* (*Betrothing*),

but not completed. The practice of Divorce was afterwards checked by Law (the *Lex Papia Poppæa*). Under the Christian Emperors it was punished in various ways; but still the power remained, subject to certain forms in its exercise.

203. There is no Law of England which authorizes Divorce. Every particular case must be the effect of a Special Act of Parliament. Even the gravest violation of the Rights of Marriage, Adultery, is, by the English Law, only cause of separation *from bed and board;* it does not lead to a dissolution of the Marriage. The reason given for this by the Commentators is, that if Divorce were allowed to depend upon a matter within the power of either of the parties, they would probably be extremely frequent. The Ecclesiastical Courts, which have a portion of the jurisdiction concerning Marriages, in virtue of the religious character of the ordinance, can, upon due grounds, grant a separation, not only *a mensâ et thoro,* but a total Divorce *a vinculo matrimonii.* But this must be for causes of impediment existing before the marriage. When these are shown, the marriage is declared null, as having been unlawful *ab initio,* and the parties are separated *pro salute animarum,* that they may not endanger their Souls by living in a state of known sin. But still the Ecclesiastical Law, like the Common Law of England, grants no Divorce for any Supervenient Cause; according to Commentators*, it deems so highly, and with such mysterious reverence, the nuptial tie, that it will not allow it to be unloosed for any cause whatever that arises after the Union is made. But it is mainly moved to take this view of marriage by the authority of religion.

204. As we have already seen, the only kind of Marriage which is recognized by the Roman Law as complete, is that of one husband with one wife. Cli-

* Bl. I. 440.

mate does not necessarily occasion any exception to this Rule. Thus the Law of Justinian, promulgated by the Romans in the climate of modern Turkey, is express*: "Duas uxores eodem tempore habere non licet."

Yet the Laws of several Countries in various ways take note of other unions arising from the irregalar operation of those Desires and Affections which lead to Family connexions. There are various provisions in the Laws of Rome respecting Concubines; and in our own Laws, with regard to Illegitimate Children, or Bastards. By the Roman Law, a true marriage could only take place between Roman citizens†: "Justas nuptias inter se cives Romani contrahunt qui secundùm precepta legum coeunt." No other unions were complete marriages.

It depends upon the law, and the general structure of each State, whom a citizen is allowed to marry. He may be prohibited from taking a wife beyond a certain circle. He may be forbidden to marry a stranger. He may be compelled to marry, not only within his own Nation, but within his own Tribe.

205. On the other hand, men and women are, in almost all countries, forbidden to marry *within* a certain circle of relationship. Marriages within these limits were forbidden by the Romans as *Nuptiæ incestæ;* and the union of persons so related is *Incest.* Such unions were those of Parents and Children, Brothers and Sisters‡. "Nuptiæ consistere non possunt inter eas personas quæ in numero parentium libe-

* *Inst.* I. 10. 6. It is not lawful to have two wives at the same time.

† *Inst.* I. 10. 1. That is a true marriage which is contracted between Roman citizens who come together in the manner directed by the Law.

‡ Marriage cannot take place between those persons who stand in the relation of parents and children, whether of a near or of a more remote degree, to any number of steps.

rorumve sunt, sive proximi sive ulterioris gradus sunt, usque ad infinitum." The degrees of kindred between which marriage is prohibited have been different in different times and places. But everywhere incestuous unions have been looked upon not only with condemnation, but with horror. It has been conceived that there is a Divine curse upon them.

The chastity of woman, which, as we have seen (187), is so highly prized, requires to be guarded and supported by the sympathy and reverence of her Family for this treasure. Her relatives, with whom she familiarly lives, especially her Father and her Brothers, are the natural Guardians of her purity. In the intercourse between men and women not withheld by any impediment, the thoughts often turn to the union of sexes. Men are prone to solicit, and women apt to yield, when the union is one on which the thoughts are allowed to dwell. The opportunity and authority which near relationships usually give, would add to this tendency, if the belief of a Divine curse upon transgression did not keep the thoughts and affections in harmony with the reverence for the woman's chastity. The Law supports this tone of the thoughts and affections, by its prohibition of incestuous marriages.

CHAPTER VI.

THE RIGHTS OF GOVERNMENT, OR STATE RIGHTS.

206. We have already stated (48), that among the most powerful Springs of Human Action is the Desire of Civil Society; and that man cannot exist as man except he exist in Civil Society, under the sway of Rules of Action really enforced by some of the

Members of the Community. Those Members of the Community, whose office it thus is to enforce the Rules, through which the Community subsists, are, for this purpose, invested with Rights, which are here termed *Rights of Government.* The possessor of these Rights is spoken of as having *Authority* in the Community.

207. We have rights of this kind even in the Family; and especially in Families where the paternal Power is most ample. As we have seen (185), in some countries, the Father has exercised a power of Life and Death over the Son. We may, in such a case, conceive the Father laying down Rules for the conduct of the Family, and enforcing them by any penalties which he may appoint.

When the Children of such a Family grow up, and when they themselves marry and have children, we may still conceive the habit of obedience to the Head of the Family to remain. As the Family extends, it becomes a Family in a wider sense; a House, a Tribe, a Clan, a Nation; but it may still continue to recognize a Supreme Right to obedience in the common parent. Such is a *Patriarchal Government.* The Right of Government is here vested entirely in the Patriarch. The other members of the Community have only the Obligation of Obedience towards him.

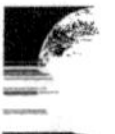

208. The Patriarchal Government is naturally broken up by the death of the Patriarch. We may suppose a Patriarchal Government to be continued generation after generation, by some agreement in the Family, as to who is to inherit the Patriarchal Authority: but such a government, though it may exist as an Institution, is no longer the natural result of the Family habits of affection and obedience. To obey a brother, a nephew, or a remoter relative, is not a natural, necessary, and universal rule. The Patriarchal Form of Society being broken up, the mixtures of Families, their migrations and various for-

tunes, still further loosen and destroy the bonds of Patriarchal Government, and form men into Nations, according to various conditions of race, dwelling-place, and history. The *National Government* then takes place of the Patriarchal.

209. The person or persons in whom the Supreme Authority in each nation resides, are determined in every case by the History of the nation (97). The whole past History of each nation has terminated in the Fact of its present Government. In the Course of History, the Governing Authorities of Nations have passed into various hands, have been variously distributed, and have assumed many various forms. Nations which were formerly separate, are now united under the same Supreme Authority: Nations which were formerly united as one, have now separate governments: the Lines of Succession of Governors, the modes of appointing them, the way of their exercising their authority in each nation, have changed. The Laws by which they govern have also changed. But in every nation, so far as it is subjected to Rules of Action; so far as its members really possess Rights and Obligations; there is some *Supreme* Authority, in which the Rights of Government are vested.

210. The Supreme Authority may reside in one Person, or in many. It may be exercised by one Person, under conditions depending upon the consent and co-operation of others. In almost all nations, there is a *Difference of Ranks*, connected with the conditions of the exercise of the Supreme Power. Besides the highest Governor, (King, Consul, President, or in whatever other name he governs,) there are Nobles, Senators, Lords, Citizens, Aliens, often Slaves. Some of these Ranks have Authority, which, like that of the highest Governor, is the result of the History of the Nation. They have Rights with refer-

ence to each other, determined by Laws and Customs, traditionally received, or historically instituted.

The structure of a Society considered with regard to this Difference of Ranks, is its *Political* Structure. The Laws and Customs which determine the Rights of different Ranks, and their share in the Supreme Authority, are the *Constitution* of the Nation.

In every Constitution, the Supreme Authority is termed also the *Sovereign* Power. As the Constitution places the Sovereign power in the hands of One, or of a few men of Rank, or of the General Body of the Citizens, the State is a *Monarchy*, an *Aristocracy*, or a *Democracy*. These are the *Simple Forms* of Government.

The Sovereign Power executes the existing Laws, and on all occasions, both in reference to the citizens within the State, and to persons and states without, acts for the State. These are the *Executive* Functions of the Government.

211. It is the existence of a Supreme Authority, or Government, which gives reality to the other Rights;—the Rights of the Person, of Property, of Contract, of Marriage. The Government acts as the *State* (94), and carries into effect the Laws by which Rights and Obligations are defined. The Government, also, by means of its tribunals and Judges (94), decides disputed questions which arise among its citizens concerning their Rights and Obligations. These are the *Judicial* Functions of the Government.

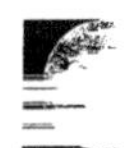

But the Definitions of Rights and Obligations, though given by the Law of each nation, are not arbitrary and capricious (105). They are intended in all nations to be *right;* that is, conformable to the Supreme Rule of Human Action. They are intended to be *just*, that is, conformable to the Moral Idea of Justice, as well as to the actual Fact of Law. Such Moral Ideas will be the subject of our consideration hereafter.

212. Offences against the Rights of Government are *Rebellion*, when subjects openly and by force resist the Governors: *Treason*, when by combination and contrivance they seek to dispossess them: *Sedition*, when they attempt to transfer some of the functions of Government from the Governors to other hands. In many free states, where the citizens have a considerable share in the government, they are divided into *Parties*, which act upon opposite or different maxims in the administration of the State. When a Party acts not for the good of the State, but for its own advantage as a Party, it is a *Faction*.

213. Since, in all Nations, the Definitions of Rights and Obligations are intended to be right and just, it is natural that there should be much that is common in the views and determinations of all nations on these subjects. That which is common in the determinations of all Nations respecting Rights and Obligations, is called *Jus Naturæ*, or *Jus Gentium*. That which is peculiar in the Law of a particular State or City, is called *Jus Civile*, or *Jus Municipale*. We may distinguish these two kinds of Jus as *Natural Jus* and *National Jus*. *Jus Civile*, *Civil Law*, is often used to denote *Jus Civile Romanorum*, the *Romam Law*.

214. Nations or States are, for the most part, independent bodies, with no common authority to which they can refer. Each is a *Sovereign State*, acknowledging no Superior. Hence there is no Authority which can define or enforce their Rights which they claim against each other. But the general rules and analogies of Natural Jus (212) lead to determinations of the Rights and Obligations of Nations, which form a body of acknowledged Law. This body of Law is *Jus inter Gentes*, and may be termed *International Jus*.

215. Though the existing Government in each Nation is a Fact, the result of preceding historical

Facts (209), it is not *merely* a Fact. Governments for the most part claim to exist by Justice, as well as by Power. They recognize the Rules of National Jus and International Jus of which we have spoken; and assert themselves to be Governments *de jure* as well as *de facto*. Moral Ideas, and the Sentiments combined with them, have great force among the springs of action (56); and thus the opinion, generally prevalent, that any person or body of persons does or does not possess the Government of a Nation *de jure*, will very materially effect the support and obedience which men will render to it, and will thus determine the historical fact of its standing or falling. The existing Government is a Fact; but it is a Fact determined by the previously operating Idea of Justice. Its power rests on the general opinion of its Authority. Might does not make Right; the opinion of Right makes Might; and the Might thus generated determines all subordinate questions of Right.

216. Although we at first, while treating of Jus, consider the Laws of each State as absolutely fixed and given (105), yet Laws are intended, as we have said (211), to be just. Hence the State has, for one of its offices, to remove out of the Laws all that is unjust, so as to make them more and more just. That part of the Governing Body which is by the Constitution (210) thus invested with Authority to make and alter Laws, is the *Legislative Body*, or *Legislature*. The Executive and Judicial branches of Government, of which we have already spoken (210, 211), and the Legislative Branch now spoken of, form the three great Members of every Constitution.

217. It will be our business hereafter to consider the Moral Idea of Justice, and its consequences; but we may already easily discern cases in which the general analogy of Natural Jus would lead to a modification of Laws. If, for instance, one Nation have made war upon another, invaded the Country,

and reduced the inhabitants to slavery: (as in ancient times was the Rule of International Jus;) when the conquered inhabitants have lived as slaves for many generations, it would be agreeable to Natural Jus to annul the Laws which keep the slaves in bondage (this being done, of course, by the proper legislative authority). For the ancient conquest, in which the condition of the slaves was founded, was a transitory and accidental event, and cannot properly be the basis of an eternal Law. Indeed, the progress of time not only obliterates the effect of such events, but overthrows even the Rules of International Jus by which the events formerly produced such effects: for it is now no longer a Rule of International Law, that when one nation conquers another in war, it makes slaves of the inhabitants.

By following such changes, States may aim at constantly making their Laws continually more and more just. In doing so, they tend to bring together the *Idea* of Justice and the *Fact* of Law. The Laws are rendered just; and they are actually carried into effect because they are the measures of Justice.

218. The Idea and the Fact cannot be separated. We cannot have Justice without Law, that is, without actual historical Law. For Justice requires us to give to each man his own, and Law alone determines what is each man's own. If we draw inferences from the notion of Justice, without taking account of the traditions of Law and History, we shall be led to contradiction and confusion. Thus, if we say that Justice implies Equality, and if we thereupon attempt to make the Property of all citizens always equal, we destroy the conception of Property. If, on the like ground, we declare that no man shall lose by a Contract, we destroy the conception of a Contract. Justice implies Property, and Property implies permanent actual possession, historically established. Justice implies Contracts; and a Contract implies that a

transaction which takes place at one time, determines arbitrarily what follows. If we do not take the historical definitions of Property, Contract, and the like, the things themselves disappear; and there is no longer any material for the Idea of Justice to act upon.

And on the other hand, we cannot be content with the mere Fact of Law, without the idea of Justice. Power without authority, Might without Right, give Possession, but do not give Property. In order that Law may be looked upon as Law, it must be combined with Justice.

219. Actual and fixed Laws are requisite as means for the moral education of the members of the State (104). For the Moral Ideas are educed in man by his being made to understand the Terms denoting Moral Conceptions; and these Terms become intelligible by being applied under definite conditions. Moral Conceptions cannot be applied, without assuming the jural Conceptions of Property, Contract, Marriage, and the like. A child cannot learn that he ought not to take what is not his own, except he be made to understand what is, and what is not, his own. The Laws being, as in many States they are or have been, familiarly made known to young persons, form an important part of their education. And the Reasons commonly given for the Laws, involve the Idea of Justice, and serve to educe that Idea in the minds of the citizens.

220. Among the ancient Romans, the earliest Laws, and the Maxims and Formulæ of Laws, were thus inculcated in the earliest years of life. Their children were made familiar with these expressions, as our children are with Nursery Rhymes. Cicero says* to his brother: "A pueris enim didicimus *Si in jus vocat*, atque ejusmodi alias leges nominare." And

* *De Leg.* II. 4. From the time of our boyhood we learnt, *If a man sues you at Law*, and other Laws of that kind, by rote.

again*: "Nostis quæ sequuntur; discebamus enim pueri XII (Tabulas) ut carmen necessiarum." And it was the office of the higher class of Romans to expound the application and interpretation of the Law to their clients. The familiarity with the Law, thus generated, joined with a belief that the Roman Law was the perfection of justice, constituted a Moral Education for the Romans.

In like manner, the habitual use of expressions implying moral qualities and moral sentiments, calls up moral notions and moral sentiments in those who thus learn the language of morality. But moral notions and moral sentiments can have no definiteness and fixity, except the Rules by which their objects are determined are definite and fixed; and these Rules are Law and Custom.

Each successive generation, deriving its education from the existing Laws and Customs of the Nation, and being imbued with a belief that these Laws, and the Maxims which they imply, are right and just, will transmit the same education to the next generation. And thus the stability and consistency of the State will be preserved.

221. Thus the Laws of each country must be in a great measure fixed and permanent, in order that the Moral Education of the citizens may go forwards consistently, and in order that the Stability of the State may be preserved. But the Laws, if they are to be just, cannot be absolutely fixed; because if they were so, they would involve arbitrary elements, depending entirely upon the accidental events and Institutions of former times; and this mixture of an Arbitrary Element is inconsistent with the Idea of Justice.

The Idea of Justice, so far as it has operated in

* Id. II. 23. You know what follows, for when we were boys we learnt the Twelve Tables like a familiar rhyme.

forming the Laws of any State, has operated in each generation upon the materials which the existing state of the Community supplied, and has thus more or less modified the Laws in each generation. It would not be the Idea of Justice, if it did not produce such modifications; for it is not just that there should be *arbitrary* inequalities among men. But *differences* among men and classes of men, arising from the events of former times, can never be removed; because the present condition of man is, in all cases, determined by their past condition: and among the features of this present condition, are their convictions as to their Rights and Obligations, which necessarily are derived from the past. For example, it is not just that there should be *arbitrary* differences in the distribution of Property. But there must be vast *inequalities* in the distribution of Property; for Property being a permanent thing, the inequalities of its distribution go on accumulating for ages; and this is not unjust. Yet still, these Rules of permanence in Property must not be regarded as absolutely fixed. Justice or Humanity may require such fixed Rules to bend; as we have seen that fixed Rules of Law bend in cases of necessity, as self-defence and the like (118 and 152). And it may be just or humane, not merely to make an exception to the Law, but to alter the Law; and the Law itself may thus become more just and more humane.

222. Thus the Law, in so far as it is a given fixed Fact, is a means of Education, by giving shape and substance to our Ideas. But again, it is to be a means of *Moral* Education, and is to give shape and substance to our Ideas of Justice: and for this purpose it must be fixed only so far as Justice makes it fixed. The Law must perpetually and slowly tend towards the idea of Justice;—slowly, because it must always be fixed enough to afford a standing ground for our thoughts and a means of education;—perpet-

ually, because there will never cease to remain some portion of the arbitrary historical element, on which it is its office still to operate.

Since we are thus brought to views in which the Idea of Justice comes under our consideration, (and by the like reasonings we should be led to other Moral Ideas,) we shall now proceed to the part of our subject to which these Ideas belong,—Morality.

223. Before we proceed, it will be proper to observe that there are other Classes of Rights, which we have not yet considered, because they are of a less extensive and fundamentel kind than the Five Principal Classes. Also, they involve Moral notions and offices of the Reason not yet treated of. Of these we may briefly notice the Right of Reputation.

The Right of Reputation.

224. We have noticed the Desire of Esteem, and the Fear of Condemnation and Infamy, as Springs of Human Action (55). Although the objects to which these Desires tend are notions which are not unfolded in our minds without the operation of reflection; they are, still, so universal, that the tranquillity of man in society cannot subsist, except the objects of these, as of other Desires, are established as Rights. Contumely, the expression of condemnation and scorn, naturally provoke acts of violence; and may often, on that account, be prohibited, as the first step in a violation of personal Rights. To take away a man's Good Name, or Good Repute, may prevent his neighbours trusting him, and may bring on him great loss. Hence the law forbids such acts*. "Si quis librum

* *Dig.* XLVII. 10. 5. If any one shall have written, composed, put forth, or by any trick cause to be written, composed, or put forth, any book tending to the defamation of another, even though it be put forth in the name of another person, or without a name, he may be proceeded against.

ad infamiam alicujus pertinentem scripserit, composuerit, ediderit, dolove malo fecerit, quo quod eorum fieret, etiamsi alterius nomine ediderit, vel sine nomine, uti de eâ re agere liceret." But the Commentator adds, that this is punishable only if the infamy be undeserved* : "Eum qui nocentem infamaverit, non est bonum æquum ob eam rem condemnari; peccata enim nocentium nota esse et oportere et expedire." But a man's good Reputation, when deserved, is protected as a personal right† : "Est enim famæ, ut et vitæ, habenda ratio." In like manner, the English Law takes cognizance of injuries affecting a man's Reputation, committed by malicious, slanderous, and scandalous words, spoken, or otherwise published, and tending to his damage and derogation. The Rule with regard to the words which the Law thus considers injurious, is, that they are such as may endanger a man by subjecting him to the penalties of the Law; may exclude him from Society; may impair his Trade, or may affect him as a Magistrate, or one in public Trust. But it is added by the Lawyers, that mere Scurrility, or opprobrious words, which neither in themselves import, nor are in fact attended with any hurtful effects, are not punishable by the common Law. Such Scandals are however cognizable in the Ecclesiastical Courts; as for instance, to call a man an adulterer or a heretic. By the Common Law, words uttered in the heat of passion, as to call a man Rogue or a Rascal, if productive of no ill consequences, are not punishable. Nor are words of advice or admonition punishable, in consequence of any ill spoken of the person admonished; for, say the Lawyers, they are not maliciously spoken. More-

* *Dig.* XLVII. 10. 18. For defaming a guilty man, it is not right and fit that a man be condemned: for the crimes of guilty men ought to be known.

† *Dig.* XLVII. 10. 18. For reputation, as well as life, is to be protected by Law.

over, if the person who has spoken ill of another, be able to prove the words to be true, he justifies himself, even though special damage have ensued; for then it is no slander or false tale; as we have seen is the provision also in the Roman Law.

BOOK III.

MORALITY.

OF VIRTUES AND DUTIES.

CHAPTER I.

OF MORAL PRECEPTS

225. By the constitution of our human nature, we are necessarily led to assume and refer to a Supreme Rule of human action; and to conceive human actions, our own and those of other men, to be absolutely right, when they are conformable to this Rule. In order that such a Rule may have a definite form, in human Society, men must have rights; and must also have their Obligations, corresponding, in each man, to the Rights of others. The real existence of Rights and Obligations is a condition requisite for the definite application of the Supreme Rule of Human Action: for, by the existence of Rights and Obligations, the objects of human desire and affection assume such a general and abstract form, that they may be made the subjects of Rules of Action. These points have been discussed and established in the First Book.

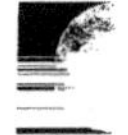

The Rights and Obligations which really exist among men are regulated by Laws, or Customs equivalent to Laws. Some of the most important of such Laws have been stated in the Second Book. Laws regard external actions only. But external actions are the result of internal actions, namely, of Will and Intention, of Mental Desires and of Affections. These internal actions are essential parts of external actions, considered as human actions; or rather, these internal actions, Desire, Affection, Intention, Will, are the only really human part of actions.

External actions, as the motions in our own limbs, and the motions and changes thereby produced in material things, and in the state of other persons, are not *our* actions, except so far as they are the consequences of *our* intention and will. When we have willed, what follows is a consequence of Laws of Nature, extraneous to us; and derives its character of right or wrong, so far as we are concerned in it, from the Will, and that which preceded the Will. Thus, if I fire off a pistol and kill a man, his pain and death, the grief of his friends, the loss to his family and his country, all follow as the consequence of the act of Will by which I pull the trigger. They are all morally included in that act of the Will. All those consequences are produced by the working of the Springs of Action within me. They may all be prevented by the operation of other Faculties, withholding me from this act of Will. Hence the Will, the Springs of Action which impel it, and the Faculties which control and direct it, must be the main subjects of our consideration, in treating of actions as right and wrong.

Will, Intention, Desire, Affection, are governed, not merely by external objects and by transient impulses, but by habits and Dispositions, which give a permanent character to the operation of the Springs of Action and of the controlling Faculties.

226. The Reason is the Faculty by which we conceive General Rules, and Special Cases as conformable to General Rules (14). It is therefore the Faculty by which we conceive Actions as right or wrong. The Moral Sentiments, Approval of what is right, Condemnation of what is wrong, are powerful

Springs of action (82), and thus impel us to carry into effect the judgments formed by the Reason. When we intentionally conform to the Supreme Rule, we speak of our actions as rightly directed by our Reason.

Actions to which we are rightly directed by our Reason are *Duties*. The Habits and Dispositions by which we perform our Duties are *Virtues*. Morality is the Doctrine of Duties and Virtues.

227. The internal actions, Desire, Affection, Intention, Will, point to external Acts; they have external acts for their Objects, and derive their character and significance, as right or wrong, from the external Acts to which they thus point. Thus the Desire of Having leads to Acts of appropriation, and derives its character, as right or wrong, from the Acts of appropriation to which it points. Hence, if this, or any other internal Act, point to external Acts of which the character, as right or wrong, is already determined in the preceding Book; these internal Acts have their characters as right or wrong determined. If the Desire of Having point to the Act of Stealing, which Act is wrong; the Desire itself is wrong. For, as we have already said, it is the internal Springs of Action from which the Act derives its character of wrong. If it be wrong, it is so because the Desire and Intention which produce it are wrong.

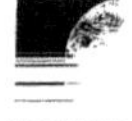

The character of actions considered with reference to the internal Springs of Action from which they proceed, is their *Moral* character.

The Moral character of actions is governed by their jural character. To steal is jurally wrong; it is contrary to universal natural Law. Hence the Volition which aims at theft is morally wrong. The Intention which points to theft is also morally wrong. The Desire of that which belongs to another is morally wrong. These internal acts are wrong, even if the external act do not take place. It is wrong to put my hand in a man's pocket in order to pick it, even if I find nothing there. It is wrong to intend to do so, even if I am prevented making the attempt by the presence of a looker-on. It is wrong to desire another man's money, even if I do not proceed to take it.

228. As there are Laws, which express Rules of external action, there are also *Moral Precepts*, which express Rules of internal action; that is, of Will and Intention, of the Desires and Affections. Thus the Law is, *Do not steal;* the Moral Precept is, *Do not covet*, or *desire* what is another's.

Such Moral Precepts express our Duties. They may be put in various forms. Thus the Precept, Do not covet, may be expressed by saying, It *is wrong* to covet: We *ought not* to covet; We *must not* covet; We *should not* covet; We *are not to* covet; It is our *Duty not* to covet; We are *morally bound* not to covet; We *must not be guilty* of covetousness.

229. As the Laws which describe our principal Obligations have reference respectively to the principal Desires and Affections of our nature, the Moral Precepts which respect those Desires will correspond to each of our principal Obligations. Hence we shall have Precepts of Duty corresponding to each of the Classes of Rights, of which we have spoken in the last Book.

Thus there are Rights of the Person, and a corresponding Class of Obligations. We are bound by Law to abstain from inflicting any personal harm on any one through anger, malice, or negligence. We are therefore bound morally to abstain from the affections which aim at any such harm, and the habits of mind which lead to it. It is our Duty to avoid Anger, Malice, and the Carelessness which may lead to another's hurt. The Moral Precepts are; Be not angry with any man: Bear no Malice: Neglect no one's safety.

There are the Rights of Property, and a corresponding Class of Obligations. We are bound by Law not to meddle with the Property of another; not to take or appropriate what is not our own. We are morally bound to abstain from the Intentions and Desires which point to such appropriation. It is our Duty to avoid the Wish to possess what is another's. The Moral Precept is, Do not covet.

There is a Class of Obligations which regards Contracts and Promises. We are bound by Law to perform our Contracts; not to break our Engagements. We are morally bound not to wish to break our Engagements. And as the moral obligation is not confined by mere legal limits, we are morally bound to perform our engagements, whether or not they are legally valid as Contracts. It is our Duty to perform our Promises: not to deceive or mislead any man by our words. The Moral Precepts are, Do not break your word; Do not deceive.

There is a Class of Obligations which regards the Marriage Union. We are bound by Law not to meddle with the person, or seduce the conjugal affection, of her who belongs to another. There is a Class of Duties which regard the Desires and Affections on which this Union is founded. We are morally bound not to allow these Desires and Affections to point to unlawful objects. The Moral Precept is, Do not lust after her.

There is a Class of Obligations which regard the Governors and the Government of the State to which we belong. We are jurally bound to obey the Governors, and to conform our actions to the Law. We are morally bound to conform our Desires and Intentions to the Law. It is our Duty to submit to positive Laws, as the realization and definition of the Supreme Law. The Moral Precepts are, Do not desire what the Law forbids. Do not desire to violate general Laws.

The Moral Precepts just stated: Be not angry: Bear no malice: Do not covet: Do not lie: Do not deceive: Do not lust: Do not desire to break Law: are to be applied to the whole train of our affections, desires, thoughts, and purposes, and to the whole course of actions, internal and external, which make up our lives. By their application to the various circumstances of human character and condition, the Classes of Duties, thus pointed out, are further particularized and defined.

CHAPTER II.

OF THE *IDEA* OF MORAL GOODNESS.

230. THESE Moral Precepts, as now stated, are negative. They prohibit certain kinds of internal actions. They point out certain Conceptions which we are to avoid: Anger, Malice, Covetousness, Lying, Deceit, Lust, Law-breaking. These are internal acts from which we are morally bound to abstain. These are points *from* which the Forces of morality tend.

But negative Precepts and repulsive Forces cannot suffice to express the character of Morality. The Supreme Law of Human Action must be positive. It must command as well as prohibit. It must direct us what to tend *to*, as well as from. It must not merely repress and control the Affections, Desires, and Intentions; it must direct them to their proper objects, and enjoin steadiness and energy in them, thus directed. The Supreme Law of our Actions must be a Law for all the Powers of Action. It must include the whole of our nature. Its rule for Affection and Desire must be, not that they shall be extinguished, but that they shall be right Affection and right Desire. And the Reason, which has for its office the formation of Conceptions to which the Mental Affections and Desires tend, must form Conceptions to which the right Affections and right Desires may tend.

231. The Conceptions *to* which Morality directs our Desires and Affections, may be collected, in a general way, from what has been said of the Conceptions *from* which the impulses of Morality urge us. As Morality calls us from Anger, Malice, Covetousness, Lying, Deceit, Lust, Law-breaking; she impels us to an opposite set of qualities:—Mildness, Kindness, Liberality, Fairness, Truthfulness, Humanity, Temperance, Chastity, Obedience. These Conceptions must enter into the Idea of the End of Human Action. These must be included in the Supreme Law of Human Action. These points indicate the place to which the lines of Duty all tend. The Supreme Law of Human Action must be found in the point to which all such lines converge. It may be conceived as the *Ideal Center* of such special moral tendencies as we have spoken of; and, thus, as the *Idea* of Morality.

232. We may proceed somewhat further in the determination of this Ideal Center, or Idea of Morality. The Supreme Law of Human Action must be a Law which belongs to man as man; a thing in which all men sympathize, and which binds together man and man by the tie of their common humanity (69). It excludes all that operates merely to separate men; for example, all Desires that tend to a center in each individual, without any regard to the common sympathy of mankind; and especially, all Affections which operate directly to introduce discord and conflict; as we have seen, accordingly, that it excludes Malice and Anger, and directs us to Mildness and Kindness. The absence of all the affections which tend to separate men, and the aggregate of the Affections which unite them, may be expressed by the

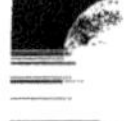

term *Benevolence,* understood in its largest and fullest sense, as including all the ties of Love which bind men together. We feel and conceive the affection of Love, at first as binding together the members of the same Family, or of the same Community: but man is capable of extending his Love to all mankind; in proportion as there is unfolded, in his mind, the conception of the community of their nature and his own; —of their common affections, reason, and moral sentiments in which all mankind participate. With the development of this conception, he is led to a love of man as man, and a desire of the good of all men;—an affection in which all mankind are ready to sympathize, and which binds together man as man. This Affection, then, of Love to man as man, is a part of the Supreme Law of Human Action: and the *Idea* of a complete and universal *Benevolence* is a point in the direction of the Ideal Center, or a part of the Idea of Morality of which we have spoken.

Again; in the Supreme Law of Human Action we must exclude, as we have said, all Desires that merely tend to their center in the individual, without regard to the common sympathy of mankind. The Desire of Property is, in its original form, of this kind. Each man desires Property for himself alone. But the nature of Morality, as we have seen, points out Liberality and Fairness as the proper guides of action, in opposition to Selfish Covetousness. Liberality partakes of Benevolence; but Fairness may be conceived as the Desire that each person should have his own. And this Desire may be conceived in its most complete and comprehensive form as *Justice:* and the *Idea* of *Justice,* thus fully understood, is part of that Ideal Center or Idea of Morality above mentioned.

Again; among the necessary conditions of a Rule of human action, is the existence of a Common Understanding among men, such that they can depend upon each other's actions. Lying and Deceit tend to separate and disunite men; and to make all actions implying mutual dependence, that is, all social action and social life, impossible. Such acts are accordingly excluded by the Supreme Rule, and Truthfulness and Honesty are pointed out as proper guides of Moral Action. These qualities, conceived in their most complete form, as extending from the Acts to the Words, and from the Words to the Intentions, may be termed *Integrity*, as implying an entire consistence of external and internal acts; or may be termed *Truth*, as implying an agreement of the verbal expression with the thought; and the *Idea* of *Truth*, in this full and comprehensive sense, is a part of the Central Idea, or Idea of Morality.

Again: the bodily Appetites and Desires, still more than the mental ones, tend to their center in the individual, and thus operate to disunite and oppose men. The Affections make the bodily Desires, in some measure, operate towards the union and sympathy of men; but still more towards their conflict and disunion, except so far as both Desires and Affections are governed by Obligations. The Supreme Rule requires that they should be so governed as not even to tend to violate Obligations;—that they should be conformed to Precepts of Duty; and therefore, that they should be controlled and directed by the Moral Sentiments and the Reason. The Control of the Appetites by the Moral Sentiments and the Reason is recommended to us by Morality, under the Conceptions of Temperance and Chastity. In our moral view of the Springs of Action, we conceive the Appetites and Desires as elements which ought to be thus controlled. Appetite and Desire are the *Lower Parts;* Moral Sentiments and Reason are the *Higher Parts*, of our Nature: and the Precepts which recommend to us Temperance and Chastity may be expressed in a general form by saying, that the Higher Part of our

Nature ought to control and govern the Lower. We may express this Control and Government in the most general and comprehensive way by the term *Purity;* and the *Idea of Purity*, thus completely and comprehensively understood, is a part of the Ideal Center, or Idea of Morality.

Again: the Supreme Law of Human Action, in order to operate effectively upon men's minds, must be distinctly and definitely conceived, at least in some of its parts and applications. But all distinct and definite conceptions of Laws of Human Action must involve a reference to the relations which positive Laws establish. Hence Moral Rules, in order to be distinct and definite, must depend upon Laws; and must suppose Laws to be fixed and permanent. It is our duty to promote, by our acts, this fixity and permanence; and the Duty, of course, extends to our internal actions, to Will, Intention, Desire and Affection, as well as to external act. We must conform our Dispositions to the Laws; obey the Laws cordially, or administer them carefully, according to the position we may happen to hold in the community. This disposition may be denoted by the term *Order*, understood in a large and comprehensive sense. But further: not only positive human Laws, but subordinate moral Rules, are necessary conditions of morality. We cannot conform our actions, intentions, desires, to the Supreme Rule, without having in our thoughts subordinate Rules, which are partial expressions of the Supreme Rule; and to such subordinate Rules, it is our Duty to conform our Intentions and Desires. The disposition to do this may also be included in the term *Order*, taken in its largest sense. We thus denote, by this term, a disposition to conform, both to positive human Laws as the necessary conditions of this, and to special Moral Rules, as the expression of the Supreme Rule. And the *Idea* of *Order* in this com-

prehensive sense is part of the Central Idea of Morality.

233. Thus we have five Ideas, *Benevolence, Justice, Truth, Purity*, and *Order*, which may be considered as the elements of the Central Idea of Morality, or as the Cardinal Points of the Supreme Rule of Human Action.

We are not to conceive these Ideas as distinct and separable, but rather as connected and combined in a fundamental and intimate manner. Thus, we have already mentioned moral qualities which partake of more than one, as Liberality partakes of Benevolence and Justice: Honesty, of Justice and Truth. And all these dispositions, Benevolence, Justice, Truth, Purity, Order, may be conceived to be included in a Love of *Goodness*. The Disposition enjoined by the Supreme Law of Human Action is the Love of Moral Good as Good, and the desire to advance towards it as the ultimate and only real object of action. To this object, all special affections, all external objects, and the desires of such objects, all intercourse of men, all institutions of society, are considered as subordinate and instrumental. And thus, this Love of Good includes, excites, nourishes, and directs to their proper ends, those more special Affections and Dispositions of which we have spoken.

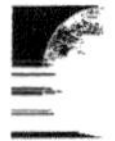

In order to describe the character and conduct conformable to the Supreme Rule, we may speak of it as the character and conduct of a *good man*. That is right which a good man would do. Those are right affections which a good man would feel.

234. Benevolence, Justice, Truth, Purity, Order, have been considered as Dispositions in man. But these Dispositions may be conceived as Desires or Affections, tending to certain abstract mental Objects or Ideas. Thus, Benevolence is a Desire or Affection which has for its Object the Good of all Mankind. This object may be expressed by the

term Humanity. Humanity, which is thus the ideal object of Benevolence, is also a term used to describe the disposition itself, as it exists in man, who is the subject of this affection. We have thus an *objective* and a *subjective* Humanity. In like manner, Justice is a Desire which has for its Object the Rule, To each his own. This Rule is itself described as Justice, ("I ask for Justice"); and thus we have subjective Justice, the Disposition, and objective Justice, the Rule. In like manner, Truth, the Disposition as it exists in man, its Subject, assumes and tends to an Objective Truth, the agreement between the reality of things and our expressed conceptions of them. Purity, the Disposition, has for its Object an Ideal Purity, free from all blemish and taint of mere desire. Willing conformity to Law, which is subjective Order, has, for its Object, Law itself, which may be described as Objective Order. Thus, some of the most common and familiar abstract terms, Humanity, Justice, Truth, Purity, Order, are used to describe both subjectively, the Disposition, and objectively, the Idea to which it tends.

235. There are, however, other terms by which the two significations of each of these words is separately expressed. Thus, as we have seen, subjective Humanity is *Benevolence;* objective Humanity is the Good of all Mankind, the Welfare of Man, and the like. Perhaps one of the most usual modes of describing the object of Benevolence, in its largest sense, is to say, that it is the increase of *Human Happiness*. Justice is used with equal familiarity for Subjective Justice, the Disposition, and Objective Justice, the Rule. Subjective Truth is called Truthfulness, *Veracity;* and under certain conditions, Faithfulness, Fidelity. Special portions of objective Truth are *Truths:* and are also termed *Verities.* Purity in its subjective sense may be distinguished, as *Purity of Heart*, from Purity used objectively, as

when we speak of the *Love of Purity*. Subjective Order is Orderliness, *Obedience*, or, as we have said, willing Conformity to Law: Objective Order is *Law*, Rule, which includes Special Laws and Rules, as Truth includes special Verities.

236. These five terms, in their Subjective Sense, Benevolence, Justice, Truth, Purity, Order, are Dispositions conformable to the Supreme Law of Human Action: they are therefore Virtues (226). And inasmuch as they are the leading points to which we have been led, by our analysis of human springs of action, and human obligations, we may term them *Cardinal Virtues*: although they are different from the list of Cardinal Virtues as usually given, Temperance, Fortitude, Justice, and Wisdom. This latter list is too unphilosophical a division to be employed with any advantage in Morality. But the Virtues which have names in common language, are all conceived as Virtues, in consequence of partaking of one or more of our five Cardinal Virtues, Benevolence, Justice, Truth, Purity, and Order; and we may arrange the Virtues in general according to their affinity with these five.

The five Cardinal Virtues may be variously combined with the Springs of Human Action; but yet each of these Virtues has its more peculiar sphere of operation in our nature. Benevolence is mainly concerned in guiding and governing the Affections; Justice, in controlling and correcting our Mental Desires; Truth, in directing the Mutual Understanding of men; Purity, in regulating the Bodily Desires. Order engages the Reason in the consideration of Rules and Laws, by which Virtue and its opposite are defined.

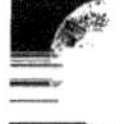

237. The opposite of Virtue, or the want of it, is *Vice*: and the language of all nations supplies us with a long list of Virtues, arising from the combination of the Cardinal Virtues with the various springs and conditions of human action, and of the antagonist Vices. These names of Virtues and Vices are Ab-

stract Terms, and have Adjectives connected with them, by which the varieties of human character and disposition are familiarly designated. The limits of Virtue and Vice, however, are far from being manifest and obvious. It is often very difficult to say where Virtue ends, and where Vice begins. To define such limits, when it is possible, must be our business, when we come to treat of Questions of Duty. But it is necessary for us to employ the names of Virtues and Vices in a general and usual sense, before we thus attempt to define their limits. The names of Virtues and Vices are the Vocabulary of Morality; and of this Vocabulary, we shall give a brief account; arranging the Terms, as we have said, according to their affinity with the Five Cardinal Virtues.

CHAPTER III.

VIRTUES AND VICES.

1. *Virtues of the Affections.*

238. Benevolence is the Virtue of the Affection of Love. This Affection is variously modified, according to the persons to whom it is directed, and the accompanying circumstances. Thus there is Conjugal Love, the Love of Husband and Wife; Parental (Paternal and Maternal) Love; Filial Love; Fraternal Love, and other kinds of Family Affection; Friendship, the Love by which Friends are especially drawn to each other; our Love of our Fellow-Citizens; of our Fellow-Countrymen; finally, the Love which we bear to the whole Human Race and to every member of it. All these Kinds of Love are Springs of Action, and Sources of Emotion, which it is the business of Morality, not to resist and destroy, but to govern and

direct. When these natural affections are directed to their proper objects, and regulated by Reason, they are *virtuous* Affections. Those in whom they are wanting are blamed as *without natural affection*. They are all included in the general term, *Benevolent Affections*. They are spoken of figuratively as the *Heart*. A man's *heart is hard*, or *cold*, when these affections are feeble and dull in him; he is *warmhearted*, when they are strong; and *openhearted*, when they are readily bestowed on those around him.

239. Benevolent Affections are called *kindly* affections, for they knit us to our Kind, the Human Race. Hence *kind*, the adjective, describes the disposition of a person full of such affections. A man is *estranged* from his friends, when those affections cease; he is *unkind*, when the opposite prevail; he is *unsocial*, when he shuns the occasions of kindly intercourse with companions.

When a benevolent affection turns our attention upon its object in a tranquil manner, it is *Regard*. *Love*, is the affection in a more marked form. It is *Tenderness*, when it implies a sensitive and vigilant solicitude for the good of its object; *Fondness*, when it absorbs the thought, so that Reason is disregarded. When this is the case, the affection is no longer a Virtue: still less is it so, when Love becomes *doting*, *overweening*, *passionate*.

Love towards a person, growing out of good received from him, is *Gratitude*. A grateful person expresses his emotions in Words, which are *Thanks*; but he is also desirous of doing Acts of gratitude; of returning Good for Good. Gratitude is a natural and virtuous Affection; but the Acts which it prompts must be limited by Rules of Duty. A man who does what is wrong in return for benefits received, makes his Benefactor the director of his actions, instead of directing them himself, as Morality requires. Hence he is said to *sell himself*; and to be *venal*.

240. The manifestations of the benevolent affections, in their influence upon the habitual external Behaviour, have various names. Such affections, regarding a particular person, and not necessarily leading to action, are *Good-will*. When they produce a current of cheerful thoughts, they are *Good-humour*. When benevolent feelings lead a man to comply readily with the wishes of others, or to seek to give them pleasure, we have *Good-nature*. When this Disposition is shown on the part of a superior, we term him ***gracious*** and ***benign***. When a person's Good-nature makes it easy to address him, he is *affable*. If, in his behaviour, he avoid all that may give offence to others, he is *courteous*. This Disposition is conceived to have generated in the inhabitants of cities, Habits of behaviour which are termed *Urbanity* and *Civility*. The opposite of these is *Rudeness*.

241. Good-humour may often be disturbed by the Provocations which offences and outrages occasion; but there are virtuous Dispositions which support our benevolence under such provocations. Such dispositions are *Gentleness, Mildness, Meekness*. Under the influence of these, we repress or avoid the resentment and anger, which offences against us, and insults offered to us, tend to produce; we preserve benevolence, tranquillity, and good-humour in our minds; and manifest such a disposition in our behaviour. With these dispositions, if men act wrongly or foolishly, we are *tolerant* and *indulgent*; if they offend us, we *pardon* and *forgive* them. We are ready to do this; we are *placable*. To be *intolerant, unforgiving, implacable*, is a vicious Disposition.

242. The Benevolent Affections are also modified by a regard to the circumstances of the object. We naturally share in the emotions which we witness in men: we have a *Fellow-feeling*, a *Sympathy* with them. When this Disposition leads us to feel pain at the sight of pain, it is *Compassion:* we *commiserate*

the object. This feeling, being strongly confirmed by Piety, came to be called *Pity*. Such a Disposition, as it prompts us to abstain from adding to the pain felt, is *Mercy*, or *Clemency;* as it prompts us to remove the pain or want which we see, it is *Charity*. But this word has also a wider sense, in which it describes Benevolence, as it makes us abstain from judging unfavourably of other men. All these are virtuous Affections, and lead to the performance of Duties of Benevolence.

243. *Admiration* can hardly be called a benevolent affection towards its object; for we admire what does not draw our Love; as when we admire a great geometer. But if we admire a man as a good man, we also love him (91). *Esteem* is the benevolent affection which we entertain towards that of which we approve. Persons whom we esteem, but to whom we are not drawn by love, we *respect*. When, with such a Disposition, we look at them as our Superiors, we *reverence* them; in a higher degree, this Affection is *Veneration;* when combined with Fear, it is *Awe*. Reverence assumes, in its object, Authority and Power, combined with Justice and Goodness.

244. The irascible Affections are, for the most part, opposed to the virtue of Benevolence; and therefore are to be repressed and controlled. Yet these Affections also have their moral office, and give rise to Virtues. They act as a Defence against harm and wrong; and hence, in their various modifications, they may be termed *Defensive Affections*. As opposed to harm, inflicted or threatened, they are Resentment; as directed against wrong, they are Indignation (56). And these Emotions may be blameless or praiseworthy; as when we feel *natural* and *proper Resentment*, or *just Indignation*. Such Sentiments are an important and necessary part of Virtue; not of Benevolence, strictly speaking, but of Justice. Without Indignation against cruelty, fraud, falsehood

foulness, disorder, the Virtues have not their full force in the mind.

But Anger, in order to be virtuous, must be directed solely against moral Wrong. *Malevolent Affections* directed towards Persons are Vices; *Antipathy, Dislike, Aversion* to any person, independently of his bad character and conduct, are vicious. It is vicious to be *displeased, irritated, incensed, exasperated* at any person, merely because his actions interfere with our pleasures and desires. The proneness to such Anger is *Irascibility*. Still more vicious are our Emotions, when they swell into *Rage* and *Fury*, or settle into *Malice* and *Hatred*. The term *Rancour* denotes a fixed Hate, which, by its inward working, has, as it were, diseased the Soul in which it exists. *Spite* implies a vigilant desire to depress and mortify its object. All these malevolent Feelings are vicious.

245. Moderate Anger, arising from pain inflicted on us, is *Offence;* which term is also used for the offensive Act. A person *commits an offence*, or *offends*, in the latter sense; and *takes offence*, or *is offended*, in the former. If the Act be one which violently transgress common rules, it is an *Outrage*. Anger at pain received, impelling a man to inflict pain in return, is *Revenge*. This term also implies the object or aim of the feeling, as well as the feeling itself. A man is *stimulated by Revenge*, and *seeks his Revenge*. The same may be said of the word *Vengeance*, another form of the word, but of the same origin. The man who admits into his heart this Affection, and retains it, is *revengeful, vengeful, vindictive*.

246. The Malevolent Feelings, as manifested in the external behaviour, have various names. As they affect our disposition to a person, without necessarily leading to action, they are *Ill-will*. When they disturb the usual current of cheerful thoughts, they are *Ill-humour*. When malevolent feelings lead

us to speak or act with a view of giving pain to others, they are *Ill-nature*. When they make us rejoice in another person's pain, they are *Malignity*. If the pleasure, which a malignant man takes in another man's pain, be unchecked by compassion, when the pain is evident, he is *cruel;* and as such a disposition shows a deficiency in the common feelings which bind men together, he is *inhuman*. If this character be strongly marked, the man is *savage;* he approaches to the character and temper of wild beasts; he is *brutal*.

The Malevolent Affections are also modified by a regard to the circumstances of the object of them, as compared with our own circumstances. Malevolent Pain at the Good which happens to another, and at our own Want of this Good, is *Envy*.

247. *Contempt* can hardly be called a malevolent feeling; for we may despise persons without hating them. Contempt consists rather in an estimate of a man as below a certain Standard of Character, to which our Esteem is given. We despise a man for Cowardice, because we admire Courage. The verb *despise* (*despicio*, to look down upon,) shows that such a view is implied. The word *Scorn* implies a condemnation of this kind, so strong that it approaches to Indignation. The expression of contempt, in a marked manner, is an *Insult*. If the discrepance of the contemplated character with the assumed standard be extravagant, so as to excite a sudden and poignant feeling of Incongruity, our Contempt expresses itself in *Laughter*. The character is regarded as *ridiculous*.

248. There are various modifications of character and conduct which arise from the greater or less Energy of the affections, and appear as Virtues or as Vices. The feelings of Love of Right, and Anger at Wrong, in a permanent and energetic form, are virtuous *Zeal*. Courage, the habit of mind which rejects Fear, is allied to this virtue; as is *Fortitude*, the

habit of not yielding to Pain. From such dispositions of mind, arise *Energy* and *Activity* in action; which are important virtues when the action is virtuous.

249. Though Hope and Fear are not Affections, they operate in increasing or diminishing our energy and activity, as the Affections do. The Disposition in which the emotion of Hope predominates is also termed *Hope*, or *Hopefulness*. *Joy* and *Joyfulness* describe rather Delight produced by some special event, than any permanent Disposition; but *Cheerfulness*, like Hopefulness, is rather an habitual Disposition; and when governed by Rules of Duty, is an auxiliary Virtue. A tranquil yet cheerful flow of the spirits keeps the thoughts and feelings in a condition suitable to virtuous action. The want of activity and energy is *Sluggishness, Sloth, Idleness, Laziness, Indolence;* which are habits alien to virtue, and connected with the Vice of Apathy, the absence of lively affections and desires. As the influence of Fear predominates, the character becomes *timid*, and tends to *Cowardice*, the opposite of Courage. Such habits are at variance with the Rules of Duty; for these Rules often direct us in a course which leads through danger, either to the Person or Fortune of the Actor, or to the Good-will which others feel for him. In order that a man may act rightly, he must act *freely, independently*. Men wanting in Independence of Character, and seeking the favour of others, without regard to moral Rules, are *slavish, servile, obsequious, cringing, fawning;* they are *Flatterers* and *Sycophants*. Such dispositions make men *abject* and *base*. The want of cheerfulness and hopefulness is *Despondency, Dejection, Sullenness, Melancholy, Gloom;* which are habits of mind adverse to active virtue. The theo logical moralists have made *Acedia* (ακηδία), Apathy with regard to Good, one of their seven deadly sins.

250. We have placed here the Virtues and Vices which are connected with Energy or Zeal, be-

cause these qualities depend very much upon the strength of the Affections. They depend also, however, upon the Habits of Mind by which the intention is directed. The energetic man decides soon and conclusively what course to take. This is *Decision.* Energy also manifests itself in *Fixity of Purpose.* When the purpose is once formed, the energetic man's course is *determined;* his doubts are *resolved;* and he goes on in spite of difficulty and danger. This is *Determination, Resolution.* A man who adheres to his purpose, in spite of strong motives to draw him away, is *firm;* but if the motives which he resists are reasonable, he is *obstinate.* Firmness implies a good cause; Obstinacy a bad one. Energy and Zeal may also become extreme, so as to trespass upon Benevolence. In this case they are *Overzeal, Vehemence, Harshness, Impatience.*

Zeal, operating through the Reason, is *Earnestness,* which leads to *Seriousness.* With this quality, Cheerfulness is not inconsistent, but *Levity* is. *Care* sometimes implies only so much attention as Earnestness requires; at other times, it implies more than is consistent with Cheerfulness. It is right *to take Care,* but it is not necessary to be *full of Care.* It is wrong to be *careless, reckless.* A disposition to attend to Trifles only is *Frivolity.*

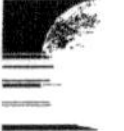

251. Connected with the pleasures of Cheerfulness, there are pleasures which show themselves externally in good-humoured Laughter; as the pleasures of Jesting and the like. These arise from intellectual acts, and may be spoken of hereafter; but we may here remark, that under the influence of Levity, they lead to mere *Merriment, Buffoonery, Folly.*

2. *Virtues of the Mental Desires.*

252. Property is the Conception about which the cardinal virtue of Justice is especially concerned; and hence the dispositions and habits of mind which regard Property, have Justice for their leading virtue. Yet Wealth, and Property of all kinds, may be used as a means of Benevolence; and from this use, arise Virtues; as *Charity*, already mentioned, *Liberality* (a willingness to give), and the like. Wealth may be desired as a means either to such ends, or to different ones. Hence the Disposition which aims at acquisition, may be virtuous or vicious, according to the ulterior object. A man may desire Wealth as a means of Luxury and Sensuality; and in such a case, the Desire of Wealth is opposed to Temperance, rather than to Justice.

The Desire of the means of Subsistence is an universal and necessary Desire. A Wish for a Competence—for so much property as may free a man from solicitude respecting common needs and common enjoyments,—is not opposed either to Justice or to Temperance. The prospect of *Poverty* and *Penury;* the pressure of *Privation* and *Want;* the sense of *Dependence* upon others;—greatly tend to disturb the influence of virtue in the mind. The Fear of these evils is not a vice. Also wealth may be desired as a means of benevolent action, or of right action, in many other ways. A person's power of doing good, of many kinds, depends much upon the Station and Influence which wealth bestows.

253. But though wealth may be desired for ends which make the Desire virtuous; the progress of men's habits is such that, when sought at first as a means, it is afterwards desired as an end. The Desire to acquire money is then unlimited; and **is** *Covetousness*, *Avarice*. The man's greediness in

desiring, is *Cupidity:* his eagerness in taking, is *Rapacity*. He scrapes and hoards. He spares carefully and spends unwillingly; he is *parsimonious, niggardly, penurious*. His solicitude and privations make him miserable. He is a *Miser*.

On the other hand, such habits of care, with regard to sparing and spending, as may tend to avoid Poverty and Privation, are reckoned as Virtues: such virtues are *Economy, Frugality*. By these, a man *thrives*, or grows in his possessions; he is *thrifty*. A person who is destitute of these qualities is an *Unthrift*. A willingness to give is Liberality, Generosity, Bountifulness; which are reckoned Virtues. But this disposition may be excessive: the man is then *lavish, extravagant*.

254. Property conveys Power to the Possessor: but there are also many other Sources of Power. Whoever aims at a larger share of Power than his neighbours possess, is, so far, regardless of Justice. The Desire of Power is *Ambition*. But the Desire of Power for good ends, and the Desire of the Power which moral excellence gives, may be termed *laudable Ambition*.

The Disposition which represses our own desires, whether of money, power, victory, or any other object; and contemplates the desires and claims of other persons with equal favour; is *Fairness*. This is a kind of personal application of Justice, to questions between ourselves and others. *Impartiality* is more commonly used for the Fairness which decides justly between two other persons.

3. *Virtues connected with Truth.*

255. We have mentioned (235) some of the names of the Virtues connected with Truth; as *Truthfulness, Veracity*. These express a conformity of our words to the reality. The conformity of our

actions to our Engagements, whether express or implied, is *Fidelity*, *Good Faith*. Thus a subject is faithful to the engagement which binds him to the Sovereign of the State. If, in such a case, Love is added to Fidelity, it becomes *Loyalty*.

A man who says what he knows to be untrue, is a *Liar*. He is guilty of *Falsehood*. A man who says what he thinks, is *sincere*. Such a man shows himself what he is. A man who conceals some important part of his feelings or thoughts, *dissembles*. When he assumes the appearance of virtues which he really does not possess, he is a *Hypocrite*. By such means men *impose* upon others, and *deceive* them.

Lies and Deceit are often used as means of *Fraud;* which is an offence against Property, and therefore contrary to Justice as well as Truth. A person who *defrauds*, *circumvents*, *cheats* any one, must be destitute both of Justice and of Truth. Property and Language may both be considered as Universal Contracts, to which the whole human race are parties; Fraud by means of Falsehood violates both these Contracts.

A man free from all fraudulent dispositions is *honest;* he is a man of *Probity*. He is not drawn aside, by the desire of gain, to act *obliquely*, *tortuously*, in a *crooked* manner. He is *straightforward*, and *upright*. His intentions, words, and actions, form a whole in which there is no inconsistent part. This is *Integrity*. A deceitful man may have two purposes; one, apparent, simulated, declared; the other secretly held, but dissembled, till it can be acted on. To have two purposes in this way is *Duplicity*. The truthful person, on the contrary, has *Simplicity* for a part of his character: he has *Singleness of Purpose*, *Singleness of heart*. He is *frank* and *open*, showing himself as he really is.

4. *Virtues relating to the Bodily Desires.*

256. The gratification of the Appetites or Bodily Desires, to a certain extent, and under certain conditions, is requisite for the continuance of the individual and of the Species, and therefore is not vicious. These Desires being mere attributes of the Body, cannot have, of themselves, a moral character. They are to be controlled by moral Rules, and made subservient to moral Affections, and thus, are the materials of Virtues. The Habits of thus controlling the bodily Desires, are the Virtues of *Temperance* and *Chastity*. The Demeanour produced by a chaste mind, especially in women, is *Modesty*.

By the establishment of Family and Social Relations, the gratification of the bodily wants is connected with the impulses of Affection and the Love of Society. The shelter of the common family roof, and the social meal, as well as the marriage-bed, are the objects of far other feelings than mere bodily desires. The Appetites are thus made subservient to the Affections. They are absorbed by the Affections, and are thus *purified*. All gratifications of the Appetites, sought as gratifications merely, are impure and vicious. Among such vices is the *Love of the Pleasures of the Table*. When the Desire of Food is gratified to excess, there is *Gluttony*, *Gulosity*. When there is an excessive solicitude about the gratification of the Taste, the man is an *Epicure*. The Love of Drink involves, not only a bodily Appetite, but a complacency in the mental condition to which certain liquors lead; namely, the condition of *Intoxication* or *Ebriety*; a condition in which the Reason loses the power of directing our actions. The Vice of falling into such a condition is *Intemperance*, *Drunkenness*.

The other leading bodily Desire, when not morally

controlled, is *Lust*. The control of this within moral limits, is *Continence*. The vicious indulgence is *Lewdness, Lechery*. Persons whose guiding springs of action are these bodily desires, are *sensual, carnal*. A chaste and modest person does not allow his eyes or his imagination to dwell on things which may excite Lust. Such images are obscene, indecent. To suggest such images in speech is *Obscenity*. All such filthy conversation *pollutes the mind*. A man who makes pleasure the object of his actions is a *Voluptuary*. Such men generally cast off moral restraint, and are hence *dissolute, profligate*. A woman who thinks lightly of chastity is *a Wanton*.

When the arts of life are employed to gratify artificial wants and desires, those who give their attention and solicitude to obtain such gratifications are *luxurious*. Luxury is often employed to describe the aggregate of such gratifications; but the Solicitude employed on the means of gratification, rather than any special Class of such means, appears to be essential to our conception of Luxury. Things which are Luxuries in one stage of society, become universal Wants, and consequently Necessaries, in another stage. Linen garments, glass windows, tea, were Luxuries a few centuries ago in this country. They are now Necessaries of life.

5. *Intellectual Virtues.*

257. The Disposition by which we accept Law and Rule as the necessary guides of human action, is that which we have termed Order. This Virtue is also, as we have said (235), termed *Orderliness, Obedience*, and the like. But it is a Virtue to govern carefully, as well as to obey cordially, according to the position we hold in the community.

A virtuous governor must be guided by Justice; but Justice itself must be defined by specific Rules.

Laws and Rules must be apprehended by the Intellect, and must be expressed in terms of general conceptions constructed by the Reason. Hence, the Virtues connected with Order especially include operations of the Intellect, and may be termed Intellectual Virtues.

258. The abstract Conceptions of the objects of our mental Desires, as Property, Power, Society, require operations of the Reason for their formation. By the further operation of the like Faculties, we form still more abstract and general conceptions of objects of action, as Good, Wellbeing, Happiness, Expediency, Interest, and the like. Rules of Action, dependent upon such Conceptions, may be conceived and expressed. Various moralists have stated various Rules, thus expressed. Different individuals govern their conduct by one or other of such Rules, more or less clearly apprehended. One man looks to Interest as his object, another to Happiness, another to Wellbeing, another to the Happiness of Mankind, and so on.

One or other of such objects being assumed as the end of human action, *Prudence* is the Intellectual Virtue by which we select the right means to this end. A man is prudent, who acts so as to promote his own Interest, if his Interest be assumed to be the proper Object of action: but if we conceive Happiness to be a higher object than Interest, he is prudent, if he disregard mere interest, and attend only to his Happiness. Prudence supposes the value of the end to be assumed, and refers only to the adaptation of the means. It is the selection of right means for given ends.

259. In the notion of *Wisdom*, we include, not only, as in Prudence, a right selection of means for an assumed end, but also a right selection of the end. However prudent a man may be in seeking his Interest, he is not wise, if, in doing this, he neglect a truer end

of human action. Wisdom is the habit by which we select right means for right ends. We approve and admire Prudence relatively to its end: we approve and admire Wisdom absolutely. We commend the prudent man, as taking the best course for his purpose; but we do not necessarily agree with him in his estimate of his object. We venerate the wise man, as one knowing, better than we do, the true object of action, as well as the means of approaching it. Wisdom is a Cardinal Virtue, like Benevolence, Justice, Truth, Purity; and with reference to the first, as well as the other four, human Dispositions are good, as they partake of the Cardinal Virtue. Wisdom is the complete Idea of Intellectual Excellence; as Benevolence, Justice, Truth, and Purity, are of Moral Excellence.

260. Prudence is, etymologically speaking, the same word as *Providence*, that is *Foresight*. But we do not call a man *prudent*, except he not only see the bearing of actions on a distant end, but act upon his foresight. A man who gambles, with a clear foresight that gambling will ruin him, is not prudent. Prudence is a virtue, not of the Speculative Reason, which contemplates Conceptions, but of the Practical Reason, which guides our Actions.

The guidance of our Actions by Reason, requires us to attend both to the present and to probable future circumstances; it requires *Attention*, and *Forethought*, or *Forecast*. It requires, too, the employment of Thought upon the Circumstances of the case. A virtuous man must be *thoughful, considerate*. The want of thoughtfulness is a part of that Levity which we have already noticed as involving a Vice of the Affections.

In order to act prudently, we must not only have Prudent thought, but have it at the right time for action; this is *Presence of Mind*. *Cunning* is a lower kind of Prudence, that seeks its ends by means, of which the end is not intended to be seen by others, when they are used.

By our Intellectual Faculties we are able to apprehend and know Truth, that is, Objective Truth (234); and especially, Truths which bear upon our actions, and which must be taken into account in framing Rules of Action. Truth is the proper object of Reason; that is, of the universal Reason of mankind: and the Supreme Rule of human action which belongs to mankind, in virtue of their universal Faculties, must depend upon the Truths which Reason makes known to us. The Love of Knowledge impels men to aim at the Knowledge of such Truths: and the *Love of Truth,* which thus contributes to a Knowledge of the Supreme Law, is a Virtue.

The progress which each man makes in the Knowledge of Truth, depends in a great measure upon himself; upon his Observation; his Diligence, Attention, Patience, in seeking the Truth. His progress depends also upon external circumstances; upon the Intellectual and Moral Development of the Society in which he lives; and upon his own Education, in the largest sense of the term. But there are also differences of the Mental Faculties, between one person and another. One man excels another in Acuteness and Clearness of the mind, when employed in observation or in reasoning; one man has a quicker or a more tenacious Memory than another. There are various degrees of Sagacity; various kinds of Imagination. Some men have Genius. These Faculties are not properly termed Virtues, but *Gifts, Endowments, Ability.* They may be used as means to right ends, and hence they are termed *Talents;* by a metaphor taken from the Parable in the New Testament, which teaches us that a man is blameable, when he does not use the means of right action assigned to him.

6. *Reflex Virtues and Vices.*

261. We may place, among the Intellectual Virtues and Vices, those which depend upon our apprehension of other men's sentiments concerning us. For such Virtues and Vices imply reflex thought. We have already enumerated (57) among the springs of human action, the Reflex Sentiments, in which we form a conception of other men's sentiments, by the image of our own; and of ourselves, as the object of those sentiments. Such are the Desire of Esteem, the Desire of Admiration, the Love of Fame, and the like.

There is a difference to be made between the Desire of Esteem and the Desire of Admiration. Esteem is given to what is deemed right and good. Admiration and Applause are often bestowed upon qualities which have no moral character; as strength, skill, beauty, wit, and the like. The want of such qualities is a ground, among many men, of Contempt; and if the deficiency appear suddenly and glaringly, of Ridicule. Ridicule implies that the object which excites it is so palpably below the standard which we apply to it, that the comparison is extravagant and absurd. The Desire of Admiration produces a Fear and Dread of this Contempt and Ridicule. But the Desire of being admired, for other than moral excellences, has in it nothing of Virtue. He who desires the Esteem of others, desires them to regard him as good; and will, for the most part, be disposed to sympathize with them in their admiration for what is good. The *Desire of Esteem* therefore is easily consistent with Virtue.

The *Desire of Admiration* produces a ready belief that we are admired, and a Joy and Elation of Mind accompanying such belief. This Disposition is *Vanity*. One who is treated with marks of general esteem among men, is brought to *Honour*. One who is pointed at as an object of general disesteem, is brought to *Disgrace;* and, if he feel the Disgrace, is put to *Shame*. But Honour and Shame likewise indicate, subjectively, the Sensibility of the man to those indications of general Esteem and Disesteem. We speak also of *False Honour*, and *False Shame;* meaning Dispositions to be influenced by Applause on the one side, and Blame or Ridicule on the other, even when they are not rightly bestowed. *True Honour* is a Regard for what is right and good, considered especially as the object of sympathy and esteem among men. A *man of Honour*, an *honourable man*, has an especial abhorrence of the Vices of Fraud and Falsehood. The Desire of Admiration in another form is the *Love of Glory*. In Civil Society are established marks of Public Honour, as Rank, Titles, Decorations, and the like. Dispositions, for the most part, allied to Vanity, fasten upon these objects; and thus we have the *Love of Rank*, or the like. But such marks of honour are often accompanied with Political Power; as when, in England, a man is made a Peer. In this case, the Desire of Rank may be Ambition, rather than Vanity.

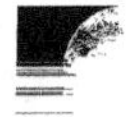

262. When I have formed a conception of *myself*, I am led to regard myself as the object of my own moral sentiments. If I approve my own character, I feel *Self-esteem*. If I am the object of my own Admiration, without requiring the Sympathy of others, this feeling is *Pride;* a Vice which estranges me from other men. The Satisfaction which is felt in my own Admiration, is *Self-complacency;* a feeling which blinds men to their true character.

I ought to render my Character such as to deserve esteem, and therefore, such as to deserve my own esteem, if I contemplate my own character. If I do this, I may reject wrong acts and emotions, as unsuited to the character which I thus ascribe to myself. The

Disposition to do this, appears to be what is meant by a *Proper Pride:* but this way of regarding one's own character appears to involve a share of *Self-complacency.* Men reckon among virtues, the *Magnanimity* which disregards small dangers and small injuries or offences. The opposite term, *Pusillanimity,* denotes cowardice; a quick sensibility to offences is *Captiousness.*

Pride is, in its tendency, at variance with the Benevolent Virtues, Meekness, Reverence, Courtesy. But the virtue which is especially opposed to Pride, is *Humility.* He who is humble in his estimate of himself, is also *modest* in comparing himself with others; but, as we have said (256), Female Modesty has a more especial meaning. When Pride is manifested so as to imply Contempt of others, it is *Haughtiness, Disdain;* if Unkindness be added, it is *Insolence.* The insolent man is *overbearing, domineering, arrogant.* Self-esteem, so far as it regards the Operation of the Intellect, is *Self-opinion.* When this excludes all mistrust of one's self, it is *Self-sufficienccy;* and, as taking much for granted, it is *Presumption.* When Pride fastens upon special points, it is *Conceit.*

263. The Habits of mind by which we resist the impulses of desire and affection, so as to conform to rules of virtue or prudence, are *Self-control, Self-command, Self-watchfulness; Self-mistrust;* when the desires which we control are so lively that we cannot suppress them, though we resist them, it is *Self-denial.* When we seek our own gratification, in disregard of more virtuous objects, it is *Self-seeking.* When we let our Will take its course, in spite of manifest warnings of prudence, it is *Self-will.*

The Habit of making ourselves the principal object of our attention and solicitude, is the Vice of *Selfishness.* A man is selfish, if the Desires which tend to himself (the Desires of the Body, the Desire of Property, and the like), rather than the Affections, are his leading

Springs of Action. These may be termed *Selfish Desires.* The term implies an Excess in the attention which we give to ourselves, a Defect in that which we give to others; and is always used in an unfavourable sense. Hence the term is not applied to the predominance of those Desires which do not interfere with the claims of others. We call a man *selfish,* in whom the Love of Money or of Bodily Ease prevails, because such Dispositions make him disregard the claims of others; but we do not call a man *selfish,* in whom the Love of Knowledge or of Society is strong; for my pursuit of knowledge takes nothing from other persons; and my love of society implies an acknowledgment of some kind of merit or value in other men. Pride and Vanity are selfish dispositions; for the proud man is too much occupied with his own admiration of himself, and the vain man with admiration of himself proceeding from other men, to regard, with due attention, the claims of his neighbours.

The Selfish Man thinks only of himself: hence he has no *Consideration for others:* no due care for their feelings, condition, and claims. This Virtue is required in all; there is a higher degree of it, *Unselfishness;* the disposition of a person who pays no regard to his own gratification when that of another person comes in competition with it. A still higher degree of such virtue is *Self-devotion;* the virtue of him who willingly incurs pain, danger, or death, to procure benefits for another.

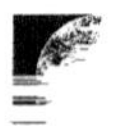

264. There are some dispositions regarded as Virtues, which are conceived to go beyond the standard of common characters. Such virtues are called *noble;* and when elevated still higher in our thoughts, they are *heroic* or *heroical. Heroism* generally implies great Fortitude or Courage, combined with Self-devotion. History is full of heroic acts; as that of Regulus, who refused to counsel his countrymen to peace, and returned to Carthage to die in tortures;

that of Virginius, who stabbed his daughter to preserve her from dishonour; that of the elder Brutus, who, as judge, condemned his own sons to death; that of Lucilius, who saved the younger Brutus by offering himself to the pursuers as Brutus; that of Socrates, who preferred to receive death in obedience to the Laws of his country, though escape was offered him by his friends. The acts of *Martyrs*, who died for the Truth, when they might have saved their lives by denying it, are heroical.

265. The Moral Vocabulary of which we have taken a survey, the Collection of Terms describing Virtues and Vices, is used to express the judgments of mankind in general, respecting the Dispositions and Characters of men. The approval or disapproval implied in each Term is, for the most part, so well understood, that the mere use of the term pronounces a moral sentence on the subject to which it is applied. And the moral judgment of mankind, thus expressed in a recognized form, is very efficacious in forming the moral sentiments of each person; and hence in modifying the characters and affections of men. The Vocabulary of Virtues and Vices is a constant moral Lesson; perpetually operating to bring each man's moral sentiments into agreement with the general judgment of men. Every man is taught, by the use of moral language, to admire Gratitude and Filial Love, to condemn Revenge and Cruelty; and the like.

For the most part, this Lesson agrees with the Lesson of true Morality, and points rightly to the Supreme Law of Human Action. This may be readily understood. For the Supreme Law of Human Action must be a Law in which all men, as men, sympathize (98). Hence the common moral judgment, of which we have been speaking, which is expressed and communicated by the moral language commonly in use among men, will, in general at least, conform to tne Supreme Law. What are universally held as Virtues, must be dispositions in conformity with this Law. What are universally reckoned Vices, must be wrong.

And a man, in so far as he is taught and formed by the general judgment of men, thus conveyed in the language of the Morality universally recognized, will be rightly taught. A man whose character contains what all men reckon Virtues, and is free from what are universally reckoned Vices, will be a good man. His affections and desires being thus regulated, he will tend to the possession of the Operative Moral Principles of Benevolence, Justice, Truth, Purity, Order; which we have stated as the Elements of the Supreme Law.

266. To the doctrine, that the common judgment of mankind respecting Virtues and Vices agrees, generally, with true Morality; it may be objected, that there are dispositions which we reckon vicious; and which yet, in many ages and countries, have been esteemed laudable, as Revenge. To this we reply, that men do not conceive themselves pronouncing the moral judgment of mankind when, under the influence of strong emotion, they speak of the satisfaction arising from Revenge, or appeal to the sympathy of other men alike moved. No Moralist speaking calmly, and in the Name of Mankind, would say that boundless Revenge is good and virtuous. So far as he could praise or defend the Disposition, it would be by identifying it with the Punishment of Wrong, that is, with Justice. Men speak of Revenge as "a kind of wild Justice;" and approve it only so far as it partakes of the nature of Justice. And in like manner, all other dispositions are reckoned Virtues, even in the common judgment of mankind, only so far as they agree with, and partake of, the Cardinal Virtues, Benevolence, Justice, Truth, Purity, and Order.

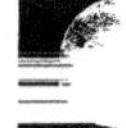

CHAPTER IV.

MORAL PRINCIPLES.

267. It is the business of our Reason to frame Rules of moral action, which are more or less partial expressions of the Supreme Rule (231, 257). When we have an assemblage of such Rules expressed in words, they may be variously connected, by means of the Conceptions which they involve; and Rules may be deduced, one from another, by reasoning; some being of a more general, and others of a more special nature. But such connexion and such reasoning must rest ultimately upon certain fundamental general Rules, which we may term *Principles;* just as in Geometry the reasoning rests ultimately upon the Axioms and Definitions. In order, therefore, that we may be able to express Moral Rules in words, we must state certain Moral Principles as the foundation of such Rules.

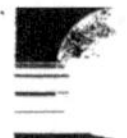

Then Moral Principles, being the expression of the Supreme Rule of Human Action, must coincide in their effect with the Ideas of Benevolence, Justice, Truth, Purity, and Order; which, as we have seen (230), are the Elements, or Cardinal Points, of the Supreme Rule. In order to lay down such Principles as we speak of, we have to express those Cardinal Ideas.

268. The term *Principles* is variously used. Springs of Action, as Affections, Desires, Dispositions, are often termed Principles of Action; especially when they operate in a steady and consistent manner. We put such steady *Principles* in opposition to transient and casual *Feelings*, which may be inconsistent with themselves. Our Feelings may prompt us to be kind to one person, and harsh to another; but Benevolence, operating as a Principle, would make us kind

to all. We have hitherto avoided speaking of "*Principles* of Action;" and have called the Affections and Desires Springs of Action (24). Custom allows us to term Benevolence, and the other Cardinal Virtues, Moral Principles, when they operate in any man steadily and consistently, even though they be not expressed in words. But we must distinguish the term *Principles*, used in this sense, from the fundamental Rules, the basis of other Rules, which we have also more especially called *Moral Principles*. We may call the former *Operative Principles*, the latter, *Express Principles*. The former are *Principles of Action*, the latter are *Principles of Reason*.

In order that a man's Character should conform to the Supreme Rule, it is requisite that Benevolence, Justice, Truth, Purity, and Order, should be in him Operative Principles. In order that he should express his Rules of Action so that they may be contemplated by the Reason, and communicated from one person to another, it is requisite that he should arrive at Express Principles.

269. Express Moral Principles must, as we have already said, be the expression of those Ideas which are the elements of the Supreme Rule. We have already been led to attempt to obtain such expressions, in speaking of these Moral Ideas.

We have seen (231) that the Idea of Benevolence is, that of an Affection, which makes man, as man, an object of love to us. We may therefore state it as a Moral Principle, that *Man is to be loved as Man*. We may term this the *Principle of Humanity*.

We have seen that the Idea of Justice is, that of a Desire that, of external things, each person should have his own, without any preference of ourselves to others, or of one person to another. We may state this also as a Moral Principle, that *Each Man is to have his own;* and this we may term the *Principle of Justice*.

We have seen that the Idea of Truth (as a Cardinal Virtue) is, the Idea of a Conformity to a Universal Understanding among men, which is involved in the use of language, and according to which Understanding, each may depend upon the representations of the others. Hence we may state it as a Moral Principle, that *We must conform to the Universal Understanding among men which the use of Language implies*: and this we may call the *Principle of Truth.*

Again, we have seen that the Idea of Purity implies the contemplation of mere Appetite and Desire, as the Lower Parts of our nature, which are to be governed by, and made subservient to, the Moral Sentiments and Reason, the Higher Parts. We may state this as a Moral Principle, that *The Lower Parts of our Nature are to be governed by, and subservient to, the Higher*. This is the *Principle of Purity.*

Again, we have seen that the Idea of Order implies a conformity, both to positive Human Laws, as the necessary conditions of morality, and to special Moral Rules, as the expression of the Supreme Rule. We may therefore state it as a Moral Principle, that *We must obey positive Laws as the necessary Conditions of Morality;* and this is the *Principle of Order.* We need not state it as a Principle, that we must obey subordinate Moral Rules: for the claims of such Rules may be established in virtue of the Primary Moral Principles which we are now stating.

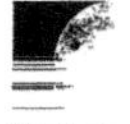

270. These five Express Moral Principles may be further unfolded; and the Conceptions by which we designate them, Humanity, Justice, Truth, Purity, and Order, may be further defined hereafter. But we do not fully express the import of the Cardinal Virtues of Benevolence, Justice, and the like, without adding some further Principles to those which we have mentioned. Benevolence must be strong, as well as general: vivid in its degree, as well as universal in its application. And the same is true of the

other Affections rightly directed. As we have already said (229), the Supreme Law must not only direct the Affections and Intentions to their proper objects, but require steadiness and energy in them thus directed. The recognition of this condition of the Supreme Rule is shown in the place which Zeal, Energy, Earnestness, hold among the Virtues (250). In order to express this, we may therefore state, as a Moral Principle, that *The Affections and Intentions must not only be rightly directed, but energetic;* and this we may call the *Principle of Earnestness.*

271. Again, it is not enough for the character of virtue, that each person should confine his desires to those objects which Justice assigns to him. His desires are not virtuous, if they terminate in the objects themselves. The Supreme Law of Human Action requires us (232) to consider Moral Good, as the object to which all other objects are subordinate, and from which they derive their only moral value. Morality cannot allow us to desire external things, as wealth, power, or honour, for their own sake, but only as means to moral ends. And we may state this as a Moral Principle, that *Things are to be sought only as means to moral ends;* and this we may term *the Principle of Moral Purpose.*

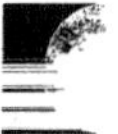

272. To the *Express Principles* which we have thus stated, correspond *Operative Principles* of Benevolence, Justice, Truth, Purity, Order, Earnestness, and Moral Purpose; which exist in each man's character, in so far as the Express Principles above stated become his habitual guides and springs of action; in so far as these express the tendencies of his affections and purposes. In this sense, as Operative Principles, a man is also said to have a *Spirit* of Benevolence, of Justice, and the like.

It may be proper hereafter to state other Moral Principles, in addition to these seven: but these seven will enable us to lay down many Rules of Duty.

which is the purpose for which we put them forwards. We must now speak of Duty; and in the first place, of the distinction between Duty and Virtue.

CHAPTER V.

DUTIES.

273. We have already stated, that Virtue and Duty differ, as the Habit and the Act; as the internal Disposition, and the outward Manifestation. Acts do not prove the existence of the Dispositions to which they generally correspond. A man may frequently give relief to a person in distress, without being really compassionate; he may habitually perform what he has promised, without real integrity. Such is the case, for instance, when a man gives alms to avoid importunity; or pays his debts to escape disgrace. Acts do not even prove Habits; for an Act may be solitary; like that of her

Who paid a tradesman once to make him stare.

But notwithstanding this, Acts of Duty are both the most natural operation of virtuous Dispositions, and the most effectual mode of forming virtuous Habits. Hence, Acts of Duty are requisite, both as the manifestations of Virtue, and as the means of becoming virtuous. The Virtues belong to a deeper part of our nature than the Duties, being the sources out of which our acts of Duty spring. But duties are more capable of definite description and determination than Virtue not exhibited in Act; and hence Duties are the more especial subject of the Moralist's discussions. The Virtues are what we are; the Duties are what we do. It is more important what we are, than what we do; but it is more easy to speak of what we do, than of what we are; and moreover, what we are, gives rise to what we do; and what we do, shows what we are.

274. Duties, in their general form, coincide with virtues. Justice is a Virtue; Justice is also a Duty. But they are generally conceived with this difference; that Virtue is more of an unconscious Disposition; Duty implies more of Conscious Thought. Our Virtues exist and operate without our thinking about them; we perform an act of Duty, *thinking* that we ought to do it. To think an Act a Duty, is to think we ought to do it; it is to think it right; to think it conformable to the Supreme Rule of Human Action.

To think an act right, is to think that there is a Reason for it, by which it is shown to be conformable to the Supreme Rule. Such Reasons are given, when we show that acts are conformable to the Moral Principles which have just been laid down (269); for these Principles express parts of the Supreme Rule. Hence, Rules of Duty are to be established by a reference to those Principles, as their Reasons.

275. Virtue is a Habit of the Desires, Affections, and Will; Duty involves an operation of the Reason, by which the Desires, Affections, and Will, are directed and governed. By the frequent performance of such acts of direction and government, they become habitual, easy, familiar, and finally cease to be objects of consciousness; and thus Duty becomes Virtue.

276. We may make a further distinction between Duty and Virtue; indicating that we carry the notion of Virtue farther than that of Duty. We speak of *Heroic Virtues*, as we have seen (264), but never of *Heroic Duties*. Heroic Virtues are Virtues beyond the range of Duty. Duty implies Rules of Duty, but Heroic Virtue soars above Rules.

277. The act of conscious thought by which we recognize our Duties, turns our attention upon ourselves as the objects of the Moral Sentiments of Approbation and Condemnation (262). The habit of regarding ourselves as worthy of Condemnation when we do wrong, and as consequently liable to Punishment, the consequence of deserved Condemnation, in a world in which the Supreme Law is really administered, is the *Sense of Responsibility*. This Habit of Thought is not explicitly recognized in our notion of Virtue, but it forms part of our conception of Duty; and is often termed the *Sense of Duty*.

278. A further feature in our Conception of Duty is, that it includes the notion of Actions determined by external Relations and Circumstances, as well as by internal Dispositions. Duties depend upon the social position of men, and other like conditions. There are Duties of Parents and Children, of Husbands and Wives, of Friends, of Neighbours, of Magistrates, of Members of various Bodies and Professions. Men's Virtues manifest themselves in various Acts of Duty, according to these conditions. The descriptions of Duties must include a reference to those varieties of circumstance and condition. There belong to each man the *Duties of his Station*. Our Duties, so far as they regard our special Relations to particular persons, may be termed *Relative* Duties.

279. It has already been seen, that there are Obligations which depend upon these same conditions. Every man has his Obligations which belong to his Station. Duties extend beyond Obligations, and direct the Affections, Desires, and Intentions, as well as the Actions. Duties give a Moral Significance to Obligations. Thus I have Obligations as a Father, or as a Son. And these Obligations determine certain good offices which are to take place between the Father and the Son. But my Duties as a Father, or as a Son, must give a Moral Significance to these good

offices. They must make them the manifestation of an internal Spring of Action; that is, of an Affection which binds together Father and Son. Such a tie of Affection is the Moral Meaning of the Paternal and Filial Obligations; for such a tie of Affection will constantly give rise to mutual good offices. Again, I have Obligations as a Master or as a Servant; and these determine certain acts of service and of guidance; but my Duties as a Master or as a Servant suppose the relation of the two to be a bond of good-will, producing cordial and considerate service and guidance. Service and guidance, in order to be Duties, must proceed from internal affections, and must thus have a Moral Meaning.

This Maxim, that there is a Moral Significance in our Social Relations, will often serve to point out our Duties. All acts relative to other men, in order to be moral, must proceed from an internal Spring of Affection; our Obligations, being what we ought to do, are also Duties. But in order that they may be Duties, there must exist an Affection which is the natural Source of such acts; and this Affection is itself a Duty.

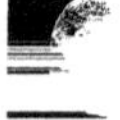

280. The Affections from which Duties thus proceed, will be, for the most part, those Affections which naturally grow up in the bosoms of men, so far as they are influenced by the common moral judgments of mankind; they will be Virtuous Affections; the Affections which belong to a good man (232, 265).

Our Duties are determined by the General Notions of the Virtues on the one hand, and on the other, by the Social Relations, special Circumstances, Conditions, Rights and Obligations of men.

So far as Duties depend on the Notions of the Virtues, they will admit of a Classification corresponding to that of the Virtues, already given. We shall have Duties of the Affections; Duties respecting Property and other Objects of Desire; Duties connected with

Truth; Duties connected with the Bodily Desires; Duties connected with Order. Each of these Classes contains Duties which may be distinguished according to the Social Relations with which they are concerned.

CHAPTER VI.

DUTIES OF THE AFFECTIONS.

281. THE Supreme Law of Human Action adopts and authorizes the Benevolent Affections, as a part of human nature which binds men together, and depends upon their common humanity. This we have expressed, by laying down the Principle of Benevolence as one of our fundamental Moral Principles (269). But further; the Supreme Law requires that the Affections thus authorized be vivid, strong, and permanent. This we have expressed, by stating the Principle of Earnestness as one of our fundamental Moral Principles (270). Now the more general Benevolent Affections which bind men together cannot be vivid and strong, except the special Benevolent Affections, determined by family relations, and other external circumstances, be also vivid and strong. For the Affection of Universal Benevolence is only the expansion of the Love belonging to narrower circles of relation. The Affection of the most General Benevolence is expressed by saying that we love all men as our *Brothers*. The heart learns to love, by its contact with its nearest objects of love, and by the occasions arising out of its intercourse with neighbouring men. If it do not begin its lesson of Duty in that school, it will never be able to apply it in a more comprehensive sphere. The Natural Affections are the proper moral School of the Heart.

The lessons of the benevolent affections are further inculcated by the general moral judgment of mankind; for the universal voice of man commends Gratitude, Family Affection, Compassion, and the like, as Virtues. Hence a good man, in his progress towards the sympathy with man as man, which is implied in the Supreme Rule, will be led to possess the Affections thus universally regarded as Virtues (265). Moreover, such Affections are requisite to give to the obligations of Family, and the like, their moral significance. They are therefore Duties (279).

Hence the special kinds of benevolent Affection, Gratitude, Compassion, Reverence for Superiors, Filial Affection, Parental Affection, Conjugal Affection, Fraternal Affection, are all Duties. They are Affections in which all men sympathize. They are Natural Affections. Those who have them not, are universally condemned as without natural affection. Such men have not found admission into the Moral School of the Heart. They have not made the first steps towards that Universal Benevolence, which is a Fundamental Moral Principle. Such men must be destitute of that warmth of right affections which the Principle of Earnestness requires. Such men cannot give to the Obligations of their Station that Moral significance which Morality requires.

We will consider this further, with regard to the above kinds of Affection in particular.

282. *Gratitude to Benefactors* is a Duty of the Affections. To render advantage for advantage, is often a matter of mutual contract; to render good-will for good-will, is the Duty which gives a Moral Significance to the Obligations of such contracts (279). Gratitude, that is, Good-will in return for benefits conferred with good-will, is a natural feeling, and is universally acknowledged as a Virtue (280). He, therefore, who does not feel this, has made little advance in the natural progress of the benevolent affec-

tions; he is little influenced by the sympathy of men in favour of Virtue. The ungrateful man disregards one of the most manifest lessons of morality; that in which the common understanding of mankind apprehends mutual good-will, as the proper signification of good offices, given and received. He violates this understanding; and is necessarily looked upon with repugnance and alarm, as one on whom the common ties of Humanity have no hold. He transgresses a Rule which all men can and must sympathize in approving; and which draws men together by the common recognition of the significance of external relations. Thus he is a violator of a Duty.

Hence, Gratitude is a Duty of the Affections. A man who is devoid of gratitude cannot be a good man. And the Affection of gratitude, which is thus a Duty, will tend to express itself in acts. But no special acts are directed by this Rule of Duty. Gratitude is one Rule for the Affections, but the Rules of Action must be governed by the consideration of all the Rules of the Affections, and all the Moral Principles. The actions which gratitude prompts may be prohibited by other Rules of Duty, derived from the Principle of Benevolence in other bearings, or from the principles of Justice, Truth, Purity, and Order, and their combinations.

283. *Reverence for Superiors* is a Duty. Reverence is a Benevolent Affection, which assumes in its object Superiority of Condition to ourselves, combined with Justice and Goodness. Obedience to Law and Authoirty are Obligations; and these Obligations, like all others, have a Moral Significance (279), when the Law is just and the Authority rightful. They require in the Inferior Party, a Spirit of Obedience (272); an Obedience of the Heart. When the person, thus invested with Authority, is also invested with Goodness, the Heart joins, and ought to join, with its Obedience, the Love which belongs to Virtue

(91). And thus, this union of the Spirit of Obedience and Love, Reverence for Superiors, is a Duty.

This Sentiment is fostered by a sympathy with the natural feelings, and with the common moral judgments of mankind, expressed by means of terms implying Virtue and Vice. That Reverence for Superiors is a natural feeling, we see in the willing submission with which, in all ages and countries, Superiors have been treated by their Inferiors; and in the cordial submission rendered to Laws. Man has, among his natural feelings, a Reverence for Something better, wiser, more stable, more permanent than himself. He readily believes in the existence of something of this nature; and has, in his mind, a ready Sentiment of deferential Regard for it. And this feeling is fostered by the general sympathy of men. The common moral judgment of mankind appears in the commendation bestowed upon such dispositions. Disloyalty to the Sovereign, Disobedience to Authority, Sedition, Treason, Rebellion, are, in themselves, looked upon with feelings of Dislike and Indignation. If a person does not participate in these feelings, he is not likely to possess Benevolent Affections at all. If he have no sympathy with these emotions, his Affections cannot be conformable to that Supreme Law, in which all men, as men, sympathize. If Goodness and Justice, joined with Superiority of condition, are not regarded by a man with Reverence, he has not that feeling towards Goodness and Justice by which virtuous men are bound together. A participation in this feeling belongs to a good man. And this feeling is requisite to invest with a moral significance the obligation of Obedience to the governing authorities of the State. For such Obedience must be a Duty, as well as an Obligation, in order that it may have a moral character. But if Obedience be a Duty, Reverence, the Obedience of the heart, which is the internal spring of external obedience, must also

be a Duty. And this Reverence, being a part of the natural feelings of a good man, and a necessary condition of the Duties of Obedience, is itself a Duty.

If it be said, that in the actual constitution of the world, it may happen that Superiority of social condition is not joined with goodness and justice, and that thus this affection has no proper place; we reply, that however this may be the case in particular instances, human government is requisite as a general condition of morality, and especially as a condition of justice and order. The Governors of Society are therefore, so far as this condition requires, the representatives of Justice and Order; and reverence to them, under this aspect, is still a general Duty: A Reverence for Superiors and Governors, as the representatives and cardinal points of justice and order, is requisite, to give a moral significance to the structure of human society. Reverence in inferiors, and Benevolence in superiors, are ties of affection which alone can bind together a community in which there are superiors and inferiors, so as to give them moral relations. And in every community, those who are, by its constitution and nature, the depositaries and sources of law and government, must be looked upon as superiors, and are, in that capacity, proper objects of reverence.

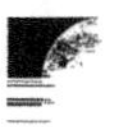

284. *Filial Affection*, the Affection of the Child towards the Parent, is a Duty of the Affections. The Supreme Law of our nature requires us to possess the Operative Principle of Benevolence; but it is unlikely that we shall possess this Principle, if we do not possess those benevolent affections which are the most natural and universal; which are commended to us and urged upon us by the sympathy and common judgment of mankind; and for which there are strong and manifest reasons. Filial Affection is pressed upon us in all these ways. It is a natural and universal affection among men, failing to show

itself only under very peculiar circumstances. It is everywhere regarded as a Virtue. A child wanting in love toward his parent, is looked upon with abhorrence, as an unnatural child. And this affection is supported by the strong and evident reasons, of its being agreeable to the Duties of Gratitude and Reverence. For, in the common course of events, children receive from their parents far more kindness, and far greater benefits, than from any other persons. And the sentiment of deferential regard and conscious dependence, which is natural to man; and for which he naturally assumes in his thoughts, as an object, a person wiser and better than himself; is, by the natural condition of man, directed, in the first place, towards the Parents. The child, who learns from them his lessons of what is good and wise; who sees and feels himself to be dependent upon them, and weak and ignorant in comparison of them; sees in them the necessary and proper objects of Reverence. This Sentiment gives a Moral Significance to the Family relation. Such an affection in the child towards the Parent, combined with Parental Affection on the other part, are ties of affection which must exist, in order that the Members of the Family may have moral relations to each other, such as correspond to the obligation of obedience in the child, and support and care in the parent (279). If this Affection be not a Duty, there is no Duty on the part of the child; for Duty extends to the Springs of Action, and therefore to the Affections. Hence Filial Affection is a necessary portion of the Benevolent Affections which a good man must possess; and being conformable to the Duties of Gratitude and Reverence for Superiors, and essential to the existence of Filial Duty, it is itself a Duty.

This Affection tends to govern the Actions. Under the influence of Filial Affection, Obedience to Parents tends to become an Obedience of Love.

Such an obedience is not merely a submission of our wishes and desires to those of others; but an identification of our wishes and desires with those of the persons whom we love and obey. We wish what they wish. Our intentions anticipate their commands. The pleasure of giving them pleasure, is a more powerful Spring of Action, than any pleasures obtained in opposition to their wishes.

285. The Duty of *Parental Affection* is shown on the like grounds. This Affection is a necessary portion of our benevolent affections. It is natural and universal; and commended by the common judgment of mankind, who loudly condemn an unnatural Parent. If a person do not feel an affection thus urged upon him, the Operative Principle of Benevolence must be entirely wanting in him, or greatly defective. Such an affection is requisite to give a moral significance to the Family relation. The Obligation of Support and Care on the part of the Parents, is necessary for the preservation and well-being of the Child. These good offices are generally secured by the impulse of a strong and almost universal affection, supported by the general sympathy of mankind. This Affection gives a moral significance to the Obligations of the parent; and constitutes a tie which is requisite, in order that the parent and child may have a moral relation to each other. If this Affection be not a Duty, there is no Duty on the part of the Parent; for Duty regards the Affections. Thus the Parental Affection is a part of the Benevolent Affections which a good man must necessarily possess; and inasmuch as it is the natural Security for the most essential Obligations of man, and requisite to the existence of Parental Duty, it is a Duty.

286. *Conjugal Affection* is, in a like manner, a Duty. This affection produces the marriage union, or grows out of it, where it is not repressed by ad-

verse feelings. It is supported by the sympathy and approbation of mankind; for all admire and praise a husband and wife, so far as they are bound together by a strong and steady mutual affection. It is this affection which alone gives moral significance to the legal union. Without the supposition of this tie of affection, there can be no moral relation between the two; no Duties, no Moral Claims; for duties and moral claims belong to the affections. Moreover, the married condition involves a Promise of such affection; and therefore the want of the affection, in that condition, implies a breach of promise, as well as a coldness of heart; and violates the Principle of Truth, as well as the Principle of Benevolence. Thus, the conjugal affection is a part of the benevolent affections which a married person must possess, in order to be good; and being required by the Principle of Truth, and essential to the existence of Conjugal Duty, it is itself a Duty.

287. *Fraternal Affection* is a Duty. Such an affection is natural; it readily grows up under the usual circumstances of Family intercourse. Not to have this affection, implies a want of that warmth and tenderness of heart, out of which Family Affections are unfolded by the conditions of the Family. If a man is wanting in this disposition, we conceive that his Benevolence, in its more comprehensive bearings, will be feeble and cold. If he do not love his brother, he is little likely to love a stranger. This affection gives a moral significance to the mutual good offices which a Family requires and gives rise to. These good offices between brethren cannot be Duties, except the affection which prompts them be a Duty. And thus Fraternal Affection is a part of the Benevolent Affections which a good man must possess; and being essential to the existence of Fraternal Duties, is itself a Duty.

288. *The Love of our Fellow-citizens* is a Duty.

This is a Fraternal Affection of a wider kind. A Community, a Tribe, a Nation, may be considered as a wider Family. The benevolent affections fasten themselves upon that part of mankind with whom we principally converse, and with whom we share many common influences. A common descent, a common history, a common language, common manners, common laws, draw fellow-citizens together, as, in a narrower way, the habits and common conditions of a family draw together the members of the family. And the mutual services and knowledge of each other, thus produced, tend to generate a mutual affection. This Affection gives a moral significance to all mutual Services; for the mutual Services of Fellow-citizens cannot be Duties, except their mutual Good-will be a Duty. And thus a Love towards his Fellow-citizens is part of the Benevolent Affections which a good man will necessarily possess; and being necessary to the existence of social and civil Duties, it is itself a Duty.

289. In the same manner, it is seen that we have Duties of Benevolent Affection towards all persons who are connected with us by any less comprehensive social relations; as to our Servants, our Masters, our Dependents, our Employers, and the like.

290. A Duty of the same kind exists towards the whole human race. There is a Duty of *Universal Benevolence* which we ought to bear to men as men. We have already (231) stated, that in considering the conditions of the Supreme Law of Human Action, we are led to the Idea of absolute and Universal Benevolence, as a part of that which the Law must include. And we have stated the express Principle which represents this Idea (269), that we must love man as man. This Principle now comes before us as an expression of a Duty. In taking this view of it, we imply that the Principle is requisite to give a moral significance to our social relations; for this has been noted as a character of Duties (279).

This character will now be seen to belong to the Affection of Universal Benevolence towards man as man. We have Duties to all men: Duties of Justice and Truth are to be performed towards all men. But these Duties cannot be performed as Duties, except they proceed from an internal Spring of Action. They must be the results of Affection. And thus an Affection towards all men, being essential to the existence of all other duties towards them, is itself a Duty.

291. As our love of the members of the same family, or of the same community, is unfolded by our being led to see and feel what their nature has in common with ours: so our love of mankind in general is unfolded by our being led to see and feel that they have a human nature, which is identical with our own. We are by degrees led to look upon them as Members of the same Race; as Children, along with ourselves, of the *great human Family*. And thus, we love them with an extension of the love which we bestow upon our brothers. We look upon all Mankind as our Brothers.

292. But this Duty of the Love of Mankind goes further. We come to feel a love for all mankind, of which we have spoken, by having brought before our thoughts the common human nature which they share with us. But there is a kind of love which we far more readily feel for those who offer themselves to our notice, as under the infliction of pain or grief. There is (242) a natural impulse of *Compassion*, which draws, to such persons, our benevolent regard; and which prompts us to do them good offices by which their distress may be relieved. This Compassion for the Afflicted, merely as afflicted, is a feeling which the whole human race sympathize in, and which is by all commended and loved. It thus naturally exists, among the benevolent affections which are unfolded in a man's bosom as he becomes more

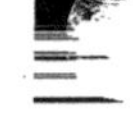

and more fully possessed of those Operative Moral Principles which belong to the Supreme Rule of Human Action, and in which man, as man, universally sympathizes. And the Acts which proceed from this affection of Compassion, are part of that course of action, which the Supreme Rule, drawing together all men, in virtue of that which belongs to all, directs and enjoins. Hence, Acts of Compassion are what men ought to do. They are Duties. But these acts cannot be Duties, except the Affection from which they proceed is a Duty. And thus Compassion, which, as we have seen, is a part of the benevolent affections possessed by a good man, being essential to the Duties of Charity, is itself a Duty.

And thus, we have established as Duties, the Affections of Gratitude, Reverence for Superiors, Filial, Parental, Conjugal, and Fraternal Affection, the Love of our Fellow-citizens, and the Love of Man as Man, and Compassion.

CHAPTER VII.

OF THE MORAL CULTURE OF THE AFFECTIONS AS A DUTY.

293. It has been shown that Gratitude to Benefactors, Reverence to Superiors, Compassion to the Afflicted, are Duties; as also are Filial, Parental, Conjugal, and Fraternal Affection, the Love of our Fellow-citizens, and the Universal Benevolence which embraces all men as men. These Affections we ought to possess. Such Affections therefore we ought to acquire. We ought to foster, cherish, cultivate them. We ought to establish these Affections in our Minds; to direct our Affections by these Forms

of Duty. We ought to form our character in such a way that these Benevolent Affections shall belong to it.

To this doctrine, it may be objected, that we have not the power of doing what we are thus enjoined to do. It may be said, that we have not the power of generating or directing our Affections, and of forming our own character. It may be urged, that we cannot love a particular person, or love under particular circumstances, and with a particular kind of love, merely because we will to do so. Love, it may be said, cannot be thus compelled by command. Character cannot be thus formed by Rule.

But we reply, that the objection, thus stated, involves much too large an assertion. It is very far from being true, that we have no power over our own affections or our own character. The universal voice of mankind recognizes the existence of such a power, by the condemnation which it awards to the want of the affections above mentioned. If a child do not love his parent, a father or a mother their child, a brother his brother: all men join in condemning the person thus destitute of natural affectionr. He offends against the common nature of man. And in like manner, all men look with repugnance and disapprobation upon the ungrateful or pitiless man. All men blame him who is irreverent towards a just and good Master. These, and the like moral judgments of mankind, imply that a man's affections are, in some way, his own act. The affections are thus declared to be part of that internal action for which he is responsible. He is a proper subject of praise or blame for what he feels; and so far, his *feeling* is his *doing*.

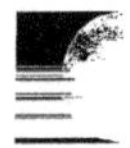

294. And we can perceive that we have, in various ways, power over our feelings. Even immediately, by the power which we possess of directing our train of thoughts, we can foster or repress an affec-

tion. We can call before our minds, and dwell upon, those features of character and situation, which tend to impress on our minds one Sentiment or another. We can, for instance, think on all that our parents have done and suffered for us, and can thus move our hearts to a love of them. And above all, the recollection that affections are natural and right, will fix and promote them. We shall constantly approximate to those benevolent affections, which we constantly regard as recommended by the universal sympathy of mankind, and as conformable to the supreme law of our being. While, on the other hand, coldness and hardness of heart,—still more, malevolence or perversely directed affection,—perpetually dwelt upon in our thoughts, as feelings which estrange us from our kind, make us a natural object of their abhorrence, and violate the very essence of our nature,—will be, by this means, repressed and extinguished.

295. The course of thought by which the virtuous affections are promoted, may sometimes be traced, in the progress of special Conceptions, and in the significance of the terms by which they are denoted. Thus the clear apprehension of a common internal nature in all men, which suggests the use of the term *Humanity* to designate this common nature, leads, further, to the benevolent affection towards man as man; which affection is also termed *Humanity.* Thus, the apprehension of objective Humanity tends to promote subjective Humanity (235). We shall hereafter consider the progress by which some Conceptions of this kind have arrived at clearness and comprehensiveness of signification. We shall thus be led to see some of the steps by which the affections are cultivated.

296. Moreover, the Benevolent Affections impel us to endeavour to do good to the objects of them. We wish to promote the wellbeing of those whom we love. This, their wellbeing, thus becomes the object

of our desires and intentions. But the conception of the Wellbeing of other persons, which we thus place before us as our object, may be variously modified and transformed by the operations of our thoughts. We may conceive it as merely their Pleasure, or as their Interest, or as their Happiness. And as some of these are truer and more moral views of Wellbeing than others; we may, by the exercise of our Faculties, advance from those which are false and wrong, to those which are true and right. This possession of true conceptions of the ends to which our benevolent affections must direct us, is a part of our character: and this, depending upon our own course of thought, is in a great measure in our own power.

297. And besides this direct operation of thought upon the affections, there are many circumstances and conditions which have an influence in the formation of our character; and which, being in our power, put the formation of our character also in our power. As we have already said, Acts of Duty generate Virtues: and our acts depend upon our will. We can, by directing our Acts, form our Habits; and Habits of external action extend their influence to the internal feelings. Each link of this chain may be in some degree loose; and yet the whole will exert a constant pressure upon the character, drawing it towards the line of Duty. The Acts of Duty may be imperfectly done; the good Habits may be imperfectly formed; the internal Feelings may imperfectly correspond to the Habits; but yet, by the steady performance of Acts of Duty, the cultivation of a virtuous character is perpetually promoted.

298. It may be objected, that when we have done all that is possible in the formation of our character, still there will remain in it much of good and evil, the result of our original native qualities which we cannot alter, and of external circumstances over which we have no control; and thus, that our char-

acter and disposition is not in our own power. To this we reply, that, as we have before said, our character and disposition is in our own power, so far as to be a subject of praise or blame. For if praise and blame are not applied to character and disposition, to what can they be applied? We are endeavouring to define those dispositions which are the proper objects of approbation. An opponent, whose objections imply that *nothing* is a proper object of approbation or disapprobation, has no common ground with us; and with him, therefore, it is useless to reason. But further; when it is said that there will remain in our character much that is good and evil, the result of its native elements, even when we have done all that is possible to repress the evil, and promote the good; we reply, that we never can be said to have done *all that is possible*, in the improvement of our character. So long as life continues, thoughts of Duty, and acts of Duty, by which our internal being may be improved, are possible: and so long, therefore, we are responsible for not labouring to remove the evil which remains, and to forward the good.

299. We thus see, that as there are certain Affections which are Duties, so is it in our power to foster and cherish those affections; to form and improve our character, so that those dispositions shall make a part of it; and to continue this course of self-improvement to the end of our lives. This course may be termed our Self-cultivation, or Moral Culture; and the effect which it produces upon our character is our Moral Progress. This Progress is carried on, as we have seen, by giving earnestness and vividness to our Moral Affections, generality and clearness to the conceptions by which such affections are regulated, steadiness to our habits of Moral Action. It also requires us to give consistency to our Rules of Duty; and generally, to give consistency, comprehensiveness,

and completeness, to the whole of our intellectual and moral being.

300. Our Moral Culture and Moral Progress can never be terminated in our lifetime: for we can never reach a condition in which there is no possibility of giving more earnestness and vividness to our moral affections, more generality and clearness to our conceptions of moral objects, more steadiness to our moral habits. The formation of a human character is never ended. There will always be some part of it which does not fully conform to Virtue. It will always be possible to go further in these respects. The Supreme Law of our Being, by which we are directed to Duty and Virtue, is not satisfied, except the whole of our Being conform to it. Hence this Law demands a perpetual Moral Progress; and such a perpetual Moral Progress is necessary, in consequence of other changes also. New persons, new objects, are constantly presented to us: new thoughts, new views of ends and means, constantly arise in the mind. And as these arise, the feelings which they occasion, ought constantly to be conformed to the Supreme Law. The Affections must constantly expand and modify themselves, according to these developments of the mind, so as to remain in harmony with the Moral Ideas. The current of thought is constantly flowing, and constantly receiving accessions from fresh rills, put in motion by the course of the outer world. It thus becomes constantly wider and deeper through life, except when it is narrowed and constrained by external obstacles. The whole of this current of thought must be tinged by the virtuous affections; and there must, therefore, be a constantly flowing source of moral goodness to preserve the moral colour of the stream. As there is, in the head, a fountain of perpetual internal change; there must be, in the heart, a fountain which shall give to every change a character of good.

301. Thus there is a Duty of Moral Self-culture, which can never be interrupted nor terminated. With reference to that part of Morality of which we are now speaking, this is the Duty of the Culture of the Affections. It is our duty constantly to cultivate the Affections which have been described as Duties; Gratitude; Compassion; Reverence; Family Love; the Love of our Fellow-countrymen; the Love of our Fellow-men. This Culture of the benevolent affections is a Duty which never stops nor ends.

302. Further; the Duty of thus cultivating these Affections includes the Duty of possessing such affections; and may often, in our consideration, take the place of the Duties which we have mentioned. The Duty of cultivating Gratitude and Compassion includes the Duty of feeling Gratitude and Compassion. That we are to cultivate such Affections, is a reason for feeling them, which is added to the other reasons, but which includes them all. We are to feel Gratitude and Compassion, because it is right; we are to cultivate them, because it is right to feel them; but we cultivate them by feeling them. The Duty of Self-culture enjoins upon us the same feelings which the Duty of Gratitude and the Duty of Compassion enjoined before.

303. The constant and interminable moral culture of the affections which is thus a Duty, and includes the other Duties of the Affections, may suffer interruption and reverse. The progress at which such culture aims, is thwarted by every act which is morally wrong. The moral progress of our affections is *interrupted* by every malicious act, by every feeling of malice, by the want of love on occasions when the circumstances and relations of our position call for it. Our moral progress is *reversed* when such malice, or such coldness of heart, becomes habitual. The *transgression* of moral precepts, whether they regard external acts, or internal springs of action, is a suspen-

sion, and may be a termination, of our moral progress. And this effect of transgression, as being a contradiction of our moral culture, adds greatly to the importance of its moral aspect.

304. We may further add, that in this aspect of *transgressions* of Duty, that they interrupt or undo our moral progress, we have the aspect of them which most determines their moral weight; so that those transgressions are considered most grave, which most interrupt our moral progress. As the interruption or inversion of this progress becomes more decided, the transgression becomes *more grievous*. This subject will be pursued afterwards.

We may likewise remark, as a point which will be hereafter pursued, that Moral Progress, the Supreme Law of our nature, must necessarily be the way to *Happiness*, the Supreme Object of our nature.

305. It may perhaps appear to some that there is nothing gained in Morality by the view just presented; since the Duty of Moral Culture is identical with other Duties already spoken of. But this is not so. By presenting to our minds the Conception of Moral Culture, our Duties often assume a different aspect from that which they have when considered separately; and we are able to establish Rules of Action, of a wider and completer kind than those to which the contemplation of more partial Duties would lead. For instance, the Duty of Compassion assumes a new and larger aspect, when we consider every compassionate act and compassionate feeling to be not only a relative Duty towards the distressed object, but a means of softening and improving our own heart: and this aspect of the Duty may be a better guide for our actions and feelings than any narrower view would be. And thus our Duties, when regarded as parts of our Moral Progress, may be looked upon as higher objects of moral desire, and higher aims, than more special objects and more partial aims could be.

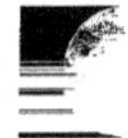

306. Although Moral Culture can never reach its termination, it may be conceived as a Progress towards an Ideal Object by which its tendency is marked. Our Moral Progress may be conceived as a constant tendency towards an Ideal Point of complete Moral Perfection;—the same Ideal Centre of Morality of which we have already spoken (231). The Elements of this ideal Moral Perfection are, as we have already said, the Cardinal Virtues, Benevolence, Justice, Truth, Purity, and Order. To these we are constantly to tend. We are to establish them in our minds as Principles: that is (268), as Operative Principles—the Operative Principles of our Being. To do this, we may look upon as the Highest Object of our actions; as the *Greatest Good* of which our moral nature is capable.

For the present, we are considering only the Moral Culture of the *Affections;* which requires us to make Benevolence an Operative Principle of our Being, so that it may manifest itself in all its modifications, according to our condition and relations to other men. But what has been said of the Duty of Moral Culture, and of its bearing upon more Special Duties, and upon violations of Duty, applies equally to the other classes of Duties, as well as to those of the Affections. We now proceed to those other classes.

CHAPTER VIII.

DUTIES RESPECTING PROPERTY AND OTHER OBJECTS OF DESIRES.

307. The Rules of Duty with regard to external things, as objects of possession, are consequences of the Principle of Justice, that Each man is to have

his own; and of the Principle of Moral Ends, that Things are to be sought only as means to moral ends.

The Rule that each man is to have his own, is a Rule which regulates all external acts relative to Property. It thus prescribes external Duties. But these external Duties imply also an internal Duty, directing the Desires and Affections. We must desire that each man should have his own, and must desire things for ourselves, only so far as they are assigned to us by this rule. And this Duty enjoins a perfect Fairness and Evenness in our views of external possession; an Equality in our estimate of our own claims with those of other persons; and an absence of any vehemence of Desire which might disturb this equality. The Duty of a Spirit of Justice excludes all Cupidity or eagerness in our desires of wealth; all Covetousness, or wish to possess what is another's; all Partiality, or disposition to deviate from equal Rule in judging between ourselves and others. The Rule of action is, Let each man have his own; but the Rule of desire is, Let no man seek his own, except so far as the former Rule directs him to do so. Justice gives to each man his own: but each ought to cling to his own, not from the love of riches, but from the love of Justice. It is the love of equal and steady laws, not of possessions, which makes a good man appropriate what is his. This rule does not require us to abstain from the usual transactions respecting property:—buying and selling, getting and spending; for it is by being employed in such transactions, that property is an instrument of human action,—the means by which the characters and dispositions of men manifest themselves. A rich man may employ many men in his service by means of his wealth; nor does morality forbid this; but then, they must be employed for moral purposes.

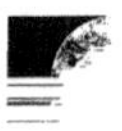

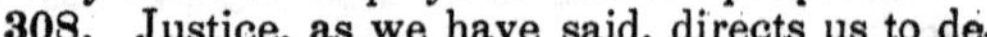

308. Justice, as we have said, directs us to desire external things only in so far as an equal and steady Rule assigns them to us as our own. But further: even when they are our own, our desires must not turn to external things, as ultimate and independent objects. We must not seek them for their own sake, but as Means to moral Ends. We must not desire gold and lands, as things in themselves desirable; but as things which will enable us to do good. We are not forbidden by morality to use our possessions in upholding and carrying on the usual relations of society; as those of Employer and Workman, Master and Servant; for the duties of men suppose the existence and fixity of these relations; but we must consider these relations, also, as means of our duty; and must maintain and direct them, only in such a manner as that they are such means of duty. We must in all things regulate our desire of wealth and its results by the Spirit of Moral Purpose.

Thus we are directed by Morality to regard Property only as a mean of doing good. In the eyes of the Moralist no possessions are absolute and unconditional property; the possessor holds them only *in trust* for moral and benevolent purposes. He is a *Trustee* (152) for the general benefit of mankind; and the Condition of the Trust is, not merely that he shall give something, in cases where benevolence directs; but that he should employ the whole so as to promote moral ends. Not only in giving, but in buying goods, paying wages, saving or spending, he is bound to act morally. When the proprietor asks, Have I not a Right to do what I will with my own? the Moralist replies, No; you have not a moral Right to do what is wrong with your own.

The same may be said of the other Desires. A good man may seek Rank, or eminent station in the State, and may desire the Power which Rank and Station give. But then, he will seek these his Objects only in entire fairness of act and spirit; and he will desire them only as means of doing good.

309. Thus, the Duties of the Desires are determined by the Principle of Justice, and the Principle of Moral Purpose. But these Principles, in order to have their proper place in the character, must become complete Operative Principles. The Spirit of Justice, and the Spirit of Moral Purpose must pervade the whole of the good man's being, must regulate all his thoughts and wishes. This is a condition of ideal moral perfection, towards which we may tend, but to which we can never fully attain. Yet, that we have it in our power to make some advance in this direction, is plain. We have it in our power to become in some degree just and morally minded; for if this were not so, we should deserve no condemnation for being unjust and sordid minded. Since, then, we can make progress towards the possession of these Principles of Justice and Moral Purpose, in which a large portion of our Duty is contained, our Duty requires us to make such Progress. There is, in these respects, as in the case of the Affections, a Duty of Moral Progress and of Moral Culture.

310. The conception of our Moral Culture being placed before us, as an object of our desires and endeavours, our Duties with regard to Wealth, and other external things, assume a new aspect, by which light may often be thrown upon the course of our Duty. We are to use Wealth only as a means of our Moral Culture and Moral Progress. Hence, though, as we have said, if we are rich, we may use Wealth in most of its ordinary applications, as in maintaining many servants, or in employing many workmen; we must take care that there is not, in our affections to such dependents, or in the occupation thus given to our thoughts, or in the results which we intend or expect, anything which prevents our moral progress. And since benevolence to our

dependents is a part of moral excellence, we must give to our relation to them such a character as promotes their welfare.

311. As the rich man is bound in Duty to seek and to use wealth for moral ends only, and to make it a means of his moral culture; so the poor man, who has to labour in order to provide himself with the necessaries and comforts of life, is also bound to abstain from all labours that are immoral; and to combine, with a care for his bodily wants, a care also for his moral progress. A man may not, because he is poor, engage himself in the service of vice; or sell, for his own gain, what is committed to him as a trust. And however large a portion of his time and thought, a man's necessary labours may demand; he must always recollect that he has a mind, which is to be instructed and morally cultivated, as well as a body to be supported. The poorest, as well as the richest man, is a moral agent; and does not conform to the aw of his being, except he make all other ends subservient to moral ends. He who seeks a mere livelihood, must still seek to make acting rightly, and doing good, the ends of his living. He who has the largest superfluity cannot live for a higher purpose, and may not live for a lower.

312. The power which wealth bestows upon its possessor, and any other power or influence over his fellow-men, which any one may possess, must be used for their welfare, in obedience to the Principle of Benevolence, as we have already said. The welfare of men may be contemplated under various aspects; as Interest, Happiness, and the like. But our contemplation of the good of other men cannot be complete, except we include in it that which we consider as the highest good for ourselves; namely, Moral Progress. Our Benevolence, therefore, will not be consistent with our moral views, except we seek to

promote the Moral Culture of those over whom our power extends.

The Moral Culture and progress of Man, considered as an object which we may endeavour to promote, includes many comprehensive and complex conceptions; the Liberty, the Education, the Civilization of Man, may all be considered as elements of their moral culture, which we may make our objects in our efforts for their welfare; and above all, Religion may be looked upon as including the most important part of such culture. In order to follw, into further detail, the Duty of the Moral Culture of men, we must unfold into particulars and consequences these Conceptions of Liberty, Education, Civilization, Religion. This it will hereafter be our business, in some measure, to do. In the mean time, we proceed to another class of Duties.

CHAPTER IX.

DUTIES CONNECTED WITH TRUTH.

313. THE Duties connected with Truth, are those which result from the Principle of Truth already stated (269); that we must conform to the universal understanding among men which the use of language implies. This Principle is expressed more briefly by saying, that we must not Lie; for a Lie is a violation of the universal understanding of which we speak. This Rule of Duty is in agreement with the universal moral sympathy of mankind, which condemns the Liar as hateful and despicable. That a Lie is a violation of the general understanding of mankind, is the reason why the Rule, *Lie not,* is universally accepted by mankind as an absolute Rule, even when a

Lie infringes no positive Rights. The other absolute Rules, *Kill not, Steal not*, and the like, are requisite for the establishment of Rights of the Person, of Property, and so on. A Lie violates no Right, except the Right of knowing the truth; which is not a jural Right, though it may be a moral claim. But the Rule is acknowledged by men as absolute; because a Contract to speak the Truth is implied in the use of Language; and a Right to know the Truth is conveyed, by every speaker, to the person to whom he addresses his assertions.

Accordingly, when the common understanding among men is not violated, a declaration is not a lie, although in the common meaning of the term it would be false; as when a man says at the end of a letter, "I am your obedient Servant," though the letter itself may contain a refusal to obey or to serve the correspondent.

314. Not only Lying, but every mode of conveying a false belief, is prohibited by the Principle of Truth. This especially applies when we convey a belief of our own intention in a matter affecting him whom we address; that is, when we make a Promise. We are bound by the Duty of Truth to promise only what we intend to perform. All Deceit, Fraud, Duplicity, Imposition, is excluded by the Duty of Truth.

But if I have promised what I intended to perform, and afterwards change my intention, does it cease to be my Duty to perform my Promise? It is plain that it does not. To break my Promise is to break the understanding between the *Promisee* and me. The understanding established between us was, not a doubtful understanding; namely, that, if I did not change my mind, I would do thus and thus; but an absolute one, that I would do thus. If a Promise were capable of arbitrary revocation by the Promiser, it would establish no common understanding, and could be of no use in enabling the Promisee to regulate his actions. At the time I make the Promise, I have the power of determining my future actions, by retaining my present intention. The engagement I make is, that I will retain it; and this the Promisee must be able to reckon upon, in order that the Promise may mean anything. It is therefore a universal Duty to perform Promises.

315. The Duty of performing Promises is an extension of the Obligation of performing Contracts. A Contract is a Promise, sanctioned by the formalities which the law prescribes, as necessary to make it valid. It is a Duty to perform Contracts, as well as a legal Obligation; but the Duty is not limited by the formalities which limit the legal Obligation. The legal Obligation depends upon the external form, as well as the intention; but the Duty depends upon the intention and mutual understanding alone; and therefore the Duty of performing Promises must exist, wherever the mutual understanding of the Promiser and Promisee existed.

It follows from this, also, that Promises are to be performed in the Sense in which they were made and received, by the mutual understanding of the two parties, at the time.

316. It is a Duty to avoid all Falsehood, Deceit, Fraud, Duplicity, Imposition. Hence it is a Duty to have the internal spring of action which impels us to avoid such acts. It is a Duty to hate Lying, Deceit, Fraud, Duplicity: to have no wish to deceive or impose upon any one: to profess and assume no intentions different from those which we really entertain. Singleness of Heart, Simplicity of Character, Openness, Frankness, are the virtues which ought to give rise to our words and actions. We ought to have in us the Operative Principle, or Spirit, of Truth.

317. And as in the case of the other Principles, because we ought to have this Principle in operation within us, we ought to cultivate and encourage it in

our hearts. Our Moral Culture in this respect also is a Duty.

The Spirit of Truth is to be cultivated by Acts of Truthfulness. That we have it in our power to be truthful, is evident. The difficulty and need of exertion, indeed, are on the other side. To say that which we know not to be true; to assume the appearance of that which we are not; requires effort, invention, and contrivance. Truth is the first thing that comes to our lips; and we must do some violence to ourselves, to substitute anything else for it. In this respect, then, in order to cultivate a Spirit of Truth in ourselves, we have only to obey our natural impulses, and to say what we think and feel. But yet there are many desires, purposes, and motives, which are constantly impelling men to falsehood and deceit. Men use language as a means to ends;—not always, nor principally, as the simple declaration of what they think and feel; but with a view to the effect which it will produce upon the person addressed. And as a falsification or distortion of the real state of the case, often seems likely to answer their purpose, better than a true representation, the natural impulses of Truth are checked and overpowered by other Springs of Action. Now the Moral Culture of the Principle of Truth in us, requires that all such working of our desires should be suppressed. To lie, to deceive, for any purpose whatever, is utterly inconsistent with any care for our moral progress.

It is impossible that the Operative Principle of Truth should acquire that place in our character which morality requires, if we allow it to be thrust aside by the desire of pleasure, or gain, or power, or the like. The only way in which we can advance towards the moral standard, at which it is our Duty constantly to aim, is by a steady and solemn determination, under no circumstances, to be guilty of falsehood. A man earnestly aiming at his own moral progress, will be true in his assertion, true to his promises, true to his implied engagements, true in what he says, true in what he does. No prospect of any object of desire, or of any advantage, can sway him to any deceit or fraud; for objects of desire have no necessary tendency to further his purpose; whereas deceit and fraud are in direct contradiction to it.

318. We have spoken of a steady and *solemn* determination not to be guilty of falsehood, as means of moral culture. This expression supposes, that which our consciousness as moral beings assures us of, that we have the power of making such determinations of our future course of action. We can determine and resolve upon a future act or course of actions. We must do this, in order that we may promise, and fulfil our promise. But we may combine a greater than ordinary degree of earnestness and self-watchfulness with this determination; a more than ordinary degree of distinctness and gravity with the promise, or declaration in which we express the determination. We may *solemnly* resolve, and *solemnly* promise. If we do this, we connect the fulfilment of our resolution and promise more thoroughly with the progress of our moral culture. We entwine the two, so that the one cannot be broken, without great damage to the other. We embark a larger portion than usual of the moral treasure of our lives in one bottom, and risk a more ruinous wreck. If we break a solemn resolution, a solemn promise, what hope can we have of any steadiness or vigour in our future moral course? How can we retain the moral hopes and aspirations which are to carry us forwards? The growth of the Principle of Truth is arrested; the Principle itself seems to be eradicated. The interruption and reverse in our moral progress is marked and glaring, and hence (304) the offence is grievous. The violation of a solemn promise is a moral offence of the highest kind.

There may be some cases in which there may be

at first a doubt what course this Rule of the Duty of Truth directs us to take; but these cases we shall consider, when we have taken a view of the remaining Classes of Duties.

CHAPTER X.

DUTIES CONNECTED WITH PURITY.

319. The Duties connected with Purity, are those which result from the Principle of Purity; that the Lower Parts of our Nature are to be governed by and subservient to the Higher Parts. Thus the Appetites and Desires, which find their gratification in meat and drink, with the accompaniments of a decent table, are to be indulged as subservient to the support of life, strength, and cheerfulness, and the cultivation of the social affections; the indulgence is to be limited by these purposes, and these purposes by moral rules. In like manner, other desires, mingled of bodily and mental elements, are to be indulged only in subservience to the affections and hopes which belong to them; and the affections and hopes are to be regulated by conditions which morality and law prescribe. In the gradation of the parts of human nature, we place bodily appetite, and all merely selfish desires, below affection; but mere blind affection we place below the moral affection which approves of goodness. The affections of the heart in some measure refine the desires of the body; but the affections of the heart may be greatly impure, if they are not regulated by the law of the heart, which morality teaches. Affection alone does not make actions moral, or remove that stain of impurity which they derive from bodily appetite. The nature of man is purified, by having a

moral character given to it. This moral character purifies the affections; and the affections, thus purified, communicate their purity to the desires which are subservient to them. And thus, Morality does not require us to extinguish the desires, or to reject the pleasures arising from their gratification. Still, she directs us not to dwell on this gratification in our thoughts, as an object; but to accept from it that influence, which it can exercise in giving energy to our affections, without being itself a direct object of contemplation. The bodily desires are made the instruments and evidences of the affections; and are thus absorbed into the affections, and made conformable to the Principle of Purity.

320. The distinction of the Lower and Higher Parts of our Nature, by means of which we express the Principle of Purity, has been rejected by some moralists, and has been termed Declamation. Such moralists contend that pleasure is universally and necessarily the object of human action; and that human pleasures do not differ in kind, but only in intensity and duration: so that, according to these teachers, there is no difference of superior and inferior, between the pleasures of appetite, the pleasures of affection, and the pleasure of doing good. Hence, say they, the only difference in the character of actions, is their being better or worse means of obtaining pleasure. But the universal reason of man assents to the opposite doctrine, delivered by Butler: who maintains that our principles of action do not differ in degree merely, but in kind also; some being, by the constitution of human nature, superior to others, and their natural governors. Thus, as he teaches, the Rule of our nature is, that Prudence shall control Appetite, and that the Moral Sentiments shall control the Affections. If we take the opposite view, we obliterate the difference between man and brute beasts. We make no distinction between the blame which we

bestow upon Error, and upon Crime; for on this supposition, Crime is only miscalculation; and merely means an erroneous way of seeking pleasure. If we follow this view, we make a bad heart the same thing as a bad head. According to this doctrine, we can have no *Supreme* Rule of Action; for if pleasure be the *highest* object of action, it is also the *lowest*. With such opinions, we deprive the words *right* and *wrong* of their common meaning; for to men in general, they do not mean right and wrong roads to enjoyment, which this view makes them mean.

321. The Duties of Purity are those which follow from such an operation of the Principle. They prohibit indulgence in the pleasures of the Table for the sake of bodily gratification alone; though they allow our meals to be so conducted, that they may not only satisfy the bodily wants of nature, but also minister to the cheerful and social flow of spirits and thought, which is a condition favourable to moral action. They prohibit, in like manner, the gratification of other bodily appetites when sought for their own sake; though they allow such gratification under the sanction of the conjugal tie, and with the hope of that extension of family affections, and family duties, which the birth of children brings.

322. As it is our Duty to regulate our actions by these Rules, it is our Duty also to acquire and possess an inward Principle, from which such a course of action will spring. It is our Duty to acquire and possess within us an Operative Principle, or Spirit, of Purity, which may of itself, and without the recollection of express Rules, direct us from all that is impure. A good man has dispositions, and habits of mind, which not only restrain him from acts of intemperance and unchastity, but repress and banish intemperate and unchaste desires and wishes.

And though it may sometimes be difficult for a man to arrive at this state of Purity of Heart and Mind; it is always the Duty of every man to aim at it. A moral Self-culture in such Purity, is a constant and universal Duty, of which the obligation can never relax nor terminate. A Moral Progress in this, as in other respects, must be the constant aim of a good man.

323. Offences against the Duties of which we are now speaking, more distinctly than in other Classes of Duties, produce their effect, of impeding our Moral Progress, and turning our course backwards. The intemperate and unchaste person becomes, by every vicious act and every vicious purpose, plainly more and more prone to Vice. These Vices affect his habits of mind in a very direct manner. The Glutton and the Epicure, eager and curious respecting the pleasures of the palate, can hardly give due weight in their thoughts to higher objects; and they often stimulate and overtask the bodily functions, till the mind is oppressed, impeded, or arrested in its intellectual and moral operations. In the man who indulges a love of intoxicating liquors, this takes place more evidently and more rapidly. He speedily reduces himself to a condition in which neither reason nor moral restraint has its due power. The indulgence of other sensual appetites stimulates the bodily desires and inflames the imagination. Lust, obeyed as mere Lust, tends to fill the mind with obscene thoughts, and to make the intellect and the fancy mere ministers of Appetite. By such courses, the heart and affections are corrupted: the imagination is polluted: the character is depraved. Any steps in such a course are the opposite of a moral progress: they are steps in a course of moral degradation, of which the end is utter depravity, filthiness, and profligacy; in short, moral ruin. Transgressions of the Rules of Duty, of the kind now referred to, especially produce their effect, as steps of a course. The act of transgression leaves a more distinct trace in the habits, than in the case of mere mental desires. The

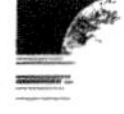

appetites become more powerful by being gratified. Their craving becomes, by indulgence, more and more importunate and irresistible. The body will not let the mind turn away from the accustomed path of sensuality. Sensual acts leave a stain of material filth upon the mind; of which it takes long and earnest efforts to remove the trace, so that it shall not afterwards give a sensual tendency to the Will. And thus, every sensual act contributes to the moral degradation of which we have spoken; and is grossly at variance with the Duty of our own Moral Culture.

324. It is very important to dwell upon this Duty of Moral Self-culture, in reference to offences of Impurity; for these offences are not mere extensions of the notion of jural wrongs, as some moral offences are. Jurally speaking, each person may be said to have a Right over his own body, provided he injure no other person; and two persons may appear to have a Right to agree to unite in acts of sensuality, when no Right of a husband or a father is violated. Accordingly, Fornication, and Concubinage, have not been generally prohibited by the Laws of Ancient and Modern Countries. But yet such practices have almost always been condemned as impure and degraded. And the consideration of the Duty of Moral Self-culture, which we have insisted on, shows the propriety of this condemnation. No person can use his body for purposes of mere Lust, without utterly abandoning all aim at his Moral Progress, and all hope of it. He who thus gives himself up to the government of the Lower parts of his nature, neglects and despises the Higher. So far as he does this, he renounces his moral nature, reduces himself to the level of brute beasts, and goes on resolutely and recklessly to moral ruin. It is true, that men may continue to perform some Duties, and to aim at some Virtues, while they still do not refrain from the Vice of Impurity. But it is plain, that a man's desire of

Moral Progress must be so feeble and inconsistent as not to deserve the name, if he contentedly and intentionally pursues a course which manifestly leads to the pollution and degradation of one main element of a moral character.

325. The different constitution of the heart and mind in the two sexes, as well as the difference in corporeal conditions, lead to some special considerations respecting their Duties. The Desires and Affections of both sexes lead to the Conjugal Union: but according to the natural feelings of most persons, and the practice of most communities, the man proposes and urges the union, before it takes place; the woman yields and consents. The man is impelled by a love which he proclaims to be the object of it; and he asks for a return in which he has the character of a conqueror. The woman is lead to consent, not only by affection, but by the hope of a life filled with those family affections, and family enjoyments, for which, as her heart whispers to her, she was made. When these natural propensities operate under due moral restraint, they lead to the marriage union. But moral restraints may be disregarded in some cases; and in other cases may be so feeble, that the solicitation on one side overcomes the resistance on the other; and the woman is seduced to a bodily union without marriage. This is an act of sensuality; and thus, as we have already said, an offence against morality. And in consequence of the character and conditions of the two sexes, of which we have just spoken, after such an act, the woman continues to yield, but the man is no longer ready to bind himself to her by the marriage tie. She is betrayed, as well as seduced. In so far as the Seducer breaks the engagements which he has expressly or implicitly made, he violates the Duty of Good Faith, as well as the Duty of Chastity. But what we have here to observe is, that by the act of unchastity, he

not only renounces the Duty of Moral Culture, so far as he himself is concerned; but that he is a Violator of the Duty of Benevolence, as the author of her moral degradation; perhaps of her utter moral ruin. For, as we have already said, the Vice of Sensuality, once admitted, has an especial, and almost irresistible tendency, to extend itself over the whole character. The woman who has yielded to blind affection, afterwards, when her affections are chilled, and her character hardened, by the disappointment and treachery she has experienced, and retaining the trace of sensual desire which unchastity produces, may, as we know she often does, become a Wanton; may give herself up to lasciviousness; may sink from one degree of impurity to another, till she end in a state of utter moral ruin. There are said to be men who intentionally, and without remorse, practise the Seduction of women. It cannot but seem very strange, to a person of the ordinary kind of affections, that a human being should employ his skill and exertions in urging a woman, whom he pretends to love and admire, down this moral descent. Such conduct appears to involve a want of common humanity; for the moral degradation of the woman deprives her of almost all that is admirable and estimable, even in the eyes of her seducer himself; and would be mourned by him as the bitterest evil, and resented as the most grievous wrong, if it were inflicted upon any one for whom he has a family affection. To say nothing of the duty of purity, a man who is not restrained by his Humanity from such a course of action, must look upon the moral destruction of women with the kind of indifference with which the sportsman looks upon the death and wounds of beasts and birds which he pursues. It is difficult to conceive a more monstrous degree of inhumanity than is implied in such a view of human beings. The cruelty is greater than if the pursuer were, in wilful levity, to inflict bodily

pain and wounds: for this moral damage is, and is commonly held to be, a greater calamity than any bodily suffering. The moral ruin of a woman makes her an object of abhorrence to those who are bound to her by ties of family love; and produces in her and in them extreme bitterness of heart, and a gloom approaching to the blackness of despair.

326. The tendency of sensual indulgence to inflame the desires, defile the imagination, and corrupt the heart, makes the Duty of Purity especially important in the season of youth. Habits of indulgence, begun in that season, can hardly fail to give their impress to the character, throughout life. The common belief that this is so, appears in the contempt and condemnation which the loss of virginity in unmarried women, has in all ages and countries incurred. In its effects upon the moral culture of the character, unchastity is as destructive in men as in women. No young man who has any regard for his moral progress, will make his body the instrument of lust. And as connected with the government of his bodily desires, both in the way of cause and of consequence, he will guard the purity of his mind. He will avoid admitting into his own thoughts, or suggesting to others, lascivious images. He will avoid placing himself in circumstances of temptation or opportunity. He will watch the affections which may arise in his heart towards particular persons, in order to suppress them; well aware how vehement may become the combined urgency of unlawful affection, and sensual desire; and in what a career of vice they plunge those whom they overmaster.

327. The direction of the Affections and Desires, here referred to, towards their proper object, Marriage, is the best mode of avoiding the degradation of character which is produced by their improper operation. Virtuous love, as it has often been said, is the best preservative against impure acts and

thoughts. The Love which looks forwards to the conjugal union, includes a reverence for the conjugal condition, and all its circumstances. Such a love produces in the mind a kind of moral illumination, which shows the lover how foul a thing mere lust is; and makes him see, as a self-evident truth, that affection is requisite to purify desire, and virtue necessary to purify affection.

Other Duties arising out of the conjugal union depend upon the Principle of Order, and must be considered in reference to that Principle.

CHAPTER XI.

DUTIES OF ORDER.

328. The Principle of Order is, that we must obey positive Laws as the necessary conditions of morality (269). This Principle leads to various Duties of Obedience towards persons connected with us by various social relations; for these social relations are established and recognized by Laws; or by Customs equivalent to Laws; and are the points on which our Obligations, and therefore our relative Duties, depend: and many of these relations give one person an authority over another. Thus, by the laws and customs of nations, parents have a large amount of authority over their children. In most places, the husband has by law and usage some authority over the wife; the master over the servant; and every where, there are magistrates and governors, in whom are vested authority over the members of the community in general. There is, for all, an Obligation to submit to this Authority; and, in order that such acts of Submission may be moral, there must

be corresponding Duties of Obedience. There must therefore be Duties of Obedience of Children to Parents, of Wives to Husbands, of Servants to Masters, of Private Persons to Magistrates; and these we term Duties of Order, or more specially, Duties of Obedience.

These Duties of Obedience, in order to be moral, must arise from a corresponding internal Disposition: from a Spirit of Obedience. It is therefore our Duty to possess such a Spirit of Obedience, and a corresponding Affection towards our Superiors. We have already spoken of certain Affections,—Reverence towards our Superiors, Love of Parents, Conjugal Love, and the like,—as Duties. We have there also remarked, that these Duties involve the Principle of Order, as well as the Principle of Benevolence; and that the Affectoins, thus enjoined, show themselves in acts of willing Obedience.

329. The Rules of the Duty of Obedience, belonging to each of the Relations of Society, that of the Child, that of the Wife, that of the Servant, and the like, must depend, in part, upon the Rules which Law and Custom have established in each community. For our Duties are such as give moral significance to our legal Obligations (279); and the Obligations of the various Members of the Family to each other, must depend upon the idea of the structure of the Family, entertained in each community. The limits of Filial Obedience are very different, in the customs of different countries; and these customs must have their weight in defining the Limits of Duty. In all states of Society, in the early stages of life, the Parent is the natural guide and governor of the child; and it is the Duty of the child to obey such government and guidance. But we cannot pretend to say, generally, how far or how long this Duty extends. For instance, we cannot lay down any universal Rule to determine whether the Parent may prevent the son from selecting a wife, or the daughter a husband, by

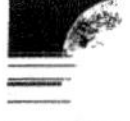

their own choice; and whether, in such a case, it is the child's Duty to obey: or whether, supposing that obedience to a prohibition in such a case be a Duty, it be a Duty also to take the husband or the wife whom the Parent selects. In some countries, the marriage of the child is a matter usually managed altogether by the parents. In such cases, it is the child's duty to bring the affections, as far as possible, into harmony with the custom. But those communities and those parents appear to provide better for that special personal affection which the completeness of the marriage union requires, who allow to young men and young women freedom of choice in marriage. Where this is the case, it is the Duty of the man to select a partner to whom his heart tells him he is likely to bear a true conjugal affection; and of the woman, also, to give her hand only when she can give her heart. But even in such cases, filial duty requires, if not absolute obedience, great reverence and deference to the wishes of parents; especially while the children are young; and while, consequently, the habit of submitting to the parent's guidance must be still in force in a family directed by Rules of Duty. In the same manner, the kind of authority which the husband, by law and custom, has over the wife, is different in different communities. In all countries, the man is the head and representative of the family, and is the person to whom political offices are assigned. But to what extent the husband, and to what extent the wife, shall rule in domestic concerns, will be regulated by local usage, or by special understanding of the parties. And in every case, the Duties of the husband and of the wife are those which give a moral significance to the Rules which usage and mutual understanding establish. While established, Duty requires the married pair to conform to the Rules; but Duty requires, too, that this should be done in a spirit of Affection and Confidence; the acts

thus performed expressing the common will of the two. And in the same way, the Obligations of obedience in Servants are variously determined by law, use, or agreement; and their Duties will vary with their Obligations: but in all cases, there are Duties corresponding to their Obligations; their offices must be performed faithfully and heartily, not with a grudging and merely formal service. And with respect to political relations, a willing obedience to the laws, an affection for his country, a love of its institutions and of its constitution, a loyalty to its sovereign, are proper feelings of a good man, in a rightly constituted state; and are Duties, except where, by some special historical facts, objects on which such feelings can be employed, are wanting.

330. A willing obedience to the Laws of the Land is, as we have said, a Duty; for the Laws define those social relations which determine the course of our Duties; the Laws establish those Obligations of which our Duties are the expansion, and to which our Duties give a moral signification. But Laws themselves aim at a moral signification; they seek to be just and equitable Laws. We shall hereafter consider the moral character of Laws; but we may here remark, that so far as they have an obvious moral signification, it is our duty to accept and obey them according to this signification. In cases where the Law is equitable, it is our Duty to conform to the Spirit as well as to the Letter of the Law.

331. There are, however, many cases in which the Law is arbitrary, and rests upon the Authority of the State alone; or in some other way, is devoid of any obvious moral signification. There are many forms, details, and magnitudes regulated by Law, merely because they must be fixed by some Rule, and Law is the proper Rule. In such cases we have no Duty, but to conform to the letter of the Law.

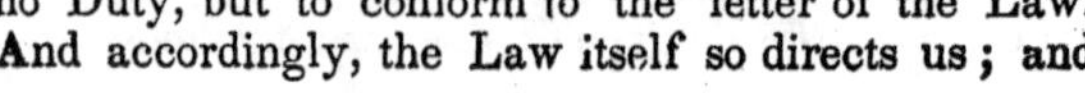

And accordingly, the Law itself so directs us; and

the Courts of Justice pronounce their decisions, according to the Letter of the Law. In such indifferent matters, we are not to seek for a Spirit beyond the Letter. The State itself, to which our Duties refer, gives us to understand that we are to guide ourselves by the Letter. Nor, in such cases, is the Intention of the Legislature the measure of our Duty. It is not with any particular Legislator or Body of Legislators that we have to do. The State enjoins the Law; and we accept the Law as the State understands it. The State must be supposed to have accepted the Law, and to understand it, according to the meaning of the words; for the State has accepted and adopted the expressed words, not the unexpressed meaning of any man or set of men. If any set of Legislators failed in expressing what they meant, the State cannot be bound by their incapacity. And thus, in indifferent matters, the Letter of the Law, and not some supposed Spirit besides the Letter, is the proper guide of our obedience. The business of Legislation is to prevent our Duties depending upon anything so vague and obscure, as the Spirit of a Law not expressed in the Letter.

332. We have spoken hitherto of Duties of Obedience; but the Duties of Order include also the Duties which exist on the other side; the Duties of Command. As it is a Duty to give a cordial obedience to just authority, with a regard to the purposes for which the authority subsists; so is it a Duty to exercise Authority for its proper purposes, and in a spirit of benevolence towards those who are its subjects. As it is the Child's Duty to submit to the guidance and government of the Parent, it is the Parent's Duty to guide the Child aright, and to govern it by Rules which the good of the child itself justifies. As far as it is the Wife's Duty to obey the commands of her husband, it is the Husband's Duty to command nothing harshly, capriciously, or unreasonably; but

such acts only as may fall in with an affectionate and confiding conduct of their united course of life. As it is the Servant's Duty to do his work willingly, and bear to his employer such respect as suits their relative condition; it is the Employer's Duty, in directing those who labour in his service, to consider their powers and their comfort. It is his Duty, also, not to make the relation of employer and servant a source of estrangement between the two classes, by a hard and repulsive demeanour; for this cannot be the true moral aspect of the relation between men, since they are bound together by the Duty of mutual Benevolence. As to their place in the social scale of a particular community, men may be called Superiors and Inferiors; but no class of men are superior or inferior to others, in their moral claim to kindness in our intention, and gentleness in our manner. So far as the relations of society receive their true moral significance, they bind together all the members of the society by a tie of benevolence; which has, for its natural results, ready and willing good offices of all to all; frank, affable, and courteous intercourse of all with all. If this feeling of benevolence had its due effect, the repulsive forces which social distinctions bring into play—the pride of rank and station, the capricious exclusions of fashion, the supreme regard of each class to its own comfort, the excessive jealousy of interference, the impatience of intrusion—would disappear before it; and, so far as the influence of such a feeling operates upon the members of a community, those repulsive elements will diminish and melt away.

333. The Duties of Order, so far as regards the State, like other Duties, include the duty of giving a moral significance to the social and civil relations with which they deal. Every man who has any power, or any function in the State assigned him, must exercise it in such a manner as to give a moral

meaning to his office. He must act, on the part of the State, as a public representative of its moral character. If he be a Judge, he must administer the Laws impartially, and so as to make them instruments of justice. If he be an administrative officer, he must carry into effect the intentions of the Community; giving to it, as far as the Rules of his office admit, the character of a moral agent acting rightly. If he have assigned to him a vote by which he shares in the election of a legislator or a governor, the vote is a *Trust* for public purposes (152); and it is grossly immoral to convert such a Trust to purposes of priate gain. All such Duties are *Public Duties;* and Public, no less than Private Duties, require us to use all our external means and powers for the furtherance of Morality.

334. The Laws and Customs which determine how far each person shall have a share in the government of the State, define the *Political* Rights and Obligations of men; and the general scheme of Government, thus constituted, is the *Constitution* of the Country. In every country, the Political Rights and Obligations of men ought to be in a great measure fixed; for otherwise the Laws could not remain fixed, and could afford no fixed points to serve as the basis of Duty. It is therefore the Duty of a citizen to use his Political Rights, so as to give to the Laws the fixity which the purposes of Morality require. This is the *Political Duty of Conservation.* On the other hand, the Political Rights and Obligations of the citizens of a State may change from time to time; for by course of time and circumstance, it often becomes possible to alter the Laws in general, and Political Laws in particular, so as better to further the purposes of Morality. It is the Duty of a citizen to use his Political Rights in promoting changes of this description. This is the *Political Duty of Progress.*

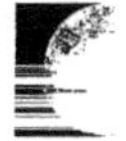

CHAPTER XII.

INTELLECTUAL DUTIES.

335. Besides the Duties of Kindness, which the Duties of Command include, there are other Duties of Command, which require our attention. He who has authority, must issue Commands, not only kind, but also prudent, and wise. He has faculties by which he is enabled to judge of such characters in Rules of Action: and he is bound to employ these faculties, as well as his Affections, in the performance of his Duty. Thus, there are Duties which belong to these faculties. We may term them generally, Duties of the Intellectual Faculties; but we may conveniently distinguish among them, the *Duty of Prudence* and the *Duty of Wisdom*.

We have already said, that we conceive Prudence as the Virtue by which we select right means for given ends; while Wisdom implies the selection of right ends, as well as of right means. Those who have authority over others, have to lay down Laws for their conduct; and these Laws may be considered as means, to ends which the Lawgiver contemplates. There are certain objects, which those who possess authority by their social position, may be assumed as having constantly and necessarily in their desires: thus, a head of a family desires sustenance for his family, tranquillity among the members of it, freedom from debts contracted by them; as an employer, he desires to have his work well and carefully done; and the like: and he manifests his Prudence by the Laws, which he lays down, or the Rules on which he acts, with reference to these objects. But perhaps a father makes it his main object that his sons and his daughters should rise to riches and

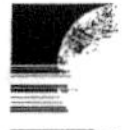

rank: and then, though he may be prudent in the means he takes for such ends, we may doubt whether he is wise in selecting these as his highest ends.

336. But we have to select the ends of action, and the means to them, for ourselves, as well as for others; and Prudence and Wisdom are concerned in this selection, in the former, as in the latter case. We may therefore consider the Duty of Prudence, and the Duty of Wisdom, without any special reference to the offices of command over others, which men may have to execute.

The Duty of Prudence, like other Duties, implies that man has a power over the faculties, which such a Duty requires him to employ. That man has some power over his own thoughts, is evident. He can retain an object of thought in his mind: contemplate it in various aspects and bearings; scrutinize it; deliberate upon it. This is Inquiry and *Consideration;* and by this proceeding, he can often discover means to an end, and consequences of an act, which escape his notice, in a more rapid and slight mode of regarding the subject. Now the means to an end have their moral character affected by the end. The consequences of an act contribute to the moral character of the act. The points which Consideration and Inquiry brings into view, may determine whether the act be good or bad. And since we must employ all our Faculties and Powers in order to conform our actions to the Supreme Law, we must exercise this power of Consideration; and thus every man, as a moral agent, is bound by a *Duty of Consideration*, including a Duty of Inquiry.

337. The Intention is directed by the various Springs of Action, including the Moral Sentiments and the Reason. Morality requires that Intention be directed rightly: that is, towards the Ideas contained in the Supreme Law; Benevolence, Justice, Truth, Purity, and Order. There is a Duty of right Inten-

tion, which is included in all other Duties. Now we have here to remark, that this Duty of Right Intention does not replace or supersede the Duty of Consideration. We must consider the means, as they are in themselves, as well as in subservience to the end at which our intention points. We must consider the consequences which will follow upon our act, as well as the act which we directly intend. For a good end does not justify the means which we employ, if a due consideration would show us that the means are wrongly selected: and that an act is in itself moral, does not justify it, if by a due consideration we might see that it would lead to evil consequences. I may have a wish to improve the character of my child: I may hastily punish him, with such an intention. But the intention does not justify the haste. If a little thought and care, bestowed upon the subject, would have shown me that these courses would make him worse, and not better, I am to blame. I have violated the Duty of Consideration. And in like manner, the Duty of Consideration is transgressed by any want of a Regard to Consequences. I may heedlessly indulge the desires of a child, or give what a man asks of me. But if the consequences of doing this be mischief to the child or to the man, and mischief which a little thought would have shown to be probable, or certain, I am culpable. Here, also, I have violated the Duty of Consideration. Haste and Heedlessness are grave offences, in cases which concern the welfare of others. We have already seen that the Law treats such offences as violations of our Obligations (114): and our Duties, in this, as in other cases, are extensions of our Obligations. If Law require in us a care and consideration for the wellbeing of our fellow-men, Morality must require such care and consideration still more; and must require more care and more consideration than the Law can enforce. Benevolence aims at the good of

those among whom we are placed: but she must take to her aid the best exertions of the Intellect, in order to determine by what means such good is to be brought about; and what will be the consequences of any acts which such a purpose may suggest to us.

338. It is in our power to deliberate; but even after deliberation, we may be mistaken. It may be asked, if we are responsible for such a mistake. Is it a violation of any Duty to select wrong means to good ends, or to err in foreseeing the consequences of actions meant for good? If we here also follow the analogy of the Law, we shall be led to conclude that, in some cases at least, such an error is blameable. A physician who administers medicaments grossly pernicious, is condemned by the Law for his error, however right may have been his intentions, and with however much thought he may have gone to his error. And the common judgment of mankind throws a like blame upon similar errors. Men are indignant against folly and ignorance, when they affect important acts; as well as against evil intention. Men feel, and express, a strong moral indignation against a father, who ruins the character of his child by bad teaching, though he may have employed much pains upon its education: against a pilot who wrecks his ship by bad steering, though he may have steered his best: against a legislator who makes bad laws, though he thought them good. And if we look into the ground of this indignation, and of the moral condemnation which it involves, we shall see that the persons, in these cases, are judged to be to blame, because they deviated from the guidance of that Reason which is the common light of all mankind. They had a Faculty which points out the difference between what is good and what is bad, in such cases; between right means and wrong means, to the acknowledged ends. They cannot have duly employed this Faculty, or they would not have gone wrong.

They acted irrationally, and in so doing, they violated a Duty; and thus we are led to recognize *the Duty of acting rationally.* It is our Duty, not only to be careful and considerate in our choice of means to ends, but also to choose rationally. We do not say that it is our Duty to choose rightly, for there may be inevitable errors: but at least, we must use our Reason in choosing, and avoid such errors as her light manifests to us.

We do not say that it is easy to determine what errors can, and what cannot be avoided: what selection of means for an acknowledged end is rational, and what is irrational. So far as such a distinction can be drawn, it will be our business hereafter to examine it. But the difficulty of doing this, does not prevent our recognizing, in general, the Duty of acting rationally, as one of our intellectual Duties.

339. The Reason directs our course in various ways: among others, by accepting Rules of action, and directing the conduct in conformity to them. Such Rules have it for their office to control and regulate the variable and discordant action of men's Affections and Desires: to render permanent and consistent the guidance, which Reason, operating without Rules, exercises, in each person, doubtfully and interruptedly. Rules are the primary expressions of Duties. The Rules, *Do not kill, Do not steal, Do not lie,* and the like, are the basis of moral action. The formation, the establishment, the acceptance of such Rules, is the mode in which man becomes a moral agent. But besides such Rules, others, of a less absolute and general kind, are among the most suitable and efficacious means of controlling the conduct in a rational and moral manner. Such are those we have just mentioned: *Children, obey your parents: Masters, treat your servants with kindness.* Such Rules, accepted as right, and retained in the recollection as the constant guides of our conduct, extend the sway of

Reason to times when, without them, we might be led wrong by passion or desire. They sustain us against the pressure of special seasons of temptation; and extend, to the worse periods of our rational and moral life, the influence of the better periods. To act by such Rules, is the very meaning of acting according to Duty. Further; not only are such Moral Rules means by which our Reason guides us, but other Rules also, not directly moral, but of a prudential character only, are among the proper means of directing our conduct rationally. Thus, we may avoid intemperance, by conforming to Rules which shall moderate our eating and drinking; we may escape debt and poverty, by conforming to Rules limiting our habitual expenses; we may suppress our tendencies to harsh and rude behaviour, by conforming ourselves to Rules of courtesy. Rules of this kind, more or less distinctly expressed in words, are the proper guides of man, as a rational being. They are the modes in which the general convictions of the Reason are brought into contact with particular cases of action. It is our Duty thus to regulate our conduct; and thus we have a *Duty of acting according to Rule.*

340. Moral Rules, in so far as they are moral, are absolute, being expressions of the Supreme Rule of human action, which nothing can overmaster or supersede. Prudential Rules, having for their object subordinate ends, may be set aside in particular cases, as these objects themselves may. They must give way, for instance, whenever they interfere with Moral Rules. Moral Rules only, are, in the highest sense, the proper guides of human life.

Hence, it is our Duty to accept or to frame Moral Rules, as the means of our guidance. This is a Duty, which has not, like the Duties of which we have been speaking, reference to any subordinate end, but to the highest; it is the Duty of Wisdom, not a Duty of Providence.

The Duty of Wisdom is the Duty of framing or adopting such Rules of action as are consistent with the Supreme Rule of Human Action. It is the Duty of having Rules of Duty: for, as we have seen, the Rules of Duty are determined, on the one hand, by those Moral Ideas which serve to express the Supreme Rule; while, on the other hand, they are determined by the various social relations and conditions of man's life.

341. By what means can we obtain Rules of Duty which are truly moral, truly consistent with the Supreme Rule? We have already been employed in laying down such Rules; and we have seen, in some measure, by what process they may be arrived at. We find that there are external conditions necessary to the existence of man as a moral being; that there are certain Rights and Obligations, according to which, as external Facts, man's Duties are regulated. There are, also, certain Ideas of Virtues, namely, Benevolence, Justice, and the like, according to which, as internal Ideas, the conceptions of Duty are regulated. By the combination of these two elements, we have endeavoured to define, in some measure, the scheme of Duties which belong to man. But we have, in several instances, been led to see that some further steps are requisite, before we can describe our Duties in a complete manner; and before we can produce Rules which shall admit of definite application, in the cases which commonly offer themselves to our notice. Among the steps which are thus pointed out to us, as required for the formation of more definite Rules of Duty, are Determinations and Definitions, more exact than we have yet obtained, of some of the Conceptions, in terms of which our Rules must necessarily be expressed; such conceptions, for instance, as Justice, Humanity, Happiness, and the like. The next step which we shall take, in the establishment of Moral Rules, will be to attempt to analyze and define, more

precisely than we have yet done, several such Conceptions as these, and to apply, in particular cases, the Conceptions thus defined. We may, in this way, best hope to obtain both Moral Truths of a general kind, and the determination of the questions which belong to special cases.

342. The precision of our Conceptions, which may thus aid us in arriving at Moral Truths, is a proper object for us to aim at, as a mode of promoting our Moral Culture. It is our Duty to aim at such an intellectual progress, as a means to our moral progress. And not only may this particular kind of improvement of the intellect, be an aid in our moral culture; but the improvement of the intellect in general, in its conceptions and operations, is fitted to have this effect. And it is therefore our Duty to aim at such improvement. Corresponding to the Duty of Moral Culture of ourselves, there is a *Duty of intellectual Culture*. To cultivate our Intellect, is, in itself, a source of gratification. The love of knowledge which we have spoken of, as one of the desires of man, impels him constantly to make his knowledge more and more extensive, more and more precise, more and more connected; and an advance of this kind is indeed a Culture of the Intellect. But besides all other Truth, to which the love of knowledge leads, and where man seeks for the satisfaction of knowing, this desire leads to Moral Truth, which is the proper guide of man's life; and which, therefore, he is impelled to seek, not only by pleasure, but by Duty.

343. Moral Truth is, as we have said, the proper guide of human life; and hence, those who have to guide others, are under a more peculiar necessity of knowing Moral Truth, and of possessing precise and consistent moral conceptions. Those especially need such Truth, such Precision, and such Consistency, whose office it is to make Rules for others, or to

teach them the Rules which they are to follow;—those, that is, who have to legislate for mankind, or to educate them. The Duty of Wisdom is especially incumbent on Legislators and on Educators.

Since the offices of Legislation and of Education especially require the possession of Moral Truth, we shall defer the consideration of those offices in detail, till we have, under our notice, those further elements of Moral Truth, which we still have to consider.

We will only observe, before we quit this part of the subject, that Legislation implies, not merely combinations of Conceptions, and mental results of Ideas, but also the external Facts, by which Law is realized. Laws are Moral Rules, clothed in an actual historical Form. The Legislator must also be a Governor; or at least his ideas must be adopted and enforced by the Governor, in order to make them be Laws.

344. In like manner, Education, so far as it teaches Rules of action, implies external facts, which give reality to the Precepts inculcated. The Educator teaches the learner the Laws of the Land, for instance, in order that he may guide himself by them; but in order that his teaching may have its effect, he must be able to speak of these Laws, as actually existing Laws; not as merely possible conceivable Rules. And when the Educator has to teach, not merely human Laws, but moral Rules, he must still be able to present these moral Rules, not merely as imaginable, but as possessing a real Authority. Moral Rules derive their substance from the Supreme Rule of Human Action, of which they are partial expressions. Hence, this Supreme Rule must have a real authority, and an actual force. The Educator teaches his pupil to do what is absolutely right; and because it is right: but this teaching supposes that its being right includes a sufficient reason for doing it; estimating reasons according to the real condition and destination of man.

The Supreme Rule of Human Action derives its Real Authority, and its actual force, from its being the Law of God, the Creator of Man. The Reason for doing what is absolutely right, is, that it is the Will of God, through which the condition and destination of man are what they are.

We are thus led to Religion as a necessary part of the Moral Education of men. But in order to complete the train of thought by which Morality leads us to Religion, we must pursue somewhat further the subject of Moral Transgression, of which we have already spoken (303).

CHAPTER XIII.

OF TRANSGRESSION.

345. In our survey of the several classes of Duties (281—344) we have seen that, beside the direct Duties of action, and of affection towards others, there are reflex Duties which regard ourselves: the Duties, namely, of unfolding within us, or establishing in our minds the Operative Moral Principles from which external Duties must proceed; the Duty of aiming at our own Moral Progress. The duty of cultivating in our own minds the principles of Benevolence, Justice, Truth, Purity, and Order. We have it for our business and proper aim, to make our Lives a Moral Progress, in which these Principles constantly become more and more identified with our habits of action, thought, and feeling. We have to form our character, so that these principles are its predominant features. We have to seek not only to *do*, but to *be;* not only to perform acts of duty, but to become virtuous (299, &c).

Further: there is an Intellectual, as well as a moral progress, at which we must aim; an Intellectual Progress, which is a means to a Moral Progress. We are to endeavour constantly to improve our powers of apprehending Truth, in order that we may be able the more readily and firmly to lay hold on that Moral Truth, which is the proper guide of our Lives (342).

346. We have to aim at this moral and intellectual progress as the Greatest Good which we can desire for ourselves (306). But further, the complete Benevolence which is part of the character at which we thus aim, and which seeks the good of others, must seek for them that good which for ourselves we esteem the greatest. Our benevolence, therefore, will seek the moral progress of others as well as our own; and intellectual progress for them, no less than for ourselves, as a means of moral progress. And thus, the complex Object, at which we shall constantly have to aim, is, the Moral and Intellectual Progress of Ourselves and of the rest of Mankind.

We may consider this as the highest object of action and thought which we can propose to ourselves; and in proportion as we make this our object, and direct our thoughts and purposes to it, we elevate our minds.

347. We have already seen (293, &c.) that we have the power, in some measure at least, of carrying on this moral and intellectual progress within ourselves. That this progress must be altogether incomplete and imperfect without the aid of Religion, we shall hereafter see; but it is at least so far possible for men to promote or neglect their own moral progress, that one man shall differ very much from another in the advance he has thus made. Two men may be, at least by comparison, one virtuous and another vicious; and by a like difference, they may be at very different stages of their moral progress; if, indeed, we may not say of some, that the course of their lives

is a constant moral degradation rather than a progress.

348. This moral progress, as we have said (300), can never terminate while we remain on earth. So long as we live, we shall have room to make ourselves better and wiser: to increase the warmth of our benevolence, to purify our hearts, to elevate our thoughts, to make ourselves more and more virtuous. To do this, is a moral growth and nurture; a moral life, which can never end, while our natural life goes on. Or if the moral progress end, the moral life is turned to moral disorder. In the moral faculties, if there be not a healthy growth, there must be a morbid decay and foul disease.

349. The Moral life is nourished by the perpetual aliment of moral actions, moral habits, moral thoughts, moral affections. All acts of Duty, and all affections which lead to acts of Duty, tend to promote our Moral Culture. On the other hand, all *Transgressions* of Duty interrupt our Moral Culture, arrest our Moral Progress, and are steps in a retrograde moral course. Unkind affections, unlawful desires, fraudulent intentions, impure imaginations, are inconsistent with our moral advancement, while they occupy us; and are proofs that we have much still to do, in giving a moral character to our being. If these things form frequent and common parts of our lives, they are proofs that we have made little moral progress; or rather, that we have made none, and are making none. If these things are acquiesced in by us, and allowed to grow into habits, we are not going forwards, but backwards, in moral character. So far as this is our case, we tend to become more and more degraded, depraved, vicious (303).

350. Thus, if wrong affections, desires, intentions, and imaginations, occur in our lives at all, they are interruptions of our moral progress; and evidences that, in our moral culture, we have still much to

do. Yet such things may occur, so long as our moral culture is incomplete; and since, during our lives, it ever must be incomplete, they may occur so long as life remains. The Springs of Action, not fully converted into Moral Principles, may, under special circumstances, tend to deviate from the Law of Duty. Desires may be inflamed, Affections perverted, Reason misled, Consideration omitted, Rules neglected, lower aims put in the place of the highest; and man may fall below the line which morality draws. The circumstances which tend to produce such an effect are *Temptations*. By the impulses of the Springs of Action, not fully controlled by Rules of Duty, man is *tempted* to transgress such Rules.

351. It is the moral business of man to *resist* Temptation. The powers by which we guide ourselves, the Reason, and the Moral Sentiments, must be employed in controlling the Desires and Affections which impel us in an immoral direction. All the results of our Moral Culture must be called to our aid for this purpose. The Express Moral Principles which we have learnt; the Operative Moral Principles which we have acquired; Consideration, Rational Action, and Rules of Duty, we must call into operation, that they may overcome the immoral impulses by which we are urged. This we must do as moral agents; although to these resources, Religion alone can give their full force.

If a man does not effectually resist Temptation; if he is overcome and yields, he transgresses the Rules of Duty; he offends against Morality; he commits a vicious act. The contemplation of man under this aspect, as liable to *Transgressions* and *Offences*, introduces us to very important and serious views of his condition and destination.

352. Transgressions or Offences are described by various terms, implying various degrees of condemnation. As defects from the standard of Morali-

ty they are *Faults;* and when we would ascribe them to weakness of Will, rather than to wrong intention, they are called *Failings*. As transgression becomes graver, more grievous, we have no term which directly expresses an enormous violation of morality (as do the latin *scelus, flagitium, facinus*). *Vice* implies the disposition to transgress; *Guilt* and *Crime* properly express the violation of human laws; and *Sin*, an offence against God. But *Guilt* and *Crime* are terms also used of the violation of moral laws; and all Transgressions are Sins. Those who commit Sins are *wicked*, which is said to have meant, originally, *under the influence of evil spirits*. Sins are described, according to their character, as acts of cruelty, of injustice, of falsehood, of uncleanness, and the like. As they excite our moral abhorrence, they are termed *hateful, heinous, atrocious, shocking, abominable, detestable, execrable*. Crimes are said, figuratively, in proportion as they are greater, to be *higher, deeper, heavier, darker*. As their criminal nature is more manifest, they are *flagrant*.

353. It may be asked, according to what Measure and Standard do moral transgressions become greater and graver. Is there a definite gradation from slight Failings to atrocious Crimes; and if so, what circumstances fix the place of each Offence in this Scale? To this we reply, that the universal voice of mankind declares some offences to be greater, some to be less; some heavier, some lighter. But yet, since the moral transgression consists in the perversion of internal affections, desires, and will; and since this internal condition cannot be fully known and compared in any two cases, at least in any two classes of cases; it must be almost impossible to declare one class of transgressions to be better or worse than another. This at least we may say; that to pronounce one kind of offences better and slighter than another, would tend to convey a false opinion

respecting the offences thus in some degree preferred and palliated. For no transgression can be said to be so much better than another, as not to be utterly bad. No offence can rightly be deemed slight, since the slightest utterly interrupts our moral progress.

354. But in this aspect of offences, that they interrupt or undo our moral progress, we have a kind of Measure, of their magnitude. Those offences are most grievous, which are most pernicious in their effect upon our moral culture. Some may interrupt our moral culture for a time, and it may nevertheless be resumed. Others may show that moral culture has no place in our thoughts; that we have no wish to be better than we are. Other transgressions may imply a recklessness or despair of moral progress; a state of mind which points to moral ruin as its natural sequel. The gravity of the offence will therefore be increased by all circumstances which indicate it to be the result of an habitually immoral state of the Affections and Desires, of settled and deliberate purpose, of a want or a rejection of moral aims. The hope that an offence may be only a transient interruption of the offender's moral progress, is favoured by its being the result of great and sudden Temptation, plainly at variance with the habitual course of the affections and will. Such circumstances, therefore, tend to make an offence less grave and mischievous to the offender.

355. I have already pointed out, of what nature the mischief is, which offences do to the offender. So long as there is a suspension of the authority of Duty, there is a suspension of the proper moral functions of man. So long as immoral thought, purpose, and affection prevail, the moral progress, which is the proper course of man's life; is arrested or inverted. Acts of Wickedness are steps towards moral ruin. Or, to resume a figure which we have already employed; the moral life is nourished by the per

petual aliment of moral purposes, desires and affections. By an immoral act, poison is taken into the human being, which tends to enfeeble, distemper, and destroy the moral life.

We are now led to ask, whether there is any remedy for this mischief. When transgression has been committed, how is rectitude to be restored? When the moral progress has been interrupted and turned back, how is the regress to be checked, the lost ground to be recovered, the progress to be resumed? When poison has been taken into our moral being, how is it to be ejected, and the powers of life restored to their healthful action?

The mode in which the poison of immoral purposes, desires, and affections, was taken into our being was, by their being *our* purposes, *our* desires, *our* affections. In order to expel their effect, they must be rejected as our purposes, our desires, our affections. They must be repudiated, so that they shall no longer belong to us. They must be changed into their reverse; desire, into aversion; love, into hate; the purpose to do, into the purpose to undo; joy in what was done, to sorrow that it was done. This change must be carried, by an effort of thought, into the past. We must recall in our memory the past act of transgression, contradicting, as we do so, the motives by which we were misled, and condemning the purpose which we formed. This change, this sorrow, this renunciation and condemnation of our past act, is *Repentance*. The transgressor must *repent*. We do not say that this suffices to remedy the evil. It does not do so. But there can be no remedy of the evil without this. This, at least, he must do. He must make the effort of Repentance, in order to cast out of his being the poison of immoral act or purpose. He, for this purpose, must see his moral regression as what it is, a dire mischief, which, if not remedied, tends to immeasurable evil.

356. But the regression must not only be lamented, it must also be repaired. We must not only reject the past offence by repentance, but we must seek to resume the course which morality points out. We must endeavour to restore our moral progress; to regain the ground which we have lost; to avoid all repetition of the errors and offences which we have committed. We must direct our Moral Culture to our recovery and renovation. We must *amend* ourselves. We must *reform* our lives. *Amendment* and *Reformation*, as well as Repentance, are the necessary sequel of transgression, in virtue of that Duty of Moral Culture and Moral Progress which is constantly incumbent upon all men.

357. The Moralist is thus led to teach, that after Transgression, Repentance and Amendment are necessary steps in our Moral Culture. But the Moralist cannot pronounce how far these steps can avail as a remedy for the evil; how far they can repair the broken completeness of man's moral course; how far they can restore the health of man's moral life; how far they can finally, and upon the whole, avert the consequences of sin from man's condition and destination. These are points on which the Moralist necessarily looks to Religion for her teaching. These questions regard the effects of Sin upon the Soul, and the concerns of the Soul belong to Religion. They regard the provision made by God for saving man from the effects of Sin, and this is also a matter belonging to Religion.

358. There is, however, one consequence of what has been said, which we may notice. We have said, that when a man has deviated from the course of Duty, he cannot resume his moral progress without Repentance and Amendment. We may remark further, that the Amendment is required by Morality to be *immediate*. If a man repents in the middle of an immoral act, he will not go on with the act. As soon

as the authority of Morality is acknowledged, the moral course of action must begin; and not at some later period, when pending acts have been completed. Duty is the perpetual rightful Governor of every man; and the man who merely promises to obey this Governor at some future time, is really disobedient. The man who completes an immoral act, knowing it to be immoral, commits a new offence. He yielded to temptation in the first part of the act; he sins against conviction, in the second.

This remark may be of use when we come to consider some cases of Duty. For instance, if I have made an immoral promise, and see my fault, it is my Duty not to complete the act by performing the promise.

CHAPTER XIV.

OF CONSCIENCE.

359. The Desires and Affections receive their Culture by being converted into, or comprehended in, the Operative Moral Principles. The Faculties which control and direct the Desires and Affections, namely, the Reason and the Moral Sentiments, must also receive their Culture, in order that the being of man may tend to its proper completeness. The Culture of these Faculties implies the formation or adoption, in our minds, of Rules of Duty, and the application of such Rules to our own actions, with the accompanying Sentiment of Approval or Disapproval of ourselves.

Thus, by the culture of these controlling and directing Faculties, we form habits, according to which we turn our attention upon ourselves, and approve or disapprove what we there discern. These Faculties, thus cultured, are the *Conscience* of each man. The word *conscious* implies a reflex attention of the mind to its own condition or operation; a contemplation of what we ourselves feel and do. We *feel* pain, but we are *conscious* of impatience. We start *unconsciously* at a surprise, but in danger we are *conscious* of fear. Our consciousness reveals to us not only our most secret acts, but our desires, affections, and intentions. These are the especial subjects of morality, and we cannot think of them, without considering them as right or wrong. We approve, or disapprove, of what we have done, or tried to do. We consider our acts, external and internal, with reference to a moral standard of right and wrong. We recognize them as virtuous or vicious. The Faculty or Habit of doing this is Conscience.

360. As *Science* means *Knowledge*, *Conscience* etymologically means *Self-knowledge;* and such is the meaning of the word in Latin and French, and of the corresponding word in Greek; (*conscientia*, *conscience*, συνείδησις). But the English word implies a Moral Standard of action in the mind, as well as a Consciousness of our own actions. It may be convenient to us to mark this distinction of an internal Moral Standard, as one part of Conscience; and Self-knowledge, or Consciousness, as another part. The one is the Internal Law; the other, the Internal Accuser, Witness, and Judge.

This distinction was noted by early Christian Moralists. They termed the former part of Conscience, *Synteresis*, the internal Repository: the latter, *Syneidesis*, the internal Knowledge. We may term the former, Conscience as Law; the latter, Conscience as Witness.

361. We have already (341) spoken of the steps by which we establish in our minds that internal Law which we call Conscience. It is established by such a Culture of our Reason as enables us to

frame or to accept Rules which are in agreement with the Supreme Law; and by the agreement of our Moral Sentiments with such Rules. *Conscience as Law*, is the expression of the condition at which we have aimed, in our advance towards a knowledge of the Supreme Law. It is a Stage in our moral and intellectual Progress.

362. The Offices of *Conscience as Witness, Accuser*, and *Judge*, cannot easily be separated; for to be conscious of having done an act, to question its character, and to know that it is wrong, are steps which usually follow close upon each other. Yet these steps may often be distinct. It may require some consideration, and some careful exercise of the intellect, to discern the important features of an act, and to apply to it the appropriate Rules of Duty. The moralists who distinguish the *Synteresis* from the *Syneidesis*, represent the acts of Conscience as expressed by the three members of a Syllogism; of which the first contains the *Law*, the Second, the *Witness*, the Third, the *Judgment*. As an example, we may take this Syllogism:

He who dissembles, transgresses the Duty of Truth;

I have dissembled;

Therefore I have transgressed the Duty of Truth.

363. We may also note a further office which is ascribed to Conscience. She inflicts *Punishment* for the offences thus condemned. For the Self-accusation and Self-condemnation, of which we have spoken, bring with them their especial pains. Repentance is sorrow; Remorse is a pang, a torment. Transgression lies like a weight on the Conscience, and makes it feel burthened and oppressed. Again, the Conscience is spoken of as the *Record* of offences committed; and as stained, polluted, blackened by our transgressions.

364. Conscience, the Judge, must pronounce its

decision according to Conscience, the Law. If we have not transgressed the Law of Conscience, Conscience acquits us. If we have violated the Law of Conscience, Conscience condemns us.

He who is condemned by his own Conscience, is guilty. He has really done wrong. He has really offended against the Supreme Rule. His actions are inconsistent with the Stage at which he has arrived in his moral progress. They are therefore inconsistent with Morality. He who acts *against his Conscience* is always wrong.

365. The question naturally occurs, whether, on the other hand, he who acts *according to his conscience* is always right; whether he who is acquitted by his conscience is free from blame. Is it enough for the demands of morality, if each person compares his actions to the Standard of right and wrong which he has in his mind? Is this a complete justification?

It is evident, that to answer these questions in the affirmative, would lead to great inconsistencies in our Morality. For, under the influence of Education, Laws, Prejudices, and Passions, the Standard of right and wrong, which exists in men's minds for the time, is often very different from that which the Moralist can assent to. Men have often committed thefts, frauds, impositions, homicides, thinking their actions right; though they were such as all Moralists would condemn as wrong. Such men acted according to their Consciences. Were they thereby justified?

366. What has already been said, may suggest a Reply to such questions. It is the Duty of man constantly to prosecute his moral and intellectual Culture (345). This requires not only that we should conform our actions to the Standard which we have in our minds for the time; but that, also, we are to make this Standard truly moral. Whatever subordinate Law we have in our minds, is to be looked upon only as a step to the Supreme Law;—the Law of

complete Benevolence, Justice, Truth, Purity, and Order. Conscience, the Law, must be constantly directed with the purpose of making it conform to this Supreme Law. We must seek for such light, such knowledge, as may enable us constantly to promote this conformity. We must labour to *enlighten* and *instruct* our Conscience. This task can never be ended. So long as life and powers of thought remain to us, we may always be able to acquire a still clearer and higher view than we yet possess, of the Supreme Law of our Being. We never can have done all that is in our power, in this respect. It never can be consistent with our Duty, to despair of enlightening and instructing our Conscience, beyond what we have yet done. Our standard of virtue is not high enough, if we think it need be made no higher. Virtue has never so completely taken possession of man's being, but that she may possess it still more completely; and therefore, any conception of Virtue, which we look upon as perfect, must, on that very account, be imperfect. Conscience is never fully formed, but always in the course of formation.

367. We may add, that in attempting to enlighten and instruct our Conscience, and to carry on our moral progress, we are led to feel the want of some light and some power in addition to the light of mere reason, and the ordinary powers which we possess over our own minds; and that Religion offers to us the hope of such a power, which will, if duly sought, be exercised upon us.

368. It appears from what has just been said, that we cannot properly refer to our Conscience as an Ultimate and Supreme Authority. It has only a subordinate and intermediate Authority; standing between the Supreme Law, to which it is bound to conform, and our own Actions, which must conform to it, in order to be moral. Conscience is not a Standard, personal to each man; as each man has his standard

of bodily appetite. Each man's Standard of morals, is a standard of Morals, only because it is supposed to represent the Supreme Standard, which is expressed by the Moral Ideas, Benevolence, Justice, Truth, Purity, and Wisdom. As each man has his Reason, in virtue of his participation in the Common Reason of mankind, so each man has his Conscience, in virtue of his participation in the Common Conscience of mankind, by which Benevolence, Justice, Truth, Purity, and Wisdom, are recognized as the Supreme Law of Man's Being. As the object of Reason is to determine what is true, so the object of Conscience is to determine what is right. As each man's Reason may err, and thus lead him to false opinion, so each man's Conscience may err, and lead him to a false moral standard. As false opinion does not disprove the reality of Truth, so the false moral standards of men do not disprove the reality of a Supreme Rule of Human Action.

369. Since Conscience is thus a subordinate and fallible Rule, it appears, that for a man to act according to his conscience, is not necessarily to act rightly. His conscience may be erroneous. It may be culpably in error; for he may not have taken due pains to enlighten and instruct it. If the conscience be in error, it must be so, for this reason, that the man's moral and intellectual progress is still incomplete; and this incompleteness is no justification of what is done under its influence. A conformity to an Erroneous Conscience is no more blameless, than an act of imperfect Benevolence, or imperfect Justice.

370. Moreover, since Conscience has only this subordinate and derivative authority, it cannot be right for a man to refer to his own Conscience, as a supreme and ultimate ground of action. The making our Conscience a ground of action, to this extent, is in itself wrong; since it is abandoning that Duty of further enlightening and instructing our Conscience.

which can never cease to be a Duty. That a man acts *according to his Conscience,* is not a reason for his actions, which can supersede the necessity of assigning other Reasons. If an action be according to his Conscience, it must be so because it is conformable to his Conceptions of Benevolence, Justice, Truth, Purity, Wisdom; and his reason for the action is more properly rendered by showing that the act does conform to these Moral Ideas, than by saying that it is according to his Conscience. To allege that an act is according to my Conscience; meaning thereby, that I act according to a rule which is already fixed and settled in my mind, so that I will no longer examine whether the Rule be right; is to reject the real signification of moral Rules. It is the conduct of a person who pursues a wrong road to the place he aims at; and refuses to have it proved that the road is wrong.

Indeed, the very use of the term *Conscience,* in rendering moral reasons for actions, may tend to mislead us, by presenting conscience to our minds as an authoritative and supreme guide. To dwell too much upon this abstraction, which, as we have said, merely denotes a step in our progress towards the Supreme Rule, may obstruct and disturb our further progress. We may confuse our minds, by fixing our consciousness too much upon our Conscience;—by reflecting upon this reflex habit. It has been said, that if I *talk* of my Humility, I lose it; something of the same kind may be said of Conscience.

371. But though a virtuous man may abstain from speaking much of his Conscience, he will not reverence its guidance the less on that account; or rather, his silence, if he be silent, will be that of reverence. For nothing can be more worthy of reverence than Conscience. It is, as we have said, the expression of the Supreme Rule, so far as each man has been able to discern that Rule. Conscience is to

each man the representative of the Supreme Law, and is invested with the authority of the Supreme Law. It is the voice which pronounces for him the distinction of right and wrong, of moral good and evil; and when he has done all that he can to enlighten and instruct it, by the aid of Religion, as well as of Morality, it is for him the Voice of God.

372. To disobey the commands and prohibitions of Conscience, under any circumstances, is utterly immoral; it is the very essence of immorality. In order to be moral, a man must be thoroughly *conscientious;* he must be careful to satisfy himself what the decision of his Conscience is, and must be resolved to follow the course thus prescribed, at any risk, and at any sacrifice. Nothing can be right which he does not do with *a clear conscience.* Whatever danger or sorrow lies in that direction, whatever advantage and gratification of the desires and affections in the other, he must not shrink or waver. Whatever may be gained by acting against his conscience, the consistency and welfare of his whole moral being is lost. His moral progress is utterly arrested. He commits a grievous transgression; and, as we have already said, morality can assure him of no means by which the evil may be remedied, and the broken unity of his moral being restored. To be steadily, resolutely, and carefully conscientious, is a Rule which every one, who aims at his moral progress, must regard as paramount to all others.

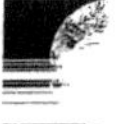

373. Inasmuch as each man's Conscience is the Supreme Law, so far as he has been able to discover that Law; and inasmuch as this discovery is a task to be performed only by a diligent and continued exercise of our faculties; there may be periods when each man is aware that the task has been imperfectly performed on special points, and may be uncertain what is right and what is wrong. In such cases, his Conscience is *doubtful.* The removal of

such doubts, is to be sought by the further use of the means by which the Conscience is enlightened and instructed. When the doubts turn rather upon special points than upon the general course of action, they are *Scruples of Conscience.*

What a person can do without offending against his Conscience, when the question has been deliberately propounded and solved in his own mind, he does with a *safe conscience,* or with a *good conscience.*

CHAPTER XV.

CASES OF CONSCIENCE RESPECTING TRUTH.

374. IT will appear from the preceding Chapter, that in all right action, the Conscience is employed, consciously or unconsciously. A man is *bound in Conscience* to do what he thinks right; but he is also bound to employ his faculties diligently, in ascertaining what is right. In cases in which he has not ascertained what is right, his Conscience is doubtful; and for the purposes of right action, it is requisite that these doubts be removed. Cases which are considered by Moralists with the view of doing this, are *Cases of Conscience.*

We are not to suppose that any particular Class of questions in Morals are Cases of Conscience. Every case of Moral action is, for the person who acts, a Case of Conscience. But in the greater part of such cases, the Rule of Duty is so plain and obvious, that no doubt arises, as to the course of action; and thus, no internal inquiry brings the Conscience into notice. In cases in which there appear to be conflicting Duties, or reasons for opposite courses of action, we must endeavour to decide between them, by enlightening and instructing the conscience; and these are especially termed Cases of Conscience.

375. Since, in Cases of Conflicting Duties, whichever way we decide, one Duty is, or seems to be, evaded or violated, Cases of Conscience, as proposed by Moralists, have often the aspect of Questions as to when Duties may be evaded or violated. To discuss such questions, has been supposed, by the world in general, more likely to pervert than to improve men's minds; and hence *Casuistry*, the part of Morality which is concerned with such discussions, has often been looked upon with dislike.

376. But the question, in every Case of Conscience, really is, not, How may Duty be evaded? but, *What is Duty?*—not, How may I avoid doing what I ought to do? but, *What ought I to do?* And this is a question which a virtuous man cannot help perpetually asking himself; and to which the answer may very often be far from obvious. In such Cases, he will be glad to know to what decision the Moralist, treating such questions in a general form, and free from the influence of personal temptation, has been led. We shall here consider a few questions of this kind.

There occur Cases of Conscience respecting all Classes of Duties: but in many of these Classes, the decision of the question may require a more exact determination of the Conceptions involved in it; for instance, in questions concerning Duties of Justice, of Humanity, which conceptions will be examined hereafter. But there are some Cases which we may consider by the aid of Rules and Maxims already laid down.

Such are particularly the Cases which respect the Duties of Truth (*Subjective Truth, Veracity*). The Rules *Lie not, Perform your Promise*, are of universal validity; and the conceptions of *Lie*, and of *Promise*, are so simple and distinct, that, in general, the

Rules may be directly and easily applied. We shall consider first some such Questions relative to Promises.

377. In what sense are Promises to be *interpreted?* We have already said (315), that the Mutual Understanding of the two parties, at the time of making the promise, is the sense in which it is the Promiser's Duty to fulfil it. This is the right interpretation of the promise, because the promise expressed and established this Mutual Understanding. If the Promiser, intending deceit to the Promisee, or to other persons, has used expressions, with a view to their being misunderstood, he has already violated the Duty of Truth. If he repent of this, his only way of resuming a moral condition is, to carry back the effect of his repentance to the time of making the promise, and to act as if he had intended what he was understood to intend.

Since the Promiser may be the only speaker in the transaction, and the Promisee may imply his acceptance of the Promise, and the sense in which he understands it, only by his silence, or by words of assent; we may state, as the Rule in such cases, that the Promiser is bound in the sense in which he believes the Promisee to understand him. For this is the only Common Understanding between them.

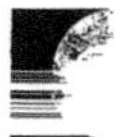

378. It may be, that the Common Understanding of what the Promiser is to do for the Promisee, includes some suppositions which are afterwards discovered to be false; and it may be asked if the Promise is still binding. This is the case of *Erroneous Promises.* And the answer to the question is, that the false supposition releases the Promiser, so far as it was included in the Common Understanding. Thus a person solicits alms from you, telling you the tale of his distresses. Your purse being empty at the time, you promise to relieve him if he will call again. In the mean time, you discover that his story contain-

ed falsehood. How far are you bound by your Promise? It is plain that if the Promise was understood by both of you to be unconditional, and the delay to take place merely on account of the state of your purse, the Promise is binding. But if the Promise was understood to be conditional, on the truth of the tale; and if the falsehoods are material; the Promiser is released. Yet it must be very difficult for the Promiser to know how far his Promise is hypothetically understood. And therefore, to avoid the moral trouble which such doubts produce, it is wise in such cases to express the condition on which the Promise is given.

379. There is one circumstance respecting Promises which must be noticed. The Duty which they create, is not an absolute, but a *Relative Duty*. It is a Duty relative *to the Promisee* only. He is the only person affected by the non-performance of the Promise. He has a Moral Claim for this performance; but he may relinquish this Claim, as he may relinquish any Right or Possession. And when he has done this, the duty of performing the promise ceases. Hence it is laid down, as a Rule of Morality respecting Promises, that *they are not binding when released by the Promisee.*

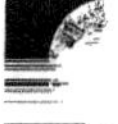

380. The principal Class of Cases of Conscience respecting Promises is, that of what are called *Unlawful Promises;* that is, Promises to do an *immoral* act; for we are not now speaking of law, but of morality.

When the immoral character of the act was known to the parties at the time, the Question of Immoral Promises is answered by recollecting what has been said (358) respecting violations of Duty. The transgressor ought to repent and amend; and as a part of his amendment, he ought not to go on with an immoral act which is begun. To Promise, and to Perform, are parts of the same connected act. If the

Performance be immoral, the Promise was so. To promise, was a transgression of Duty begun; to perform, is to complete the transgression. It is my Duty to stop in the mid course of the act, as it was my Duty not to enter upon it at first. When the question of Duty is proposed, there can be no other answer.

This applies at once to all promises to perform, or to participate in, any act of violence, injustice, fraud or impurity. In all such cases, the Promiser, by his Promise, has rejected his moral nature; and can only resume it, by repudiating his own act. Even to do this, does not leave him blameless; for, as we have said, repentance does not obliterate past guilt; but this is necessary: this is the only way in which he can avoid the continuation and further degradation of his moral condition. He offended in the Promise; he offends again in the Performance. Whatever Temptation led him to sin, in the first part of the act; he sins against conviction, if he perform his promise, when the question has been brought before his conscience.

381. But in breaking my Promise, immoral though it be, I violate my Relative Duty to the Promisee; and the case may be one in which he denies, and even blamelessly denies, the immorality of the act promised. For instance, I have promised the less worthy Candidate for an office, that I will vote for him. I cannot expect to induce him to release me from my Promise, by representing to him his own unworthiness. Nevertheless, my relative Duty to him must give way to my absolute Duty of voting for the most worthy Candidate. But though I now do what I ought, I am not therefore blameless as to the past. The violation of a Relative Duty, is an offence against the Promisee. He has good reason to complain of me; and I have reason to feel repentance and shame, for having given him a claim upon me which I can-

not satisfy. This is the unhappy consequence of making an immoral Promise.

In other cases, where the Promisee is aware that the act promised is immoral, he did wrong in accepting, as I in making, the promise. He ought to release me from the promise, not as an act of grace, but as an act of Duty. If he do not, my shame at not satisfying his claim upon me, is rightly lost in my shame at having given him such a claim.

382. When the Act promised was not immoral at the time of promising, but becomes so afterwards, it is not to be performed. For since we are asking what virtuous men would do, we are to suppose that they would not have made the promise, if they had known that performance would be immoral; and that they will release each other, now that it appears to be immoral. That the act should be lawful at the time of performance, was a part of the understanding which the promise conveyed. If a merchant promises his foreign correspondent to send him a ship-load of corn at a time appointed, and before the time arrive, the exportation of corn is forbidden by law; he is liberated from his engagement. Both parties must have understood that the promise was made, on the supposition that the act would be lawful; and that the engagement was annulled, when it became unlawful, and therefore immoral.

383. In the case where one party sees that the performance is immoral, and the other does not, the difficulty is greater; but the Rule by which we may direct ourselves is, that the promise must be understood as a promise made between virtuous men, and involving such a conditional engagement as may morally be made: and so understood, must be fulfilled.

Thus, if I promise to vote for an unworthy candidate, the promise was immoral, and is not to be kept, as we have said. But if I promise to vote for a can didate who, after my promise, becomes unworthy, not having been so before, am I bound? We say, No; for I promised on the supposition of his worthiness; and he, who ought to regard me as a moral man in making my promises, must have understood that this supposition was implied. But yet my refusal to fulfil my promise may give him ground to say, that it is not his worthiness, but my intentions, which have changed. And this must be a matter difficult of proof; at least to him; and therefore it will be difficult to show him that I have not violated my Relative Duty to him. The prospect of such difficulties, is a strong reason for not making promises respecting elections, in cases where the worthiness of the candidates, at the time of voting, ought alone to decide the election.

384. But there may be cases, in which an unconditional promise to vote for a candidate at an election may morally be given; and then it must be kept. There are cases in which the matter is left much to the discretion of the elector; and in such cases, though merit may determine his choice, he may fix his own time for making up his mind; and may promise when he has decided. Any candidate who offers himself after this, comes too late.

385. Or again, the Promise may imply an informal Contract: as when a person is elected to act on behalf of the Electors; or on the belief that he and they have a common purpose. This is the case, when the Representative of a body of men is to be elected. They look out for a person whose character fits him to act for them, and they promise to vote for him. He, on the other hand, by his conduct and his professions, pledges himself to follow a course of action which they approve. Promises thus made, are not immoral. Such a mutual understanding is requisite, between the Electors and their Representatives; and can only be established, by their promising him

their votes. The Electors are bound to elect the fittest person; but the Candidate with whom they have come to this understanding is thereby and thenceforth the fittest. The election is like the election of an Agent; and as we have said, is rather of the nature of a Contract, than of an election on the ground of merit only.

But then, in order that this Contract may morally be made, it must be for moral purposes. Such would be an understanding between the Electors and the Candidate, that he, acting as their Representative, shall aim to preserve the Constitution, or to reform the Abuses, of the body into which he is elected. But if the understanding be, that he shall give them money in return for their votes, the Contract is an immoral one. The power of electing a Representative is in their hands for the sake of some public good; it is a violation of Duty, to turn such a power into a means of private gain (311).

386. It is sometimes made a Question, Supposing such an informal Contract immorally made, whether, when the immoral end is answered, it is a Duty to perform the rest of the Contract; for instance, if a person were elected to an office of public trust on promise of sums of money to the electors, whether, after the election, it is his duty to pay these sums. We may remark, that the question, here, is not What he is to do as an innocent man; for by the supposition he is a guilty one; having been concerned in an immoral bargain. If the question be, What is he to do as a repentant man, convinced of his guilt, and wishing henceforth to do what is right, the answer is, that he must pay. There is no reason why he should add, to the violation of his absolute duty, the violation of his Relative Duty to the Promisees. If, in his repentance, he wishes not to complete an immoral transaction, he is to recollect that the immoral transaction is completed by his election. If he wish to mark

his hatred of the offence, he may signify his meaning more clearly, by expressing his repentance, and paying the money, than by keeping it; which may be interpreted as adding avarice and falsehood to the violation of public Duties.

387. Promises are immoral, which contradict a former Promise, and therefore are not to be kept; but here, as in other cases, there is a violation of the Relative Duty to the promisee; and a ground for shame and repentance, so far as regards him. And here we have another warning, of the need of being cautious in making promises.

388. Promises which it is impossible to perform, are evidently not to be kept; but then, it can hardly be that such Promises can be made, without some want of due consideration and forethought on the Part of the Promiser, which gives the Promisee good ground for complaint. If the Promiser was aware of the impossibility at the time of making the promise, he is guilty of fraud; for by making the promise, he implied his belief of the possibility of performing it.

When the Promiser himself occasions the impossibility, it is a breach of promise.

389. Are Promises extorted by Fear or Violence binding? This is a question which has been much debated among Moralists. We must apply to it the Rule which we have already laid down; that the Promise, if morally made, must be kept. If I ought not to keep the Promise, I ought not to have made it. The question, therefore, will be, whether I could morally make such a Promise. And it may be remarked, that if I could not morally make the Promise, I cannot morally derive advantage from any contract which was combined with the Promise; for to do this, is a part of the same Act, as to make the Contract. I cannot morally derive advantage from one part of the Contract, and refuse to perform another part. If I find the Contract to have been immoral, I

must undo, as far as I can, its effects; and go back, in my condition, to the state in which the Contract was made.

390. These Maxims may be applied to a case of this kind often discussed. A man falls into the power of a band of robbers, and, in fear of violence, promises them that if they will set him free, he will afterwards send them a certain sum of money. He is liberated on his promise: is he bound afterwards to send the money? According to the above considerations, if it was not immoral to make the Promise, it is a Duty to keep it. And this Rule is so obvious a one, and its application so direct, that we may wonder that any other should have been taken.

The reasons given for doubt, or for the opposite decision, are various. Thus Cicero says*, that with robbers, we have no tie of common faith or obligation. But we shall, of course, answer, that we keep our word, not as what is due to robbers, but as what is due to ourselves, and necessary to our character of truthful men: not as what is an act of obligation to them, but an act of reverence to truth. We may add, that we can hardly say that we have no ties of common obligation with them, when we have made them a promise, and have received life and liberty as a consideration for it. We make a Contract with them, though it may be an informal one. They fulfil their part of the Contract: if we do not fulfil ours, we shall take a very strange way of exemplifying our asserted moral superiority over them.

It has also been alleged, as a reason why the Promise thus given should not be kept, that their confidence in Promises will thus greatly facilitate the perpetration of such robberies;—that in this way, such Contracts may be made the means of almost unlimited extortion†. Upon this we may remark, that it is right to regard the probable consequences of our

* *Off.* III. 29. † Paley, B. III. c. 5

actions; and we must agree, that it would be wrong to contribute to maintain a state of things in which lawless banditti levy ransoms upon peaceable citizens. But these considerations, if acted on, would prevent our making the Promise. And if, notwithstanding these considerations, we have made the promise, we must consider how far it is likely that to keep our word, rather than to break it, would make us the supporters of such a habit of extortion. Is it probable that the banditti will give up their practice, simply because their captives, liberated on such promises, do not perform them? Is it not likely that, their power remaining, such disappointments would induce them to seek some more effectual mode of extortion? Do we not, by making and adhering to such contracts, prevent their adding murder to robbery? And is not the most proper and hopeful course for suppressing such robbery, to call for, and, if required, to assist, the vigorous administration of the laws against robbers, which exist in every State? Till that can be done, may it not tend to preserve, from extreme cruelties, those who fall into the hands of the robbers, that they should have some confidence in the payment of the ransom agreed upon? Even on the balance of probable advantage, it would seem that such a promise is to be kept.

But on our principles, we should not look to these results so much as to our moral culture. By keeping this promise, we cherish and exemplify our regard for truth. What moral quality do we cultivate by breaking it? If it be replied, that we thus cultivate a regard for consequences; we reply, that consequences, when both their existence, and their moral character, are so doubtful, are not the main objects for our regard. The consequences which take the shape of strict veracity in ourselves, and the consequent confidence of others in us, are proper objects of moral action The consequences which take the shape of possible inconvenience produced to robbers by our own untruthfulness, are not proper objects for us to aim at.

391. It may be asked, whether, in order to avoid thus contributing to robbers, we ought to refuse to make the promise; and whether, thus, we ought to incur violence, or even death. This is included in the general question, what we ought to do in *cases of extreme necessity*, when the adherence to the usual Rules of Duty brings with it danger of life, limb, and the like terrible consequences. And to such questions perhaps no general answer can be given. They are commonly put in this form: Whether in such cases of necessity it be *allowable* to violate Duty: and in this form something may be said respecting them hereafter.

392. If it be said, that the Law denies the validity of such engagements, by annulling Contracts made under duress; we reply, that even the Law requires that men should not allege light fears, as reasons for the nullity of a Contract. The Law makes Duress nothing less than the fear of loss of life or limb (161); and thus shows that it expects that men will show some firmness, in refusing to be parties to illegal acts. It is true, that the Law would annul a Contract made under the circumstances which we have described. It would also punish the robbers, if they were brought under its administration. But then we must recollect that Duty does not necessarily confirm the advantages to which the administration of the Law would entitle us; while Duty does necessarily confirm our obligations, and extend them, so as to give them a moral meaning. Duty interprets informal obligations, so as to make them evidence of internal principles. Duty requires the performance of promises, so as to make them evidence of a Spirit of Truthfulness.

393. Lies stand nearly on the same footing as

promises; for a Lie is a violation of the general understanding among mankind, which the use of language implies, as we have already said (313). And as has already been stated, that is a Lie which violates this mutual understanding, and nothing else. Hence the term *Lie* is not applicable, when no mutual understanding is violated. Such is the case in Parables, Fables, Tales avowedly fictitious, or nortoriously so, according to the literary habits of the time; as Novels, Dramas, Poems. A person, the most careful of his moral culture, may employ himself in such fictions. Yet there are provinces of literature in which the most rigorous attention to Truth is a Duty, as in History and Personal Narratives.

394. There are various understood *Conventions* in society, according to which words, spoken or written under particular circumstances, have a meaning different from that which the general laws of language would give them. I have already noticed such phrases as, *I am your obedient servant*, at the foot of a letter; which, though not literally true, is not to be called a Lie. The Convention is here so established, that no one is for a moment misled by it. In the same way, if, when I wish not to be interrupted by visitors, I write upon my door, *Not at home*, and if there be a common understanding to that effect; this is no more a lie than if I were to write, *Not to be seen*.

395. But if I put the same words in the mouth of a Servant, and if the Convention be not regularly established in all classes of society, the Case is different. It is a violation of Duty in me to make the Servant tell a lie: it is an offence against his moral culture (312). He may understand the Convention to be so fully established in the class with which my intercourse lies, that the words, though not literally true, convey no false belief. In this case, he may use them, and I may direct him to use them, blamelessly. But it is my Duty to ascertain that he does

thus understand the words, as a conventional form; and in order to give them this character, he should not be allowed to deviate from the form, or to add any false circumstance; as, that his master has just gone out, or the like.

396. The view that we have taken, of the nature of a Lie, suggests an answer to some of the excuses sometimes offered for lies. For instance, some men tell lies in order to preserve a secret which they wish not to be known; and allege, in their justification, that the Questioner has no Right to know the truth. To such a plea we reply, that the Questioner has a right not to be told a lie, for all men have such a Right. By answering his question at all, I give him a Right to a true answer. If I take my stand on the ground that he has no Right to an answer, I must give him no answer. I may tell him that he has no Right to an answer.

But it may be said, that to do this will in many cases be to disclose the secret which we wish to conceal. For instance, the author of an anonymous work, who wishes to remain unknown as the author, but is suspected, is asked whether he wrote the work. To refuse to reply, would be to acknowledge it. Such authors have held, that in such a case, they may deny the authorship. They urge, that the Questioner has no right to know: that the Author has a Right to remain concealed, and has no means of doing so but by such a denial. But this defence is wrong. The author has no moral Right to remain concealed at the expense of telling a Lie: that is, it is not right in him thus to protect himself. But on the other hand, he is not bound to answer. Nor need he directly refuse to do so. He may evade the question, or turn off the subject. There is nothing to prevent his saying, "How can you ask such a question?" or anything of the like kind, which may remove the expectation of an answer. If he cannot secure his object in this or

some similar way, it is to be recollected that he has drawn the inconvenience upon himself, by first writing an anonymous work, and then engaging in conversation on such terms, that he cannot escape answering questions about the authorship of the work. He has no Right, moral or other, to insist that these two employments may be pursued jointly without inconvenience. Familiar conversation is a play of reciprocal insight and reciprocal guidance of thought; and such weapons, a man may very rightly use, to guard his secret. But he may not assume that it must be guarded at any rate, by means right or wrong; by declarations true or false. On the other hand, he may seek, as widely as he chooses, for some turn of conversation by which he may baffle curiosity without violating truth. To discover such a turn, is a matter of skill, self-command, and invention. If he fail and be detected, he may receive some vexation or inconvenience; but if he succeed at the expense of truth, he receives a moral stain.

397. The like considerations apply in a case often discussed among moralists. A man is pursued by murderers who seek his life, and I conceal him. They ask me if I know where he is. Am I to say that I do not know? In this case, it is evident that I may blamelessly refuse to answer the question; but in this, as in the other case, not to answer, may be to speak plainly. I may also represent to the pursuers the wickedness of their purpose; I may call in the aid of the law. These latter courses are blameless.

But suppose that these resources fail, that the pursuers turn their fury upon me, and that they threaten to kill me, except I disclose to them the hiding-place of their victim. We have here a new case; the prospect of my own death if I do not make myself accessory to a murder, for, to give up the man to his murderers, would be to be accessory to his death. This is a Case of Necessity, and a Lie in sucn a Case is not to be judged of by common Rules.

398. *Lies of Necessity.* Falsehoods told for the purpose of saving one's life; or to avoid some other extreme peril, have found much sympathy among mankind. They are looked upon as at least excusable, and allowable. We must hereafter consider them among other Cases of Necessity. Lies of Necessity, told for the sake of saving a friend from some great misfortune, have met with a warmer admiration, in the cases in which they are narrated. Such for instance was the falsehood told by Grotius's wife to save her husband, when she represented the box in which he was contained as a box of theological books.

399. But when such falsehoods which thus save a friend from ruin are accompanied with some great foreseen calamity to the teller, they excite a still higher admiration, and may be termed *Heroic Lies:* as when Lucilius offers himself to the soldiers of Octavius to be killed, declaring himself to be Brutus. So far as such acts come under the Moralist's notice, they must be considered under a special head; for Heroic Virtue, as we have already said, is beyond the range of the Rules of Duty.

400. Though assertions, not literally true, may, by general Convention, cease to be Lies, we must be careful of trifling with the limits of such cases, and of too readily assuming, and acting upon, such Conventions. Carelessness in these matters, will diminish our habitual reverence for truth. Some Moralists have ranked with the cases in which Convention supersedes the general rule of truth, an Advocate asserting the justice, or his belief in the justice, of his Client's cause*. As a reason why he may do this, though he believe otherwise, it is said that no promise to speak the truth was given, or supposed to be given. But we reply by asking, If there is no mu.

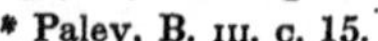

* Paley, B. III. c. 15.

tual understanding that he shall speak truly, to what purpose does he speak, or to what purpose do the judges hear?

By those who contend for such indulgence to Advocates, it is alleged, that the Profession of Advocate exists as an instrument for the administration of Justice in the Community; and that it is a necessary maxim of the Advocate's Profession, that he is to do all that can be done for his Client. It is urged, that the application of Laws is a matter of great complexity and difficulty: that the right administration of them in doubtful cases, is best provided for, if the arguments on each side be urged with the utmost force, and if the Judge alone decide which side is in the right; that for this purpose, each Advocate must urge all the arguments he can devise; and must enforce them with all the skill he can command. It is added, to justify the Advocate, that being the Advocate, he is not the Judge;—that it is not his office to determine on which side Justice is; and that therefore his duty, in his office, is not affected by his belief on this subject.

In reply to these considerations, the Moralist may grant that it is likely to answer the ends of Justice in a community, that there should exist a Profession of Advocates; ready to urge, with full force, the arguments on each side in doubtful cases. And if the Advocate, in his mode of pleading and exercising his profession, allows it to be understood that this is all that he undertakes to do, he does not transgress his Duties of Truth and Justice, even in pleading for a bad cause; since even for a bad cause, there may be arguments, and even good arguments. But if, in pleading, he assert his belief that his cause is just, when he believes it unjust, he offends against Truth; as any other man would do who, in like manner, made a like assertion. Nor is it conducive to the

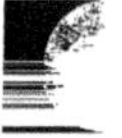

ends of justice, that every man, however palpably unjust his cause be, should have such support to it.

To the argument, that the Advocate is not the Judge, and therefore, that he is not responsible for his judgment on the merits of the case; the Moralist will reply, that every man is, in an unofficial sense, by being a moral agent, a Judge of right and wrong, and an Advocate of what is right; and is, so far, bound to be just in his judgments, and sincere in his exhortations. This general character of a moral agent, he cannot put off, by putting on any professional character. Every man, when he advocates a case in which morality is concerned, has an influence upon his hearers, which arises from the belief that he shares the moral sentiments of all mankind. This influence of his supposed morality, is one of his possessions; which, like all his possessions, he is bound to use for moral ends. If he mix up his character as an Advocate, with his character as a Moral Agent, using his moral influence for the Advocate's purpose, he acts immorally. He makes the Moral Rule subordinate to the Professional Rule. He sells to his Client, not only his skill and learning, but himself. He makes it the Supreme Object of his life to be, not a good man, but a successful Lawyer.

If it be alleged, that by allowing the difference of his professional and unprofessional character to be seen in his pleading, the Advocate will lose his influence with his hearers; the Moralist will reply, that he ought not to have an influence which arises from a false representation of himself; and that if he employ the influence of his unprofessional character, he is bound, in the use of it, to unprofessional Rules of Duty.

The Advocate must look upon his Profession, like every other endowment and possession, as an Instrument, which he must use for the purposes of Morality. To act rightly, is his proper object: to succeed as an Advocate, is a proper object, only so far as it is consistent with the former. To cultivate his Moral being, is his highest end; to cultivate his Professional eminence, is a subordinate aim.

401. But further; not only is the Advocate to cultivate and practise his profession in subordination to moral ends, and to reject its Rules where they are inconsistent with this subordination; but moreover, there belong to him moral ends which regard his Profession; namely, to make it an Institution fitted to promote Morality. He must seek, so to shape its Rules, and so to alter them if need be, that they shall be subservient to the Rules of Duty. To raise and purify the character of the Advocate's profession, so that it may answer the ends of justice, without requiring insincerity in the Advocate, is a proper aim for a good man who is a Lawyer;—a purpose on which he may well and worthily employ his efforts and his influence.

402. There are other Cases, in which the Duty of Truth may be violated by silence;—by that which we omit to say; as in selling defective wares, without notice of their faults; those faults being such as, by the universal understanding relative to such transactions, the Seller is bound to disclose. In these, as in the other cases, the Duty is, in a great measure, defined by the general understanding existing among Buyers and Sellers. In giving this Rule, we follow the guidance of the Law; which, in its decisions, recognizes such a general understanding with regard to sales. But here also Morality takes the Meaning, not the Letter of the Law, for her guide. We may apply this to a case stated by Cicero, and often since discussed by Moralists. We have already considered the case jurally (172). In a time of great scarcity at Rhodes, a corn-merchant of Alexandria arrived there with a cargo of grain. The Merchant knew, what the Rhodians did not know, that a number of

other vessels laden with corn were on their way to Rhodes: was he bound in conscience to communicate this fact to the buyers?

403. The universal Rule, that we may not deceive men, must apply in this case. The Moralist cannot doubt that it would be wrong for the merchant to tell any falsehood, in order to raise the price of his wares. It would be plainly immoral for him to say, that he did not know that any other vessels were coming. But may he, the Seller, be silent, and allow the Buyers, ignorant of the truth which he knows, to raise the price by their mutual competition? This is a question belonging to trade in general; and must, as we have said, be answered according to the general understanding which we suppose to prevail among Buyers and Sellers. In common cases, both alike are supposed to have a regard to the prospect of an increased Supply, or an increased Scarcity. The Buyer does not depend upon the Seller, nor the Seller upon the Buyer, for this information. He who has, or thinks he has, superior information on this subject, takes advantage of it, and is understood to do so: and prices are settled by the general play of such opinions, proceeding from all sides. But if a Seller possess information which he is not understood to have, and takes advantage of it, he violates the general understanding, and thus, is guilty of deceit. If the merchant in question ask such an exorbitant price for his corn, as to imply that no further supply is probable, he falls under this blame. On the other hand, he is not bound to sell his corn to-day for the price to which it may fall to-morrow, when the other vessels arrive; for, as a trader, he may take advantage of the greater skill and foresight which has brought him first to the port. We cannot say that he is generally bound to reveal to the buyer any special circumstance which may affect the market-price; as for instance, the probable speedy arrival of other vessels:

for to make this a part of his duty, would be to lay down a Rule which would place skill and ignorance, diligence and indolence, on an equality; and would thus destroy the essence of trade. But if the Buyer asks questions on this subject, the Seller may not tell a lie. And if the Seller is silent as to this circumstance, he takes upon himself the responsibility, as a moral agent, of making an equitable estimate of the gain to which his unsuspected superiority of knowledge entitles him. If it be said, that it is very unlikely that a trader will be content with this, when he can get more; we shall of course reply, that the question is not what a trader is likely to do, but what a good man, (*Vir bonus,* as Cicero puts the case,) ought to do.

404. Promises of Marriage often give rise to doubts and fears; for the Promise implies much;—no less than affection and general community of interests during a whole life. A person may well hesitate before giving such a promise, and having given it, may fear whether he is not engaging for more than he can perform. But on the other hand, the Promise, sincerely given, leads to its own fulfilment; for affection grows, in virtue of the confidence which such an engagement establishes between the parties; the marriage union adds new ties to those which drew them together; and the progress of a well conducted married life makes conjugal affection continue as a habit.

But the intention of fulfilling the engagement in this sense, and the belief of a power to do so, can alone render it right to make the Promise. A Promise of Marriage, though made, cannot morally be carried into effect, by him who does not intend thus to perform the engagement, or who despairs of doing so. If, before the Marriage takes place, he find the germ of conjugal affection wanting in his heart, the course of Duty is, to withdraw from entering upon the immoral condition of a mere external conjugal union.

But still, in doing this, he violates a most serious Relative Duty to the person thus deceived. She may have to accuse him of no less an injury, than the blighted hopes and ruined happiness of her whole life. To a man of any moral feeling, or even of any natural feeling, the remorse of having done such a wrong, by the promise of affection and livelong companionship, must be intense. And his shame also must be profound: for he may be supposed to have well examined his heart before he made the promise; and if his affections be so dark to himself, or so fickle, that in spite of his self-examination, he has remained so long in error, and has been led to such a false step at last; how can he hope ever to be justified in making a like engagement with another person? A life of remorse and shame would be the proper sequel to such a fault.

The same remarks apply when the Promise is made on the other side.

405. We may notice here a Case of Conscience treated of by preceding Moralists*. A certain person in the lifetime of his wife had promised marriage to another woman if he should ever be free. The wife died, and the woman demanded performance of the promise. The man then alleged doubts whether the promise was binding, inasmuch as it was immorally given. The question proposed has usually been, Whether the man is bound to marry the woman? But if we take the real Moral Question, Whether he *ought* to marry her? we must answer, that this does not depend on the Promise alone. If he wishes not to marry her, because he has ceased to bear her the affection which the conjugal union requires; according to what we have said, he ought not to marry her. If, on the other hand, he still wishes to marry her, there is nothing in the immoral condition of the

* Paley, B. III. c. 5. I state the case as Paley states it. Sanderson, from whom he professes to take it, states it differently

promise formerly given which need prevent it. That promise was an offence against Duty in itself, inasmuch as it implied a heart alienated from the former wife. But this does not necessarily vitiate all his succeeding dispositions to the woman to whom the promise was made. We may suppose the old promise annulled, and he may, after the first wife's death, promise the same thing without blame, and perform his promise.

406. Without there being an absolute Promise of Marriage, there are often manifest suggestions of such a common purpose, between man and woman, which lead to difficulties of the same kind. In all countries, and especially in countries in which men and women are left free, in a great measure, to choose for themselves their partners in married life, marriage is the great event of life; it is the point to which the thoughts and imaginations, the hopes and designs of the young of both sexes, constantly tend. This is still more particularly the case with women; inasmuch as their social position depends mainly upon that of the husband. Hence the manner and behaviour of young men and young women, have a frequent reference, tacit or open, to the possibility of engagements of marriage among them. Conversation, of almost any kind, may disclose features of character and disposition, by which one heart may be drawn to another; and indications of such inclination may be given, in all degrees, from the slightest to the most marked. Among such a variety of elements, it may often be doubtful how far such marks of preference, on the one side and on the other, may be equivalent to an Offer of Marriage, or to an Engagement. Nor can any general Rule be laid down; for much must depend upon the conventions of society. But we may say, in general, that Morality requires of us a most serious and reverent estimate of the marriage state; and of the union of heart and community of moral pur-

pose, by which the parties ought to be drawn together. Any behaviour, therefore, which, while it appears to tend to such a purpose, is really frivolous and unmeaning, or prompted only by vanity, or love of amusement, is at variance with Duty. Such behaviour is a very unfit portion of a life which has our Moral Culture for its constant purpose; and which looks upon the prospect of marriage, and the tone of intercourse with women, as means to this end.

The above are given as Specimens only of Cases of Conscience respecting Truth; not as a complete Collection, or even as including all the more prominent classes of Cases. But the remarks made upon the above cases may serve to show the manner in which we are led, by the doctrines of Morality, to treat them; and the like Rules may be applied to other Cases.

CHAPTER XVI.

OF CASES OF NECESSITY.

407. THE discussion of Cases of Conscience, which we were pursuing in the last Chapter, led us, in several instances, to Cases of Necessity; and these, we stated that we must reserve for a separate consideration. Cases of Conscience are those in which conflicting Duties and conflicting Rules are weighed deliberately, the time and circumstances allowing of this. Cases of Necessity are those in which a man is impelled to violate Common Duties and Common Rules by the pressure of extreme danger or fear; as when a man kills another in defence of himself or his family; or when he steals, or tells a lie, to save his life.

408. We shall first consider the Cases in which a man thus violates Common Rules under the pressure of danger *to himself.* The Law shows us that men judge such danger, when extreme, to justify the transgression of Common Rules. Thus, in the Laws of most countries, the Command, *Thou shalt not kill,* is suspended when I am attacked by a burglar or a robber; and the Command, *Thou shalt not steal,* is suspended when I am perishing with hunger. And the common moral judgment of mankind looks with indulgence upon the transgressions of ordinary Rules in such extraordinary circumstances. The Moralist must, in like manner, allow, that there are Cases of Necessity, in which the Common Rules of Duty may be transgressed. But these Cases of Necessity must be treated with great caution.

409. In the first place, the Necessity, which is the condition of these Cases, must be very rigorously understood. It must be some such extreme peril and terror of immediate death, or of some dreadful immediate evil, little short of death, as produces a pressure on the mind far beyond the usual course of human motives and passions. It is not every extraordinary emergency, when fear and other passions are excited somewhat beyond their usual bounds, that justifies acts which would otherwise be crimes. It is not a moderate danger, that justifies acts of violence and falsehood. The Law teaches us this, when it does not permit us to kill the diurnal housebreaker, or the flying robber; and when it requires, in order that a Contract, made under fear, shall be annulled, that the fear shall have been such as not a timid merely, but a firm man, might feel. To allow any looseness of signification in this condition of Cases of Necessity, would destroy all Morality. If not only the fear of death, but the fear of any great evil, would justify falsehood, there would be an end of the Duty of Truth. For any evil would appear great, when

it was impending over us; and the Duty, being confined in its influence to cases in which there were no fears of inconvenience to overcome, would have no office left. And the same might be said of the other Duties. If it be said that fear excuses the violation of Moral Rules, because it carries us out of ourselves; we reply, that so far as fear carries us out of ourselves, it makes us cease to be moral agents; and that if we allow any ordinary fears to do this, we abandon our moral character. To be thus carried out of ourselves, by fear and other passions such as commonly occur, is to be immoral and wicked. The precise office of Morality is, to condemn those who yield to such a necessity as this. We cannot make transgression blameless, merely by calling the Case a Case of Necessity.

410. In excuse of transgression of Moral Rules under Constraint, it has been said, that when man's Liberty ceases, his moral agency ceases. But to make this maxim in every degree true, the notion of a Cessation of man's liberty must be very rigorously understood. In truth, man's Liberty, as a moral agent, never ceases, till he is moved as a piece of mere brute matter. Nothing but the man's own volition can move his muscles. No force, which other men can exert, can compel him, by physical means, to utter a word, or sign his name. It is not merely being put in close prison, and scantily fed, that can deprive man of the liberty which moral agency supposes. His liberty is not a liberty that can act only when all external obstacles and influences are removed; for in fact, that can never be. Moral Liberty shows itself, not in acting without external influences, but in acting in spite of external influences. To resist fear and danger, and still to do what we will to do, is the manifestation of our liberty. If we plead the limitation of our liberty as a reason why we are not bound by Moral Rules, we cast off such Rules altogether; for our lib-

erty is always limited. It is not therefore by being deprived of Liberty merely, that we are placed in a Case of Necessity. Even when we are in prison, or otherwise under a constraint, we are bound by the ordinary Rules of Morality.

411. We have said, that the fear of *immediate* death constitutes a Case of Necessity. The fear of immediate death constitutes one of the most distinct and plain of such cases. The reason of fixing upon such a case, is that such a fear, in most persons, produces a paroxysm and agony of terror and trouble which subvert the usual balance of the mind, and the usual course of thought and action. What is done under such circumstances, may be considered as an exception to the common condition of the man's being. It has not the same bearing upon the man's moral culture as acts done in a more tranquil and deliberate manner. In cases where the condition is so extreme, we may allow a deviation from Moral Rules, without infringing their general authority. In addition to this reason for taking the fear of *immediate* death as a prominent example of a Case of Necessity, this condition makes the danger more inevitable. It may be supposed, in general, that if the threatened death be not immediate, other means of averting that result may be found by the person threatened, besides the violations of Moral Rules, which are the alternative. If, however, a death not immediate can be presented to the mind as an *inevitable* menace, it may perhaps constitute a Case of Necessity, on the grounds above stated.

412. But though the fear of immediate, or of certain, death, as the alternative, must be allowed to constitute a Case of Necessity, so far as such Cases are to be recognized; we are not therefore to conclude that such fear liberates us from all Duties, or justifies all Acts. We do not say, generally, that a man may, without blame, tell a lie, or violate other Duties, in

order to save his life. If we were to decide thus, what would become of our moral approval of Martyrs, who incur death by their open assertion of the truth? and of our admiration of virtuous men in other cases, who perform acts of Duty, knowing that they lead to their death? Even in Cases of Necessity, the violation of Rule may not be without blame; but the blame may be mitigated, in consideration of the Necessity: or, reference being had to the circumstances of the case and of the person, the act may be even excusable and allowable.

413. We shall not attempt to define or enumerate Cases of Necessity. A consideration of the peculiar character of such cases will show that the Moralist ought not to undertake such definition and enumeration. In the Act which is excused as a Case of Necessity, there must be a struggle and compunction in the mind of the agent respecting the Duty violated; although the extreme urgency of the motives which act in the opposite direction, may prevail. For we are supposing the agent to be a virtuous man; and are considering what such a one may do, in a Case of Necessity. And we cannot suppose that such a man can violate the broadest Rules of Morality, without pain and trouble of mind. If we suppose a good man to be led, under the terror of immediate death, not otherwise to be avoided, to tell a lie, or to stab the keeper of his prison; or a woman to give up her person to the lust of a man, we cannot suppose this to take place without great anguish and strong abhorrence of the acts thus committed. The intense vehemence with which man clings to life may overmaster this abhorrence; and even the best estimate which the person, at the moment, can form of the course of Duty, may direct such acts. But a person would not be virtuous who could commit them without repugnance, or look upon them with complacency. Any acquiescence in the acts, except as great though inevitable evils; any

indifference with regard to the violation of the usual Rules of Morality; is at once immoral. When the act is over, there has been a dire and mortal struggle between Moral Rules and Self-preservation; and if we rejoice that we are preserved, we must still regret that, even for a moment, the general Rules of Duty were compelled to give way. We cannot look upon lying, or homicide, or being an instrument of lust, with approbation; even if, under the circumstances, we think that the acts have been, in this case, excusable. In such Cases of Necessity, we may excuse the act, but we cannot admire it. On the contrary, in such cases, our admiration is bestowed on the other side. We admire a man who suffers death, rather than tell a lie: we admire Socrates who would not escape from unjust legal bondage and death, even when he could do so without violence; we admire a woman who suffers death rather than submit to violation. It is plain that those who act thus, conform to the law of Duty: those who, in such cases of necessity, act otherwise, may do only what, in such cases, is excusable or allowable; but the Moralist must not let them suppose that they take the course which is alone right, or eminently commendable.

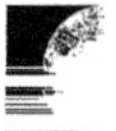

414. This being the case, we must necessarily abstain from laying down any definition of the limits of Cases of Necessity; and any Precepts for such cases. For if we were to define, beforehand, the conditions under which lying, or homicide, or submission to lust, is the proper course; those who accepted our Rules, would, when the occasion came, take that course without the reluctance and compunction, which are essential to make an act allowable in virtue of Necessity. If we were to trace a definite boundary, beyond which the Common Rules of Morality no longer hold good; men, in circumstances of temptation, would be looking out to see when they had passed this formal boundary, and were entitled to

use the license which such a position would give. They would be inquiring at what moment they were beyond the jurisdiction of ordinary Morality; in order that they might then disregard Moral Rules. Whereas this is not the disposition which the Moralist can approve or allow, even in Cases of Necessity. He requires, in order that he may give his approbation, or withhold his condemnation, a struggle in giving up what is commonly right; as well as a wish to do no more than is, in uncommon cases, allowable. He cannot wish to aid any one in looking with composure upon the shock that his moral being must receive, by the emergencies of a Case of Necessity.

415. A further reason for not defining such cases, is this; that the application of such Rules requires a calmness and fairness which cannot be looked for in a case of necessity. By the supposition of a case of necessity, the man is so thrown off his balance, that he cannot conform to the Rules of Duty in their exact and primary form. If we state these Rules in a relaxed form, Cases of Necessity will occur, in which, from the like want of balance of mind, he will transgress even the enlarged Rule. The Moralist cannot deliver, as a Precept, *Lie not except in great emergencies.* If he were to say so, to a man, under the influence of passion, small emergencies would appear great; and thus such persons might learn to lie without compunction. The Moralist says, *Lie not at all.* If an extreme emergency occurs, he grants that there are Cases of Necessity in which transgressions of Moral Rules may be excusable; and if he have to pronounce a moral sentence on the case, he will take into account the circumstances of the case and of the person.

416. He will attend to the circumstances of the person, as well as of the case. For though the man who has to act in a Case of Necessity is not likely to look to the Moralist for Rules of Action; it is very

likely, or rather, inevitable, that his course of action will depend upon his own previous Moral Culture. A man who, like Socrates, has cherished in his mind, for many years, a reverence for the laws, will wait his death from their operation, rather than evade them. A man who has carried the love of truth, a woman who has carried the love of chastity, to a high point, will die, rather than incur the guilt they abhor. Other persons, not so far advanced in Moral Progress, will yield to the present fear, and seek the allowable course, which, in such Cases of Necessity, may exist. The conduct, in such cases, is governed, not by Rules, but by the Operative Moral Principles which have been taken into the character so as to be the Springs of Action.

The conduct of a person in a Case of Necessity, as in any other case, must be considered with reference to his moral culture, in order that we may determine how far it is good or bad. Now in the case in which a person, whose moral culture has, up to that point been going on, violates the ordinary Rules of Duty in a Case of Necessity; his moral progress must, as we have said, receive a shock. There has been a mortal struggle between Moral Rules and Self-preservation; and Morality has been overcome. So far, the event is a suspension or reversal of moral culture, like any other transgression. But this has not taken place in the ordinary course of the man's being: it has been at a moment of paroxysm and agony; when by the terror of immediate death, or dreadful evil, his mind was thrown off its usual balance. This event in his moral culture, is, therefore, not to be reckoned as if it had happened at any other time. Perhaps, the struggle and the defeat of Morality, was but for a moment; and implies no real permanent depravation of the character. Perhaps, the shock, though severe, was transient. Perhaps the moral derangement was a sharp and critical disorder, brought on by special

external circumstances; which, once past, does not affect the general moral health. In Cases of Necessity, when Rules have been violated, the Moralist may be willing to hope that such is the case; and in this hope, may abstain from condemning the actor, and may thus pronounce his act allowable. In delivering such a Sentence, the Moralist trusts that, as the Moral Culture has been interrupted by extraordinary circumstances, or turned into a strange channel; it will also afterwards be resumed with extraordinary zeal, and pursued with extraordinary advantage. The man who has had to take a merely allowable course, has great reason to examine his conscience and his heart, in order to see that they have received no stain or wrench; and to remove the defect, if they have. And if any more than native aid may be obtained in such a task, he has, more than others, reason to seek for it. If he do not need Repentance and amendment after his act, at least he needs a renewed Recognition, in his heart, of the Moral Rule which he has violated.

417. We may remark, that we have spoken of cases in which the direct Rule of Duty leads to Death; as if Death were nothing more than one among many objects of human fear, although the greatest. Death is, however, also the end of our moral career, so far as this life is concerned. This consideration would not affect the merely Moral Question; which is a question concerning the Course that Duty and Virtue require, *so long as* life lasts. But Religion, which presents Death to us as, not merely the end of this life, but the beginning of another, gives a new aspect to all such questions. Still, in the eye of Religion, as in the eye of Morality, Death is only one of the events of man's being; and every man's conduct with regard to this as to the other events, must be governed by the Law of Duty.

418. It appears from what has been said, that

Cases of Necessity, in which the conflict is between Moral Rules and Self-preservation, are properly spoken of in the common maxim, which declares that *Necessity has no Law;* but the exception to Law amounts only to this; that transgression is allowable, provided the necessity be extreme.

419. In the case in which Moral Rules are transgressed, not for the sake of our own preservation, but in order to preserve some *other person* from great impending evil; we may have a Case of Necessity, which is also a *Conflict of Duties:* for to preserve another person from great evil, is a part of the general Duty of Benevolence; and when the person is connected with us by special relations, to do this, is involved in the Duties of the Specific Affections. Thus, when the wife of Grotius saved him by a lie; when Lucilius saved Brutus by falsely personating him; when Virginius preserved his daughter from pollution by her murder; when a man, in rescuing a neighbour from death, kills the robber who assails him; we have two Duties, placed in opposition to each other; on one side, the Duty of rescuing, from a terrible and impending evil, a husband, a friend, a daughter, a neighbour; on the other hand, the Duty of not telling a falsehood, or committing homicide.

These Cases of Conflict of Duties differ from the Cases of Conscience formerly considered, in having, as one alternative, death, or some extreme evil, immediately impending over a person whom we love; and hence, they hardly admit of a deliberate previous decision what we *ought* to do; but rather lead to some paroxysmal act, of which we afterwards enquire whether it was *allowable,* as in other Cases of Necessity.

420. In these Cases, as in the other Cases of Necessity, the Moralist must abstain from laying down definite Rules of decision; and for the like reasons as before. To state General Rules for deci-

ding Conflicts between opposing Duties, would have an immoral tendency. For such a procedure would necessarily seem to make light of the Duties which were thus, in a general manner, postponed to other Duties; and would tend to remove the compunction, which any Moral Rule violated, ought to occasion to the Actor. We may see these defects, in the Rules which have been proposed for such purposes. For example, it has been said by some, that the wife of Grotius and the friend of Brutus were justified in what they did, because the Duty of Truth is only a Duty to one's self; and Duties to a Husband or a Friend are of a higher order than Duties to one's self*. But the result of this Maxim would evidently be, that any Lie, however great, might be told to procure the smallest benefit to a Husband or Friend; which is a most immoral conclusion.

421. But though in such Cases of Conflict of Duties, no Moral Rules can be laid down, as of universal validity, the course taken by the Actor will depend, and ought to depend, upon his state of Moral Culture. And perhaps the best mode of deciding any particular case, is to consider how the two sides of the alternative would have affected the Moral Culture and Moral Progress of the person. Thus, in the case of Grotius's wife, Conjugal Love was in Conflict with the Love of Truth. Both of these are Moral Principles, to be cultivated in our hearts, by their influence upon our actions. If the wife had neglected an opportunity which offered itself, of saving the husband from death, the shock to Conjugal Affection would have been intense; and the irremediable evil, when it had fallen upon her, must have brought with it a self-accusation and despair, against which the recollection of scrupulous veracity could hardly have supported her. If, on the contrary, in such extreme ne-

* Eschenmayer, *Moralphilosophie.* Stuttgart, 1818. § 187 *Nothlüge.*

cessity she uttered a falsehood ; even if it had been to friends, it might have remained in her mind as an exception, without weakening the habitual reverence for Truth : but the deceit being, in fact, used towards enemies, with whom the same common understanding does not obtain, which subsists among friends, it would naturally still less be felt to be an act in which the Duty of Truth was lightly dealt with ; so that there were reasons to hope, that if any wound were inflicted on the Love of Truth by the act, it might heal readily and completely. And for the like reasons, in extreme cases, the duties of the affections may be generally preferred to the duties of truth and justice. But then this must be understood only of Cases of Necessity, that is, of death or other peril of the highest kind, incumbent upon the object of affection : for otherwise, such a Rule would destroy the duties of truth and justice altogether.

422. As we have said, in such Cases of Necessity, men will hardly, in general, look to the Rules of Moralists for the direction of their conduct. But though they may not do this, they will be determined, in their conduct on such emergencies, by their previous moral culture and moral progress. A man who, acting under a momentary sense of duty, kills his daughter to preserve her purity, must have cultivated to a high degree his love of purity ; and has probably not cultivated, in the same degree, his horror of homicide. Yet we can hardly blame him, in the same way as we should do, if immoral springs of action had overmastered a moral Principle ; for both those Principles are to be cherished in the Moral Culture of Man. If, in Cases of Necessity, the conflict of opposing Duties be decided by the energetic action of a Principle, which, though disproportioned to other Principles, is still moral, we may pronounce the act excusable ; without pretending to decide that some other course might not have been selected, by a char-

acter of more even and comprehensive Moral Culture. The predominant Principle in each character, will show itself, not only by prevailing in the struggle, when the conflict is begun; but also by stimulating the invention, and suggesting a course of conduct, which, to a more indifferent mind, would not have occurred. It was the strength of conjugal affection, which suggested to Grotius's wife the device to save her husband; it was the strength of friendship, which suggested to Lucilius the thought of presenting himself as Brutus; it was the horror of shame and slavery, which inspired in the mind of Virginius, the thought of killing his daughter. A strong Moral Principle, like any other Spring of Action, shows its strength by the activity, vigour, and inventiveness which it calls out in the mind.

423. In such cases as have been described, when the course chosen implies self-devotion, or the sacrifice of strong special affections, along with great courage or fortitude, the act becomes an *Heroic Act.* As Heroic Acts, accordingly, we have already mentioned the acts of Lucilius, and of Virginius; also (264) of the elder Brutus, Regulus, Socrates. Thus, Heroic Acts approach very near to those Cases of Necessity which involve Conflicting Duties. And they will be judged by the Moralist, in nearly the same manner as such Cases. Heroic Acts arise from the energetic predominance of some Operative Principle, which, overpowering selfish desires and affections, doubt and fear, stimulates the mind to some act out of the common course of human action. If the Principle which thus manifests itself, be a Moral Principle, although disproportioned to other Moral Principles in the character; the Moralist may, not only pronounce the acts excusable, but may even admire them, *as Heroic Acts;* that is, as Acts out of the reach of Rule. But at the same time, it must be recollected, that the Origin of Heroic Acts, in general, is a dis-

proportion in the Moral Character. To aim at Heroic Virtues only, would be an extremely bad culture of ourselves. It would lead to an entire rejection of Duties; for as we have said (276), we speak of Heroic Virtues, but not of Heroic Duties.

424. Among the Cases of Necessity, there is one Class which may be specially noticed; namely, those in which, under the pressure of Necessity, the Duty of Obedience to Government is put aside—Cases of Resistance to Governors, and of Revolutions. Such cases have occurred, in the history of almost all nations; but they are usually defended, and can only be morally defended, as Cases of Necessity. Under all common circumstances, the Duty of Obedience to the Government historically established in the Community, is incumbent upon every Citizen There may occur circumstances, in which the preservation of the Constitution of the Country, or the Welfare of the People, may make Resistance and Revolution necessary. But the Moralist must say, in such, as in other Cases of Necessity, that the Necessity must be extreme, before a violation of the Rules of Duty is allowable. All common means must be tried, all the resources of the Constitution exhausted, all other courses explored, before Resistance becomes moral. And we cannot define beforehand, at least, except in a very general way, what are those marks of Necessity which thus justify Resistance to Government. The Moralist abstains from doing this, in these, for the same reasons as in other Cases of Necessity. It would not answer the purposes of Morality, to draw lines, and mark points, to which discontented citizens might look forwards, in order to see when they had acquired the privileges of a condition free from the Rule of Obedience. We are not to class Resistance and Revolution among ordinary conditions of Society. On the contrary, they are to be looked forward to as dire calamities, whenever they come; with which the

mind is never to be familiarized, any more than with any other great transgressions of Rules, which, in Cases of Necessity, may occur.

When the Case of Necessity occurs, the Necessity will be expressed in the language of historical facts and current opinions. Both the Necessity and the expression of it, will depend upon the Moral and Political Culture which the community has attained. If, according to the historical Constitution, and actual condition of the Community, the Necessity be really extreme; and if all Constitutional courses having been exhausted, the operation of Moral Principle in the Community has produced Resistance, and led to Revolution, the Revolution may be necessary, and even glorious. But even in this case, it is conducive to Morality that the deviation from the common Rules of the Constitution should be, and should appear to be, as small as is consistent with the object to be secured. There may be occasions, on which the Moralist may have to dwell with satisfaction upon such Revolutions; and on the heroic acts by which they were brought about; but in general, it will be his province to speak of the ordinary Rules of Duty, and of their application, rather than of the difficulty and disquieting questions of Exceptions to Ordinary Rules.

CHAPTER XVII.

OF THINGS ALLOWABLE.

425. WE have been led, by our reasonings, to state that, in Cases of Necessity, certain courses of action may be declared *Allowable* or *Permitted*; even though we may not be able to pronounce them absolutely right; as to tell a lie to save one's own life, or

the life of a friend. There is a prevalent inclination among men to extend this notion of things which are permitted or allowable, though not rigorously right, to many other cases. It is often asked, with a latent persuasion that the Moralist cannot fail to return an affirmative answer, Whether it be not allowable to utter a falsehood, in order to preserve an important secret: Whether, under very provoking circumstances, anger on our own account be not allowable: Whether, in deciding a question of merit, we may not allowably lean a little to a member of our own family: Whether, a slight occasional excess of moderation, in eating and drinking, be not allowable. These, and many questions of the like kind, are often propounded: and it may be proper to consider what reply the Moralist must make to them.

The notion of what is *allowable*, is admitted in Cases of Necessity, as expressing our acquiescence in certain actions as exceptions to General Moral Rules: so that, though the general Maxims of Morality will not authorize us to pronounce them right, our regard for the condition of human nature will not permit us to pronounce them wrong. But to extend this notion of *allowable* to Cases of common occurrence, when there is no necessity, and only such a temptation as is often arising; is to annihilate all Rule. The meaning of every Moral Rule is, that it is to be obeyed, in spite of temptation to transgress. If, professing to accept the Rule as our Rule, we still deviate from it, whenever any considerable temptation occurs; the Rule is not our Rule. It is no part of the habitual conduct of our thoughts; no part of our moral culture.

426. Further: the merely propounding such questions as the above, whether deviations from the Rules of Truth, and Benevolence, and Justice, and Temperance, be allowable, of itself shows that the Moral Culture is very imperfect. It shows that the Love of

Truth, of Benevolence, of Justice, of Temperance, is not established in the mind; that the Moral Rules which express these Virtues are received as an extraneous constraint, which we would gladly escape from; not accepted as desirable means to a wished-for end. To enquire whether, under specified circumstances, violation of Moral Rules be not *allowable*, is to show that our thoughts are seeking not the way to conform to the Rule, but the way to evade it. To make a Class of Allowable Things, would be to sanction and confirm this disposition. We should place an insurmountable impediment in the way of the Moral Culture of men, if we taught them to classify actions as Good, Bad, and Allowable. For they might be led to fill their lives with Allowable actions, to the neglect of those which are Good: and it is evident that to do this, would be to remove all Moral progress and all moral aim.

427. But it may be said, there must be a class of actions which are merely Allowable: those which are not either good or bad; where a person may take one course or the other without blame: as for instance, to choose Law or Medicine for his profession: to spend more or less upon his dress and table, within the limits which his fortune prescribes: to eat more or less: to study more or less; or to study one branch of literature or another. In these, and an infinite number of others, the like matters, it may be urged that it is allowable to adopt either side. Good men constantly do both the one and the other of the things, thus put as alternatives. There is no necessary character of good or bad on either side; and either side is allowable.

Upon this we remark, that if, in such alternatives, there be not on either side any necessary character of good or bad, a man is permitted by morality to choose one side or the other according to other considerations. If this be so, the things may be described as

Things *Indifferent,* rather than as things allowable. And undoubtedly, there are, at every period of our lives, many things about us, which are, so far as we can discern, morally indifferent. We cannot see that Moral Rules are applicable to them. We cannot see that either alternative will effect our Moral Culture.

428. But we may further remark, that in many cases, in which no moral result appears at first sight, a moral result exists: and may even, by us, be discerned as probable. The choice of a profession, for instance, can hardly be a matter of indifference, in a moral point of view. We have already seen that there are wide moral questions, inseparably connected with the profession of an Advocate. Questions of the like kind might be stated, belonging to the profession of a Physician. How far either of the professions is, for each person, a moral one, must depend upon those solutions of such questions which are accepted by him. Moreover, each of these professions must, in many ways, produce a very great effect upon the moral culture of the person who exercises it. A man's profession determines the sphere and kind of his actions; and it is in the doing of these actions, that the man's moral character is to be formed. The choice of a profession, therefore, must be very far from indifferent, in its moral results, for each man.

429. But, though the choice of a profession be important in its moral bearings, it by no means follows from this, that it must be governed by any uniform Rule for all. What is good for one man, may be bad for another, according to the difference of native character and previous circumstances. The effect of a profession, as influencing the man's moral culture, will depend upon the moral culture which has taken place already. In a man's moral and intellectual progress, all the steps are connected: and his moral and intellectual Education, which has pre-

ceded his entrance upon his profession, may have made his Profession the best Sequel to his Education. We have said that, in the extraordinary exertions of moral principles, the energy of the principle stimulates the mind to select and follow out appropriate trains of thought. The same is the case, also, in the ordinary operation of the principles by which the general course of a man's life is determined. The Operative Principles which are the strongest in his character, decide him to take one course or another; and if these Operative Principles are Moral Principles, they will tend to continue his Moral Culture in the scheme of life to which they have impelled him. And thus, though we do not, in such cases, pretend to lay down Rules of choice which shall be applicable to all men alike; yet we see that the choice is, for each man, very far from a matter of indifference; that on the contrary, the congruity of his social position, with his character, and moral and intellectual condition, may influence, very favourably, or very unfavourably, his moral culture throughout his life. To decide our choice in such alternatives, is one of the great offices of Prudence and Wisdom; of Prudence, if we consider the decision with reference to any object short of the highest Moral Progress: of Wisdom, if we decide so as most to further that highest object.

430. But there are other ways in which actions, at first sight seemingly indifferent, have really a character of good or bad. They may form or foster *Habits*, which are often plainly not indifferent, though the single acts may appear so. Slight changes, daily repeated, may produce an evident modification. To exaggerate a little the events of the stories which we tell in conversation; to overpoint the antithesis of our remarks; to eat or drink to the full gratification of appetite; to give way to slight impulses of impatience or anger; may, on each single occasion, appear so

small a matter as to be allowable; and yet, in this way may be generated Habits of violating truth, justice, temperance and kindness, at least in some degree. And such Habits, existing in any degree, are necessarily very adverse to our moral culture. Habits are generated by successive acts; and, in their turn, produce a continuation of the acts; and every act in which we trifle with the suggestions of truth, justice, temperance, kindness, or any other virtue, may, and more or less must, extend its consequences to the subsequent tenour of our lives. And in the same manner, acts in which we act with a strict and special regard to truth, to justice, to temperance, to kindness, in spite of minute temptations to the contrary, in matters however apparently small and unimportant, may, by the habits which they tend to form, or to uphold, be of service to us in our moral culture.

431. Acts which are thus performed, rather from a regard to their influence in the formation of habits, than from their own value, are practised as a *Discipline*. Many of the seemingly trivial acts, which make up the tissue of our common lives, require to be regarded in this view, in order that they may be duly regulated by moral considerations. The indulgence of selfish desires in small matters; ill-humour; sharp expressions; obstinacy in trifles; must be avoided; because the contrary habits,—self-denial in small matters for the sake of others; cheerful and kind words used to them; the habit of yielding to the wishes of others in trifles;—are not only manifestations of a benevolent disposition, where it does exist; but are a discipline of benevolence, by which its growth is fostered. We must avoid colouring a story in order to produce an effect; arguing for the sake of victory only; depreciating the characters and actions of men in order to show our wit and genius; because such habits are inconsistent with the disposition of an earnest and sincere love of

truth and justice; and because such habits tend to make those who practise them, indifferent to truth and justice, in comparison of the gratification of vanity and pride. The opposite practices;—a strict fidelity in narration; a moderation in maintaining our opinion, even when we are confident we are right; an abstinence from speaking evil of any;—are a Discipline of truth and fairness. In like manner, the gratifications of the Table, even if they be not carried so far as to interfere immediately with moral action, by overloading the body, or clouding the mind, may interfere with our moral culture, by fostering a habit of self-indulgence, rather than of self-denial. Rules of living, which make the satisfaction of the bodily appetites a discipline of moderation, are the proper mode of making that part of our nature subservient to our moral culture. And as we have already said, our bodily appetites have in themselves no moral character. It is only by being thus made to contribute to our moral Discipline, that they can cease to be obstacles in the way of our moral progress.

432. In a character morally disciplined, the bodily Desires do not operate upon the actions in a direct and unmingled manner, but through the Habits. The direct operation of the desires is controlled; they are wrapt up and put out of sight, in the round of events by which the needs of the body are supplied. The more rigorous moralists have spoken of the bodily desires, as being killed, or *mortified;* and have taught that this Mortification of the Desires of the body is necessary for the full completion of our moral culture.

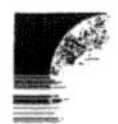

The Discipline, which consists in limiting or rejecting the indulgence of the Desires of the body, has been carried very far by some, with the view of mortifying such desires. With these persons, Discipline, *Askesis*, has been made a direct object; and they have adopted many practices to attain their object, which have hence been termed *Ascetic* Practices.

433. But it does not appear that this ascetic course, in which the mortification of the desires of the body is made a direct and primary object, is really well suited to the moral culture of men in general. The object of Discipline is not Discipline itself, but the unconscious Habits which Discipline generates. Discipline is not complete, till we do *spontaneously* the actions in which we have been disciplined. A man has not completed the discipline by which he learns to swim, till he can swim with no more effort or thought than he requires to walk. An accomplished swimmer swims spontaneously, when he finds himself in the water. A man has not completed his discipline in a foreign language, till he can understand and use it without recalling his rules of grammar; till, as it is often expressed, he thinks in the language. And such is the object, in this, and in other courses of bodily or mental discipline. The like is the case in our moral culture. Spontaneous, not Ascetic Virtue, is that which the Moralist desires to see among men. So far as ascetic practices may be requisite to generate habits of self-denial and self-control, they may be rightly employed: but we are not to forget that ascestic practices have, in themselves, no moral value. If they are good at all, they are good only as means to something else. Discipline is good as Discipline: but Discipline is completed, only by reaching the end of the ascetic struggle with inclination. In our moral culture, we are to aim, not at the means, but at the end: not at the Ascetic Struggle, but at the *Disciplined Spontaneity*.

434. What has been said of the Discipline by which moral virtues are fostered, applies likewise to the *Discipline of the Intellect*. Many employments of the mind, apparently unimportant and indifferent, are important parts of our intellectual and moral formation. Intellectual employments, which are generally pursued for the mere pleasure of the pursuit;

favourite studies; books of our own choice, and the like; can hardly fail to have a great influence upon the intellectual habits, and thus may promote or impede the development of the intellectual virtues. Studies and reading, which have in them no direct immoral tendency, may yet dissipate and distract the mind. The love of mere intellectual amusement may destroy the habit of solid thought, and interfere with those Duties of Consideration, and of acting rationally, of which we have spoken; indulgence in the literature of mere imagination, humour, wit and the like, may destroy the love of truth; the exclusive cultivation of the material and mathematical sciences may make the mind dull and captious in dealing with moral conceptions. Any course of intellectual employment, if allowed too much to absorb the mind, may check and pervert that balanced and complete intellectual culture, which is most conducive to the progress of the whole man.

435. Thus actions of all kinds, otherwise unimportant, become important as parts of a Discipline. Scarcely any thing can be said to be indifferent, when considered with reference to the effect which it may produce upon our lives, through corporeal, intellectual, and moral habits. Every act, however slight, may be good or bad, when considered as an indication of good moral discipline, or of the want of it; as, in the eyes of those who are judges of manners, every act is an indication of good or of ill Breeding.

436. For this reason, the Moralist does not readily class any act as Indifferent; or pronounce any act Allowable, which is no more than allowable. It may be difficult or impossible, to see the bearing of a single trifling act, on the actor's moral condition; and it would be unwise to lay down general rules for such acts. But the act may, nevertheless, have such an influence; and each man has it for a duty, to ex-

ercise a careful guidance and control over even trifling acts; recollecting how trifling acts grow into Habits; and how important a part of a man's moral condition his Habits are. The more entirely a man's whole being is governed and directed by Moral Principles, and the more does the circle of Things Indifferent narrow and dwindle. As the moral light grows stronger, everything assumes a colour of good or bad, between which he has to choose. Everything, however trivial or mean, affords aliment and occasions to virtue. And as all things thus become good or bad, nothing is merely allowable. If it be allowable, it is right; and is what must be done because it is right, not what may be done because it is allowable.

437. It is true, that thus to estimate every act, however trivial, as having a moral value from its influence upon our character, implies a clearness of view, as to the operation of such influences, which we can never fully attain to. This condition of mind, in which all acts are good or are bad, and none indifferent, is one which we may approximate to, but can never arrive at. When we have exercised all our sagacity and diligence, in determining what acts are right, and what are wrong; there will still remain a residue, at every period of our lives, which will have the aspect of being indifferent. Nor need we be disturbed that this is so. If, habitually referring things to a moral standard, and exercising such care and thought as a serious conduct of the business of life requires, we keep our eyes open to the good and the bad of the actions which come before us, in order to choose the good and shun the bad; we carry on our moral culture, according to the stage at which we have arrived. But in order to do this, we must, at each step, ask, not what is allowable, but what is right; not what we may do, but what we ought to do. If to these questions we can obtain, on any particular subject, no definite response from our con-

sciences, we may guide our course by the best lights of prudence which we can obtain; always recollecting, however, that our not being able to see that there is one course which we ought to take, rather than another, is an imperfection of vision, which arises from the defect of our intellectual and moral faculties; and which we may hope to see removed, when our minds are further enlightened, in a more advanced stage of our moral progress.

CHAPTER XVIII.

OF IGNORANCE AND ERROR.

438. IGNORANCE and Error are often referred to, among the causes which make actions excusable. It will be proper to consider how far Actions which are generally wrong, are, by Ignorance and Error, rendered excusable in the Agent.

We have already spoken of Intellectual Duties; and the existence of such Duties leads to some Maxims which bear upon the question now before us. We have mentioned (336—342) the Duty of Consideration; the Duty of acting according to Rule; and the Duty of acting rationally. We have further spoken of the Duty of our own Intellectual Culture; and also (366) of the Duty of constantly enlightening and instructing our Conscience. These Duties cannot be neglected or omitted, without a transgression of that Duty of Moral Culture, which is our highest and most comprehensive Duty.

439. But Ignorance and Error may arise from other Causes, besides the neglect of these Intellectual Duties; for example, they may arise from our want of information, which we have not any means of

obtaining; or from our receiving false information, which we have no reason to suspect of falsehood. In such cases Ignorance and Error are *unavoidable*: or, in the language sometimes used by Moralists, they are *invincible* Ignorance and *invincible* Error. They cannot be avoided or overcome by any obvious exertions of ours. We have performed, it is supposed, the Duty of Inquiry and Consideration (336) which is incumbent upon us, and still we remain in Ignorance or in Error. On this supposition, the actions which we ignorantly and erroneously perform are blameless. We have no way of avoiding or removing Ignorance or Error, but by Inquiry and Consideration. If we have done all that is in our power to free our actions from these defects; the defects may be considered as no longer belonging to us. If I purchase a horse, and have a suspicion that he has been stolen from a previous owner, I must inquire for the evidence of such a fact, and weigh it carefully. But if the result of my inquiry and deliberation is, to remove entirely the suspicion, I may blamelessly buy him, though he should afterwards be found to be a stolen horse. And in the same manner, I am blameless, if the circumstances of the sale are such as to banish suspicion; as for example, if he is sold in open market, it may be that this circumstance is, in consequence of the habits of the country, sufficient to remove the necessity of inquiry. In this case, Error, when it occurs, may be considered as unavoidable; and the erroneous action is still blameless.

440. But it is requisite, to the moral character of the act, that we should direct ourselves by the real inward belief to which we are led, and not merely by any external result. A mere formal inquiry, for the sake of saving appearances, or of complying with the letter of our maxims, cannot make the act moral. Such a pretended conformity to the Duty of Inquiry, is insincere and dishonest.

It will often be difficult for us to determine, whether we have been sufficiently persevering and minute in the Inquiries, which we have made, into the facts which guide our actions; and when we have been deceived, and have thus been led to do what we wished to avoid; as soon as the deceit is discovered, we may perhaps wonder that we did not detect it sooner; and may regret that we did not carry our inquiry further. Thus, when I have bought a horse, and afterwards find him to have been stolen; I may regret that I did not inquire more carefully into the Seller's story. This regret includes some condemnation of the act which I have committed under the influence of the deceit, and approaches to the character of repentance. And such sentiments of self-condemnation and repentance are well founded, when we have been negligent in our inquiries. It is very difficult to know when we have done all in our power to ascertain the truth of facts; and therefore, difficult to know when we are quite free from the blame of such negligence.

Hence we are led to this Maxim; that *Unavoidable Ignorance or Error removes the blame of the actions which it causes; but that we are to be very careful of not too easily supposing our ignorance to be unavoidable.*

441. Of course, as soon as we discover that, through ignorance or error, we have done a wrong to any one, it is our Duty to remedy the wrong. If we have bought what was stolen from him, we must restore the thing to him; and the like. Any resistance in our minds to this step, is immoral. When our ignorance ends, the excuse which it supplies to us ends. We may avoid blame, in virtue of our Ignorance or Error, but we may not receive advantage from it. We *regret* our Error; but if we retain the benefits of it, we shall have to *repent* of our Fault. There is dishonesty in resisting the consequences of the detection of our error; as there is dishonesty in willingly abstaining from detecting our error.

442. When Ignorance and Error are of such a kind that they may be avoided by Inquiry and Consideration, the actions to which they give occasion are not freed from blame by the ignorance and the error. Yet Ignorance and Error, even when they are the consequence of a neglect of the Duties of Inquiry and Consideration, may exist for a time, without producing any external action which violates Moral Rules. So long as this is the case, the fault which we have committed is the *general* Neglect of that Intellectual Culture which is requisite to our moral progress. But when Ignorance and Error, thus produced, give rise to *special* violations of Moral Rules, such transgressions are not excusable on account of the Ignorance and Error. If a man remain, through Negligence, ignorant, or mistaken, as to the amount of his income, and in consequence, contract debts greater than he can pay, he is not blameless; though Ignorance and Error are the occasion of the wrong which he does to his creditors. He is culpable for not ascertaining what he could afford to spend, before he incurred his debts. If, with the same ignorance, he had not incurred such debts, he might still be blamed for Negligence in not ascertaining the conditions under which he had to act. But when his Negligence inflicts loss on other persons, it becomes a carelessness of Justice and Honesty embodied in act; and therefore a transgression of a graver kind.

443. Still, there is a difference between *Carelessness* of Justice and Honesty, and intentional *In*justice and *Dis*honesty. Debts contracted through negligent ignorance of our income, are not so culpable as Debts contracted with fraudulent intentions. In one case, the Duty of Consideration is, for the time, omitted; but it may be resumed. In the other case, the Duty of Justice or of Honesty is intentionally vio-

lated; and the Violation must be repented of. In one case, the moral progress is suspended; in the other, it is reversed. And thus, *Ignorance and Error arising from negligence,* though they cannot excuse, *may palliate our transgressions, by excluding intentional wrong.*

444. But besides Ignorance and Error with regard to the *Facts* on which the direction of our actions must depend; there may, also, be Ignorance and Error with regard to the *Rules* by which the moral character of actions is determined. And it may be made a Question, how far such Ignorance and Error render actions excusable, which are contrary to Moral Rules. If a man be ignorant that theft is a crime, is he guilty when he steals? If a man believe slavery to be consistent with morality, is he excusable in buying and selling men? If a man think that property is an immoral institution, is he justified in disregarding the Rights of Property in other men?

To such questions, we reply, in the first place, that a person labouring under Ignorance and Error, such as are here described;—ignorant that theft is a crime; that buying and selling men is immoral; that property is an institution necessary for moral action among men;—must be in a very imperfect state of moral culture. We have shown that, in virtue of man's moral nature, property is a necessary institution, and theft necessarily a crime; and we shall be able to show, in like manner, that buying and selling men is immoral.

These Moral Truths spring from the moral nature of man, and are unfolded in an explicit form, by our moral and intellectual culture. They are virtually included in the Express Principles of Humanity, Justice, Truth, Purity, Order, Earnestness, and Moral Purpose, which we formerly stated (269). Such general moral truths, thus derived from the Fundamental Principles of Morality, may themselves be termed Moral *Principles.* And as the denial of the Expres

Principles of Morality implies a defect in the Operative Principles, namely, Benevolence, Justice, Truth, Purity, and Wisdom; so a denial of the Derivative Principles, which result from the Fundamental Principles, also implies a defect in the same Operative Principles. A person who denies the necessity of Property, the criminality of theft, and the like, must either be a person in whom the power and habit of intellectual deduction are feeble and confused; or he must be a person who denies the express Fundamental Principles of Benevolence, Justice, Truth, Purity, and Order. Denying these express Principles, he cannot possess, except in a very imperfect and obscure form, the Operative Principles which form the Cardinal Virtues of men. Hence a person who is in Ignorance and Error on such points as have been mentioned, the necessity of Property, the criminality of Theft, and the like, may be said to be *wanting in the Common Moral Principles of men.*

445. Putting off for a moment the Question how far this condition—the Want of the Common Moral Principles—may be said to excuse or exculpate actions arising from such a condition; we cannot hesitate to say that such a condition implies a low stage of moral culture. The man who is in this condition, has made a very small advance in that Moral Progress, at which, as Moral Agents, we must constantly aim. When Ignorance and Error take the form of a Want of the Common Moral Principles, they may easily suspend or reverse the Moral Progress of the Man, as much as many kinds of Transgression would do. And hence, they must produce upon the Man's Moral Being, the effects which the Suspension and Inversion of the Moral Progress does produce.

We shall not now attempt to determine what is the result of a suspended and inverted Moral Culture, when not retrieved by any subsequent progress. Perhaps Morality alone cannot decide this question; perhaps she must refer us to Religion, in order that we may learn what consequences such a final suspension and inversion of moral progress produces, upon man's destination and condition. But we must necessarily conceive thus of the result: that the condition of the man whose moral progress is finally suspended and inverted is, in some way, opposite to that of the virtuous man; and this, equally, whether the want of progress arise from transgression of moral principles, or the want of them. If Virtue lead to Happiness, as we have said it must (304), the Want of the Common Moral Principles must lead to an unhappy condition. The man who, wanting the Common Moral Principles, transgresses them, cannot be placed, by his Ignorance and Error, on a like footing with the man who knows these Principles, and conforms to them in his actions. If such Ignorance and Error be not faults, they must at least be considered as great moral misfortunes. Such Ignorance and Error belong to a conscience dark and erroneous; and a dark and erroneous Conscience is a gread moral calamity.

446. But the general judgment of mankind regards the Want of the Common Moral Principles, not only as a Misfortune and a Calamity, but as a Fault. The man who shows this Want of Moral Principles by the declarations which he makes, incurs the disapprobation and repugnance which we give to moral wrong. We abhor a man who asserts that no affection is due from a child to a parent. We do not hear with patience men asserting that they have a Right to buy and sell their brother men as if they were cattle. We condemn, as immoral, a man who refuses to acknowledge any Duty of Kindness, or Justice, or Truth, towards other men. These are Errors which we do not hold to be innocent or excusable. We think they might have been avoided, and ought to have been avoided. Each man's Reason, and the Instruc-

tion which each man receives, in the general course of Society, might, we hold, have taught him better than this. And this, our conviction, agrees with what we have said of Intellectual Duties. We require of men that they should be rational; we have seen (338) that there is a Duty of acting rationally. And as there is a Duty of acting rationally, there is a Duty of thinking rationally; for rational thinking is a condition of rational acting. And to deny, or to be ignorant of, the Common Moral Principles of Man, is to be, to a certain extent, irrational. It is to neglect or pervert the use of the human Reason, by which all men are capable of arriving at such Principles. And thus *Ignorance or Error, in the form of the Want of the Common Moral Principles of Man, are blameable.*

447. Hence, as a general distinction, Moralists pronounce *Errors of Fact*, when not accompanied with negligence, *to be exculpations* of the actions which they occasion; but *Errors of Principle, not to be exculpations.* And in this distinction, they agree with the Jurists: who lay down these two cardinal maxims: *Ignorantia facti excusat: Ignorantia juris non excusat.* Ignorance of the Fact is an excuse; Ignorance of the Law is no excuse. A man is not criminal for not directing his actions by a Fact, which he did not know from observation or testimony; and which he could not know any other way. On the other hand, ignorance of the Law cannot be accepted by the Law as an excuse. The Law is requisite for the guidance of each citizen in his social transactions, and it is his business to make himself acquainted with it so far as it concerns him. The Law is Natural Justice, with such additional regulations, as are requisite to define its application; the Law, therefore, is requisite for each man's moral guidance. It is his duty, as well as his obligation, to guide himself by it, and, therefore, to make himself acquainted with it. And the Law, in assuming a knowledge of the actual Laws, assumes

only a knowledge of that Rational Law which is the basis of Actual Laws, and of its special consequences in our own country. Such assumptions are requisite for the administration of Laws. If a man might plead ignorance of the Law, in excuse of a crime, it would be impossible to convict criminals; for men would remain wilfully ignorant of the Law, in order to avail themselves of this excuse; and even if they were not ignorant, it would be difficult, or impossible, to prove their knowledge. Hence, it is everywhere presumed that the citizen is acquainted with the Law of the State, and in like manner, it is presumed by the Moralist, that man, as a moral being, is acquainted with the Laws to which his Moral Nature directs him: and if he transgresses these Laws, or pleads ignorance, as his excuse, the excuse is generally not to be accepted.

448. But though the Moralist pronounces Ignorance and Error, when they appear as the Want of common Principles, to be blameable; and rejects such a Want, when offered as an exculpation of immoral actions, because it implies a neglect or perversion of Reason; it is still proper for him to recollect, that it is by no means easy to avoid all imperfection and confusion in the use of the Reason. It is our Duty to act and think rationally, as it is our privilege to be rational; but it is by no means easy to think in a manner perfectly rational. The orignal Endowments, internal Habits, and external Circumstances of men, make Ignorance and Error, even with regard to the Common Moral Principles of men, very difficult to avoid. Few persons are able to see, all that the light of Reason is capable of showing. Men may miss their way at many a point, in the path to and from the Fundamental Principles of Morality. We have been led to such Fundamental Principles (Express Principles (see 268)) by the examination of several abstract and general Conceptions. And we de-

duce from these Fundamental Principles, special Duties, also by means of abstract and general Conceptions. But in forming these abstract and general Conceptions, which are thus the objects of our thoughts, and the guides of our reasonings, we may perform these intellectual processes very imperfectly; and in attempting them, we may fall into confusion, ambiguity, inconsistency; and thus into Error. Abstraction and Generalization are intellectual processes which are very inexactly and obscurely performed by most persons: and in the confusion and obscurity of the general and abstract Conceptions thus formed, there is a source of a great deal of irrationality and incoherence, which thus infuses itself into the Moral Principles held by men; even when they have not been negligent, nor intentionally perverse, in their moral reasonings. Thus, if a person maintain theft to be no crime, his Error may arise from a very confused apprehension of that abstract conception, the *Right* of Property; or from a very imperfect notion of that balanced *jural* Condition of Society, in which Rights are necessary. If a person deny the necessity of Property, perhaps his Error arises from some confused notion of *equality*, applied to the quantities of men's possessions, instead of the Rights of the possessors. If a man assert that buying and selling men is not immoral, his Error may arise from a very defective conception of *Humanity*, the brotherhood of man to man; as we shall afterwards endeavour to show. In these and the like cases, it may be difficult for some men to avoid those imperfect and confused notions which thus lead to Errors, that are, in themselves, contrary to Reason.

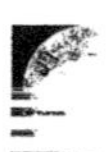

449. And this imperfection and confusion of moral notions is, in some measure, augmented and extended by the use of Moral Terms, as it prevails among men. For while many men's notions are thus defective and obscure, and on that account, as well

as on others, different, under the same name; men reason as if the same Term always meant the same Conception, and thus fall into Error. Abstract and general Terms are not only marks of our Conceptions, and thus, helps to the memory in reasoning; they are also our instruments of Reasoning. Without the names of Conceptions, we cannot reason at all; and hence, if the names are applied in a confused and variable manner, we are led to false and inconsistent Principles. Principles are established and assented to, in one sense of their Terms; and then, they are applied and urged upon our assent, in another sense. And this cause may make a man inconsistent, even with himself; for we often remember and refer to Principles expressed in words, when we do not clearly retain in our minds the meaning of the Terms which they involve. This confused use of Terms, by ourselves and those around us, leads to many Moral Errors. We live in an atmosphere of Language, by which we see Moral Truths obscured and distorted. But still we must recollect, that without the use of Language, we should not be able to see Moral Truths at all; as without an atmosphere we should have no daylight.

450. Language is not only thus a source of moral obscurity and inconsistency difficult to be avoided; but also, a source of Prejudices; for it subjects our minds to the influences of those with whom we share the habitual use of language; our families, our educators, our class, our nation. These Influences are Causes of Error difficult to avoid.

451. It will be well to recollect this, in order that we may abstain from applying to men, on account of the Express Principles which they assert, and which are contrary to true Moral Principles, that condemnation, which properly belongs to immoral Operative Principles. If, indeed, men carry out immoral Principles into immoral actions, we can

not be mistaken in condemning them. In that case, there must be something worthy of condemnation. But if, while they assert Principles, which, in their expression, are immoral, the acts which they bring forth, as examples of their Principles, are kind, just, true, pure and orderly; we may rather suppose that there is, not so much any distinct immorality in their Principles, as understood by themselves; but rather some confusion in their language, or some incoherence in their generalizations.

For, though opinion leads to practice, and false opinion seems to be the first step to wrong action; there is, in the nature of man, a very general inconsistency, which prevents this connexion from being at all certain or universal. Men who hold false general opinions, compensate an error of belief, by another error, of reasoning; and derive, from false speculations, blameless or moral Rules of Practice. The recollection that this may be so, should temper, not the promptitude of our rejection of false opinions, but the vehemence of our condemnation of those who hold these opinions.

452. So to abstain from condemning seemingly wrong Principles, is to *tolerate* them; and this *Duty of Toleration* is incumbent upon us, as we have just seen, in virtue of the imperfection of the human Faculties, and their general insufficiency for the task of constructing, in each man's mind, a perfect connected system of Moral Truth. And thus, we are led to pronounce that *Ignorance and Error, especially with regard to very general and abstract Principles, are to be tolerated.*

453. Further: Ignorance and Error, on moral subjects, may arise, not only from the imperfection of the human Faculties, but also from external Circumstances, as Education, and the defects of the National Standard of Morality. These exert an influence upon our minds, through the use of language

as we have said (450); and in other ways. The Ignorance and Error thus arising are not absolutely unavoidable; for every man may raise, by moral self-culture, his standard of Morality above that of his Education, or of his Nation; but they are difficult to avoid; for the very power of self-culture is affected by the Habits of youth, and by the national customs. Hence, we may consider the Ignorance and Error, which arise from such causes, as *difficultly vincible*: and as in some measure, involuntary. Hence, such Ignorance and Error excuse, in some degree, the transgression of Moral Rule, which they occasion. They do not remove altogether, but they diminish the blame. A youth of a savage nation, who has been bred up to look upon theft as innocent or meritorious, does not incur the same moral stain by praising an act of theft, as a boy who has been brought up amid a strict respect for property. But then, on the other hand, the moral culture of the former is very imperfect. His moral nature is very scantily unfolded; his conscience is very dark. This, as we have said, is a calamity, if it be not a fault.

454. A further reason why Ignorance and Error, when they arise from external Causes, and are hardly avoidable, may be deemed to diminish the amount of the transgression, is, that in such cases, the moral defects of the character may often admit of remedy. The defective Moral Culture may afterwards be carried further onwards, by the help of external circumstances more favourable. A bad Education may be succeeded by a better. A low standard of Morality may be superseded by a higher, when this latter is brought before the mind. The dark conscience may be enlightened; and thus, the Ignorance and the Error may be in some measure removed. Hence, the interruption or inversion of the moral progress, produced or indicated by transgres-

sions, which take place in such a condition of Ignorance or Error, are not so great, nor their remedy so hopeless, as when the transgressions proceed more entirely from the internal character, without this influence of external causes. And thus, according to what was said respecting the amount of transgressions (353), offences, arising from such hardly avoidable Ignorance or Error, are diminished in their heinousness, by their being so occasioned.

455. Ignorance and Error may be considered under one other aspect, which it is important to attend to; namely, when they are *wilful*, or as it is sometimes termed by moralists, *affected*. Such would be, for instance, these cases: A man who will not examine the Title-deeds of his estate; because he fears to find that it is not his by Right: A man who will not enquire into the amount of his income; because he fears that, when he does so, he will discover the necessity of diminishing his expenses: A man who will not attend to the proofs of the immorality of a practice which he follows; for instance, slave-dealing; A man who, really believing that negroes have human faculties, pretends to believe that they have not, in order to justify his making slaves of them: and generally, A man who either refuses to attend to the proofs of his duties, because he does not intend to perform them; or who denies some proposition, merely because it would tend to establish the proof of such duties. Such *wilful and affected Ignorance does not*, in any degree, *excuse or exculpate* the transgressions which it accompanies. Indeed, it seems rather to aggravate them: for it adds to the moral regression which the offence implies, a perversion of the intellect, adopted with a view to a consistency in immorality.

It may be thought, perhaps, that assumed or affected Ignorance or Error should be spoken of as an Offence against Truth; that is, against Truthfulness: and in

Right to land in England. The National Right is not the result, but the origin of the Right of individuals. And in like manner, of other National Rights. England, as a State, may make war upon France; and in the course of war, may kill Frenchmen, and seize French possessions. But an individual Englishman has no fraction of such a Right. Even if he declares that he will withdraw himself from a share in the national compact, and will act for himself, he is not allowed to do, on a small scale, what the nation does upon a large one. The Right of the State to make War, depends on its being the State; not on its being a Collection of Individuals.

470. The State is conceived as *one;* the Individuals of which it is composed being many: the State is conceived as *permanent*, while the individuals are born and die. Individuals derive, from the State, their Possessions, Privileges, and Condition, in the community; either directly, or by the State determining the Possessions, Privileges, and Condition of the Family, and the Laws of their derivation. The State, as a single permanent agent, in its proper functions, acts for the many constantly changing individuals, of which it consists. States have, with each other, intercourse of various kinds; making Treaties of Peace, Commerce, or Alliance with each other; and making War on each other, if the necessity arises. The State bounds the legal relations of the individual: the citizens of different states have no legal relations with each other, except through their States.

471. The State is, thus, the necessary Origin of all the Rights which exist within itself. It is an Authority, superior to all other Authorities; and from which they are all derived. This Supreme and Original Authority, thus residing in the State, is its *Sovereignty*. A state which is, in all its internal relations, independent of all other States, is a Sovereign

which assume the reality of a Universal Standard of right and wrong. They have not only Laws, which determine Rights and Obligations, but also current moral Precepts and Rules, which express the conceptions of Duties and Virtues. The assumed existence of a Standard of right and wrong shows itself in the sentiments which are associated with the conceptions and names of Virtues and Vices. Vices are, in all ages and countries, named only to be condemned. Violence, Fraud, Falsehood, Indecency, are objects of aversion at all times and places. There is no nation or language, which has not the means of expressing this; and none, which does not express it.

It is true, the actions, to which this aversion and condemnation are applied, are different in different ages and countries. In some countries, plunder of strangers, slavery, polygamy, have been regarded as blameless; to us, they are offences and vices. This difference arises from the diversity of the *Definitions of Rights* in different times and places: for, as we have seen, Rights are defined by Law, and Virtues and Duties depend upon Rights. Yet the variety of Laws, in various nations, does not prevent Rights from being a necessary element of man's condition; and in like manner, the diversity of Standards of Morality does not prevent Virtue from being a necessary object of man's approval; nor hinder Conscience, which recognizes Virtue, from being a universal attribute of mankind.

458. There must be, in all cases, a great connexion between the National Laws and the National Standard of Morality. Both the one and the other express that which is deemed right. Laws are enacted, or upheld, because it is considered right that they should be so. Actions also are approved or disapproved according as they are looked upon as right or wrong. And the consciences of individuals accommodate themselves, in a great measure, to the

law. If the national law allow polygamy, or slavery, the individual commonly practises it without self-condemnation. The exhortation of the National Moralist is, in the first place, To obey the Law. The National Moral Precepts take for granted the National Laws. The national conceptions of the various relations of society, as Property, Marriage, the Family, the State, and the like, which are the basis of the Laws, are also the basis of the Morals, of the Nation.

459. But though, in every Nation, Law and Morality are connected, they are, for the most part, not identical. The difference of Law and Morality, which we have noticed (105), is that which is generally understood: Law refers to definite external acts absolutely commanded or prohibited; Morality refers to internal springs of action; and as results of these, to acts of a less definite kind. The Precepts of Law are positive and absolute. The Precepts of Morality respecting actions, are *exemplary* and *relative*;—that is, they only *exemplify* the disposition from which the actions proceed; and they *refer* to the legal conditions of Society. The Precepts of Law, *Thou shalt not kill; Thou shalt not steal; Thou shalt not break thy promise*;—must be considered, in the first place, as fixed and absolute (105). The injunctions of Morality are to be understood as recognizing the authority of these commands; but as carrying the signification of them much further.

460. Law deals with matters external and visible, such as Objects of desire, (Things,) and Actions, and thus creates Rights. Morality has to do with matters internal and invisible; with Desires and Intentions, as well as with Laws and Rights. Desires and Intentions cannot be defined or described in any way, without some reference to Things and Actions; and therefore, cannot supply a basis of Morality independent of Law: and thus Morality, in the first place, is dependent upon Law. Rights afford the fixed

points by which moral positions are determined. Rights also supply some of the principal forces by which the moral sentiments produce their effect. Law affords a support to the frame-work of society; but Law does not suffice for the social life of man, without Morality. Law and Morality coincide in their general form and outlines; but Law is stiff and hard; Morality of a more flexible, yet more pervadingly active nature. Law is the rigid skeleton which Morality clothes with living flesh and acting muscles. Law supplies the fixed positions, on which the Machinery of Duty can rest, so as to move the world.

461. But though Morality rests upon Law, Law is subject to the Authority of Morality: Law is the Basis of Morality, but yet Morality is the Standard of Law. Law is fixed for the moment, and Morality supposes its fixity: but Morality is a supreme and eternal Rule, which Law must recognize. Law must always attempt to conform to Morality. Thus, though the Law is, in the first instance, assumed to be fixed, and though its commands are accepted as absolute and peremptory; it is not to be considered as entirely and finally unchangeable. The commands of Law are themselves liable to be judged of, as good or bad. They, and their application in particular cases, may be morally wrong, as well as right.

The Law itself acknowledges this. It puts forward its Rules and Definitions of Rights, as not absolutely fixed and universal. They admit of exceptions in extreme cases. In many such cases, there are special moral considerations, which counteract the general Reasons of the Rule, and suspend its operation. The Law, *Thou shalt not kill*, admits of exception in cases of self-defence, burglary, and the like (117): the Right of Property gives way in cases of necessity (156): and, in its general administration, the National Law either itself aspires to be the voice of Natural Justice, as the Roman Law did; or has, as in England, a jurisdiction of Equity combined with it, and proceeding by Rules of natural justice. Thus Law herself recognizes Justice, as a Standard to which she must conform her commands, and which her definitions cannot alter.

And thus, again, as Rights are to be used as instruments of Morality by individuals, so also are they by communities. Rights are built upon Law, but Law is to be subservient to Morality. Morality sanctions Law, but Law must perpetually seek the sanction of Morality. Moral Rules at first agree with Laws; but if the Moral Rules are improved, the Laws ought to follow the improvement.

462. We must consider some of the steps by which Moral Rules are improved. We have already stated, that among these steps, is the more exact Definition of some of the Conceptions, in terms of which Moral Rules are expressed. We shall now therefore proceed to consider, with a view to such a more exact determination of their import as our subject may require, some of the Conceptions of this kind; such, for instance, as The State, Justice, Humanity, Liberty, and the like.

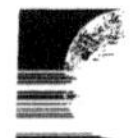

Such Conceptions, in the progress of nations, gradually become clearer and clearer among men. We may suppose that, at first, man's social and moral faculties are very imperfectly developed. His notions are mainly fastened upon objects of sense; his language refers, for the most part, to such objects. His moral conceptions are dim and vague; and the words by which they are indicated, are employed in a loose and wavering manner. Such is usually the case with all terms of moral import, in the earliest history of a language and of a nation. As the intellectual culture of the nation proceeds, abstract words are used with more precision; and in consequence, the conceptions, designated by such words, grow clearer in men's minds. Wide and general, as well as limited and narrow terms, are employed, in expressing those moral truths upon which moral precepts rest; and by which the characters of nations are unfolded and fashioned: nor can we say to what extent this intellectual and moral progress may proceed.

463. The intellectual progress of individuals follows nearly the same course, in these respects, as that of nations; although the steps of the progress may succeed each other with far greater rapidity. In consequence of the influence of the opinions of past generations upon the views of the present, through the working of literature, language, institutions, and traditions, each man's mind may pass in a short time, through successive modes of thought which, in the course of history, have been slowly unfolded one out of another. The intellectual revolutions of centuries are compressed into a few years of a man's youth; a man's moral conceptions, as they are in our time, are affected by those of the Greeks, of the Latins, and of the earlier times of our own country; not to speak here of the influence of Religion, greater than all the rest.

But though the intellectual progress of the individual is thus a compendium, and a very brief compendium, of the intellectual progress of man, the two careers are of the same kind;—a constant advance from the material to the abstract; from the particular to the general; but, in what is abstract and general, an advance from the dim and vague to the distinct and precise. And we now proceed to trace, in several instances, what the steps of this advance have been, in order to determine what they necessarily must be, and at what point we may consider ourselves as having arrived.

464. Among these steps, one of the first is the formation of a conception of a *Person*, as something having active and conscious Will and Thought, as we ourselves have: and differing, thus, from *Things*, which are unconscious and merely passive. We

have already remarked that this distinction of Persons and Things is one of the foundation-stones of man's moral nature (45).

Again; another important fundamental step in Morals, is the recognition of Things as belonging to Persons; to ourselves and others; the distinction of *meum* and *tuum* (129). This relation is at first indicated only by grammatical modifications denoting possession; such as the pronouns which have been mentioned. But Things, viewed under this aspect, are soon denoted by a general abstract Term, and are called *Property*.

Property is assigned to different persons by general Rules, and each man's Property is his *Right*. And in like manner, other Abstract Conceptions, vested as possessions in particular persons by general Rules, are Rights; as we have already said. This Conception of *Rights* is established among men, wherever there is settled and tranquil society.

Some of the succeeding steps in the progress of Moral Conceptions we must consider more in detail.

CHAPTER XX.

THE STATE.

465. In order to proceed in a distinct manner with our reasonings, we must have a Conception of *The State;* a conception which is one of the foundations of Morality (94). By the State, we mean the Community, as the Source of the Reality of Rights. The State implies a collection or aggregation of men: but it is not a mere Collection, like a herd of cattle, in which there are no Rights. The State implies Society: but not a voluntary association; for the State

is a necessary Society: man cannot exist out of such a Society. The State implies Rulers and Government: but the Rulers and the Government are not the State: for the State may change its Rulers and its mode of Government, and yet remain the same State. The State implies Laws; but the State is not the Laws; it is the Origin and Enforcer of the Laws: it is the Being whose mind and voice the Laws are. It may he said that the State, thus understood, is a mere Abstraction: but as we have all along seen, Moral Truths cannot be expressed but by Abstractions, and human life is governed by Abstractions. Law itself is an abstraction: Property, Power, Security, Life, the objects of human desire, are Abstractions: even Home, Food, Raiment, when we speak of them in the general way which moral reasonings require, are Abstractions. In like manner, the Family, the Tribe, are Abstractions; and the State is an extension of these Abstractions; including in the conception, some special attributes which belong to our subject; as for instance, that already mentioned; that the State gives reality to Rights, delivers and executes the Laws.

466. This conception prevailed from an early period. In the Jewish People, indeed, the Laws were God's Laws, supported by his sanction; and the conception of the State, as the origin of Law, was, among them, not brought into clear view. But the conception of the State as the origin of Rights and Obligations, was familiar among the Greeks. "It is manifest," says Aristotle*, "That the State (ἡ πόλις) is one of the Things which exist by nature: and that man is by nature an animal living in States (πολιτικὸν ζῶον, a political animal). A man belonging to no State, is less than man, or more. And thus we find in Homer, a savage man reviled as

* *Polit.* I. i.

ἀφρήτωρ, ἀθέμιστιος, ἀνέστιος.
A Tribeless, Lawless, Homeless Wretch." (Il. ix. 62.)

He further adds, "The State exists before the family or the individual, as the body exists before the members; for if the body do not exist, the hand or the foot is not really a hand or a foot." Where, as we find by the context, he means, that the State exists before the Individual, in the order of reasoning. The Conditions of the Individual's being, are to be derived from the Conditions of the State, and not reversely. The variety of forms of Government which prevailed among the Greek cities, and the changes of form which often succeeded each other in the same city, prevented the philosophers of that nation from confounding the State with the Governors, as was often done in long-enduring monarchies; while the strong constraint which the Laws, in many Grecian States, exercised over individual inclinations, made it unlikely that men should then view the State as a *voluntary* association; a doctrine which was adopted at a later period. That the State, notwithstanding this constraint, was an object of great reverence, not only as the Origin of Law, but the Teacher of Justice and Virtue, the reader of the Greek authors of the Republican time, will recollect abundant proofs. I may mention, for the sake of example, the expostulation which Socrates, in his dialogue with Crito, makes the State address to himself, on the supposition that he had attempted to escape from prison*.

467. The Romans were, in like manner, familiar with the conception of the State, as the condition of a society in which Rights exist. In Cicero's work *De Republicâ* he says†, "Est igitur Res publica res

* Plato. *Crito.* § 11.

† Lib. i. 25. The State, or the Commonwealth, is the Community: but a Community is not every assemblage of men, anyhow gathered together: but an assemblage connected by agreement respecting Rights, and common participation of Advantage

populi: populus autem, non omnis hominum cœtus, quoquo modo congregatus: sed cœtus multitudinis juris consensu et utilitatis communione sociatus."

468. The Conception of the State became, in later times, less clear and steady. The creation and destruction of Kingdoms and States which took place between the epochs of Alexander and Augustus; the concentration of all the powers of the Roman Commonwealth in the Emperor: the separation of the Roman Empire into new kingdoms; the further subdivision of the powers of government which prevailed under the Feudal System; the nearly absolute power of Kings in most European countries;—all tended to unsettle and confuse in men's minds the Conception of the State. On the one side, men confounded the *King* with the State, and conceived that in him was the source of Law and Authority. And in opposition to this, there grew up, in modern times, opinions in which the doctrine of the State, as the source of Rights, was rejected; and Society was represented as a mere *Concourse of Individuals*. According to this doctrine, individuals compose a State by contributing, to a common stock, the Rights which they naturally possess; sharing the aggregate of such Rights among themselves by common consent; and establishing officers, to carry their agreement into effect.

469. This latter doctrine is quite untenable. Without the existence of a State, we have no Rights; nor can the Rights of the State be at all explained, by any aggregation of the Rights of Individuals. Has the State of England its Right to the National Territory by summing up in itself the Rights of individual Landholders? Or does not, rather, each Landholder derive his Right to his Property from the State? It is plain that the latter, not the former, is the case. The Right to Land is derived from the Law of *the Land;* that is the Law of the State. Independently of the Law of the Land, no man has a

Right to land in England. The National Right is not the result, but the origin of the Right of individuals. And in like manner, of other National Rights. England, as a State, may make war upon France; and in the course of war, may kill Frenchmen, and seize French possessions. But an individual Englishman has no fraction of such a Right. Even if he declares that he will withdraw himself from a share in the national compact, and will act for himself, he is not allowed to do, on a small scale, what the nation does upon a large one. The Right of the State to make War, depends on its being the State; not on its being a Collection of Individuals.

470. The State is conceived as *one;* the Individuals of which it is composed being many: the State is conceived as *permanent*, while the individuals are born and die. Individuals derive, from the State, their Possessions, Privileges, and Condition, in the community; either directly, or by the State determining the Possessions, Privileges, and Condition of the Family, and the Laws of their derivation. The State, as a single permanent agent, in its proper functions, acts for the many constantly changing individuals, of which it consists. States have, with each other, intercourse of various kinds; making Treaties of Peace, Commerce, or Alliance with each other; and making War on each other, if the necessity arises. The State bounds the legal relations of the individual: the citizens of different states have no legal relations with each other, except through their States.

471. The State is, thus, the necessary Origin of all the Rights which exist within itself. It is an Authority, superior to all other Authorities; and from which they are all derived. This Supreme and Original Authority, thus residing in the State, is its *Sovereignty*. A state which is, in all its internal relations, independent of all other States, is a Sovereign

State. In the monarchies of modern Europe, the Supreme Power has been conceived as vested in the Monarch; and he has been looked upon as the origin of all other power. In such cases, the Monarch is termed the *Sovereign:* but in Republics, such as the United States of North America, no person is Sovereign. The term *Sovereign* has also been applied to the People; but a people, deprived of that organization which makes them a State, are not sovereign. They cannot exercise or impart authority. We can with no propriety speak of the *Sovereign People* of England; except we mean the State of England; and thus include King, Lords, and Commons, in the term *People:* if *People* denote individuals, without governors and magistrates, we can with no more propriety speak of the Sovereign People of England, than of the Sovereign People of Yorkshire. If the People of Yorkshire be not sovereign, because they are under the authority of England; the People of England are not sovereign, because, by the same rule, they are under the authority of King, Lords, and Commons. If there be any established Authority, the rule of such Authority determines where the Sovereignty resides. If we suppose all established authority annihilated, no body of men is sovereign over any individual; and each man is sovereign, with as good a Right as any other man or any collection of men.

472. If it be said that the People is really the Sovereign Authority, and the Source of Rights, because it is by the common consent of the People that the Supreme Authority is conferred upon the sovereign governors of the State: we reply, that such a transfer of sovereign power to governors, by the common consent of the members of a society, has very rarely taken place; and if in a few societies it have ever occurred, such uncommon and extraordinary events afford no grounds for the existence of Rights,

in communities in which nothing of the kind has ever taken place. And in the next place, we remark, that whenever a society have thus conferred supreme authority upon their governors by common consent, they have, in their actions, presupposed the existence of Rights derived from States. If a body of men, for instance, by common consent frame a government for the country in which they live; or for another country, which they have purchased, and into which they are migrating: they suppose, in the first instance, that the country is theirs as their native land; and in the second instance, as a purchase. But yet mere individuals alone cannot have such Property: for Property in land, as we have seen, and purchase of Land, for the like reasons, are creations of the Law.

473. Thus the Conception of a Sovereign State, as the origin and guardian of Rights, is necessary, in order that we may conceive Rights as realities. We may add, that the State is necessarily conceived as a Moral Agent; since it makes war and peace, which it may do justly or unjustly; keeps Treaties, or breaks them; educates its children, or neglects them. What are the Rules of Justice in the actions of States, we must afterwards consider: but it is plain that we must consider the State as an Agent, to whose conduct such Rules are applicable.

474. Since the State is thus a Moral Agent, we may apply to it the Rules of Duty, and the doctrines of Morality, which we have already established. The State has its Duties; Duties of Truth and Justice, as all agree; for all hold it to be the Duty of a State to observe its Treaties, to abstain from the Possessions of another State; and the like. A State has also Duties of Benevolence; to relieve its poor, to liberate its slaves, are often urged upon a State, as manifest Duties of this kind.

And, as the condition of other Duties being performed, the moral Education of its citizens, and consequently of itself, is a Duty of the State. It is its Duty to establish in the minds of its children, and to unfold more and more into constant and progressive operation, the Moral Ideas of Benevolence, Justice, Truth, Purity, and Order.

475. Thus Moral Progress is the Duty of States, as well as of individuals. States, like individuals, have a continuous existence; a series of purposes and actions; a connected course of being; a *Life*. During this Life, it is their Duty to conform their being more and more to the Moral Ideas; and this Duty extends to all their actions, and all times of their action.

CHAPTER XXI.

JUSTICE.

476. RIGHTS are, as we have formerly said, necessary conditions of man's action as man; and the State is the necessary origin and basis of Rights: the State defines them and realizes them. But though Rights are thus, in each case, what, by the State, they are defined to be; there is yet, in men's minds, a fundamental conviction, that Rights are not arbitrary. It is conceived that there is a higher Rule, to which Rights ought to conform; that they should be, not only *ordered*, but *just;* that there are not only positive Laws, enacted by special bodies of men, but a Natural Law, depending upon the nature of man.

This conception of Natural Law, appears among the Greek philosophers. "There are," says Aristotle*, "two kinds of Law; that which is proper to each community; and that which is common to all. For there is, as all men perceive more or less clearly,

* *Rhet* I. 13.

a Natural Justice and Injustice, which men in common recognize, even if they have no society nor compact with each other. Thus the Antigone of Sophocles is made to say, that it was right for her, in spite of the tyrant's command, to bury her brother Polynices, as a part of a Natural Law:

> " For this is no command of yesterday,
> But everliving Law, its source unknown."

The Books of the Laws of Plato proceed upon the same supposition; and are an attempt to draw out, in detail, the Code of Natural Law which was thus assumed to exist.

477. This Conception of a Natural Law, derived from Reason, and universally valid for all men, was still more distinctly entertained by the Romans. This appears in Cicero's Dialogues on the Laws in several places*, and still more emphatically in a passage in the work *De Republica*†: " Law is right Reason, congruous to Nature, pervading all minds, constant, eternal; which calls to Duty by its commands, and repels from wrong doing by its prohibitions; and to the good, does not command or forbid in vain; while the wicked are unmoved by its exhortations and warnings. This Law cannot be annulled, superseded, or overruled. No Senate, no People can loose us from it; no Jurist, no Interpreter, can explain it away. It is not one Law at Rome, another at Athens; one, at present, another at some future time; but one Law, perpetual and immutable, includes all Nations and all times‡."

The Law, thus described by Cicero, includes Justice, as well as Law. In the notion of Natural Law,

* *Legg.* I. 6; II. 4.

† *De Rep.* III. 22. quoted Lactant. *Inst.* VI. 8.

‡ I have omitted the concluding clause of the paragraph, " Of this Law the Author and Giver is God;" as belonging to another part of my subject.

the distinction of Obligations and Duties is not recognized.

478. But it may be said that the Natural Law, thus described by Cicero, nowhere exists. The actual Law is different at Rome and at Athens, and in every different State. And since the Natural Law, of which we speak, cannot be the same as *all* these Codes, it cannot be the same with *any;* and is actually nothing.

The reply to this difficulty is contained in what we have already said (95, 96); That the *Conceptions* of the Fundamental Rights, which Law establishes, are necessary and universal for all men; but that the *Definitions* of these Rights are Facts, which grow out of the History of each Community, and may be different in different times and places. The Second Book of this Work contains a view of this Natural Law; the Laws of Rome and of England being there employed, as exemplification, not as the necessary form, of Natural Law. We there saw, that in many instances, the Commentators on these Laws have announced Maxims of Natural Law, as the basis of the actual Law.

479. The Roman term, *Jus*, (in its sense of a body of Laws, and of Doctrines on which Laws depend), is especially adapted to denote this Natural Law; for it implies, at the same time, Law and Justice (90). The consistency of the Law with Justice, is assumed throughout the Roman Jurisprudence. Thus in the commencement of the Institutes we read*: "Justitia est constans et perpetua voluntas jus suum cuique tribuendi. Jurisprudentia est divinarum atque humanarum rerum scientia, justi atque injusti cognitio." But Justice, thus assumed as identical with

* *Inst.* I. 1. Justice is the constant and perpetual intention of giving to each his own Right. Jurisprudence is the knowledge of divine and human things, (as required for that intention): the science of what is just and unjust.

Jus in its results, is a conception which requires to be more exactly defined and developed than we have yet done, before we can so apply it. This we must now attempt to do.

480. As we have said, Law, in every form in which it exists, must involve actual Definitions, as well as the general Conception of Natural Law or Justice. These Definitions will depend upon past events. Thus, the tenure of land in each country depends upon past conquests, and migrations of the races which inhabit the country; upon many inheritances, many contracts of buying and selling, and the like, which have taken place among individuals: upon Laws which have been made, relative to such property, and such transfers; and upon various other circumstances. Justice gives to each his own; but the actual Law must define what is each person's own, according to all these circumstances. And the like may be said of all other branches of Natural Law.

481. According to our idea of Rights, as assigned by Natural Law, each person must have those Rights which it is just he should have. A person cannot have Rights which it is unjust he should have. If the actual Laws of any State give him such Rights, those Rights are unjust; and that they are so, is a reason for altering the Law, or its application. If a man has acquired a seeming Right, in violation of Justice, Natural Law rejects such Rights. According to Natural Law, *Rights cannot be founded on Injustice.*

482. On the other hand, existing Rights, in each country, as we have seen, depend upon its History: and the History of every country contains many acts of injustice. It cannot be doubted that the present Rights of Property in Land, for instance, have, in every country, been brought into being by transactions, many of which have been unjust. Shall we

say that Justice requires us to deprive persons of such Rights, when any Injustice can be discovered in their origin or transmission; however remote may be the blemish, and however blameless the present holders? If an estate were acquired by fraud centuries ago, and have since been possessed, without dispute, by generations of unconscious successors; or sold to a multitude of poor and honest purchasers; shall we say that it still, in Justice, belongs to the heirs of the defrauded person; and that, according to Natural Law, the present possessors ought to restore the property to those heirs? No one, probably, would assert it to be just to destroy supposed existing Rights on such grounds as these. All would allow that Justice is, in such a case, with the Possessors.

483. Indeed, to assert the contrary, would be to make that Law of Descent, by which the heirs of the defrauded person might claim the property, paramount over all other Laws. It would be to make that Rule of inheritance absolute and indestructible, while other Rules, as for instance, *bonâ fide* purchase, prescription, and the like, are comparatively rejected. There can be no reason, in Natural Law, for erecting any one Rule of Derivation of Rights into this absolute Supremacy over all others.

484. Thus the maxim, that Rights cannot be founded in Injustice, is not to be applied in such a way as to make every past Injustice overturn present possession. Injustice is an arbitrary act, done in disregard of Rule and Reason. Justice abhors all that is arbitrary; for it requires all things to be done according to Reason, and therefore, according to Rule. But then, the Law of Inheritance is an arbitrary thing, as well as the Act of Fraud. The Law of Inheritance is quite different in different countries; and might, in this country, have been different from what it is, if the Law had so ordered it. Justice accepts, in general, the Law of Inheritance, as her Rule; yet

not absolutely, as Supreme, but relatively, as a means to her end. Justice annuls, in general, the Effect of acts of Fraud; but still, not without limit in the contemplation of *Effects;* but only, so far as the condemnation of such effects is a means to her end. Justice cannot diregard the existing state of possessions, and turn her attention only to their origin. She cannot found her sentence on one particular past event, and take no account of the more recent events and the present conditions. On the contrary, it is the present with which she has especially to do. She has to pronounce upon existing Rights, as to whether they are valid or not; and she must look at them, as they exist. And hence, as a balance to our former maxim, we must lay down this: *Justice assigns Rights according to existing conditions.*

485. Thus Justice rejects that which is arbitrary, alike in the past and in the present. She condemns the ancient fraud, from which the present possession is derived: she limits the Rule of inheritance, on which the opposing present claim is founded. She pronounces that no Right can be founded in Injustice: but she pronounces the Right of the present holders to be founded, not on the ancient Injustice, but on the recent transactions; which are free from the stain of Injustice, and by which the ancient stain may be diluted or obliterated. A thing unjustly acquired, may, by long undisturbed possession, and *bonâ fide* tenure, become a just property: and accordingly, so the Laws of States decide (151).

486. The opposition of the two maxims respecting Justice, which have just been stated, is a result of the universal opposition of Ideas and Facts which exists in every subject of Thought (97). In the *Idea,* Justice cannot admit of anything arbitrary; for what is arbitrary is unjust. In the *Fact,* every transaction must have in it something arbitrary, for it must depend upon external circumstances, which are not

governed by our Ideas. In Idea, Justice would assign Property without regard to previous possession; but in Fact, by rejecting the regard to previous possession it ceases to be Property.

The same opposition may be remarked, in other parts of Natural Law. In Idea, for instance, Justice requires that all classes of men should have equal Rights: but in Fact, men form themselves into Classes, and by that very act make their Rights unequal. In Idea, men should make and perform their Contracts according to perfect Equality; but in Fact, the Terms of the Contract must be regarded by Justice, because Equality is too obscure and indefinite a foundation for a just decision. And the like may be said in other cases.

487. The Steps by which the Conception of Justice has been unfolded and defined among men, have involved a recognition of both the maxims which have been stated. The Laws of all Countries annul Rights acquired in violent and illegal ways; and the Laws of all Countries allow undisturbed Possession, in the sincere belief of Right, to give, at least in some cases, and after some lapse of time, a complete Right. To all men, when the origin of existing Rights is shown to be some violent and unjust act, the Rights appear to be unjust. But when it is shown, on the other hand, that the traces of this arbitrary origin are only such as inevitably exist in all Rights, the Rights again seem just. When we consider how greatly the existing tenure of Land, in this country, depends upon the violent confiscations which took place in the Norman Conquest, the Rights of many of our landlords may appear to be unjust. But when we recollect that the Saxons, whom the Normans conquered, had themselves obtained possession of the land by a similar conquest; and that the transactions respecting property in England have, for nearly eight hundred years, assumed the validity

of the Rights acquired by the Norman Conquest; we see that it would be unjust to fix our attention on that particular event, as especially vitiating Rights.

488. The remoteness of an act of violence in point of time; the complexity of the events which have succeeded it; the degree in which it has faded into oblivion; the habit of disregarding it established in the community;—all these, are circumstances which make it just to disregard the bearing of the event upon existing Rights. Every circumstance, by which the effect of a past event upon men's thoughts and actions is enfeebled, makes it less of a reality in the present condition of things; and therefore, less an element for consideration in the assignment of Rights according to justice.

489. What has now been said, agrees with what was said formerly (218) in speaking of the Idea of Justice; namely, that though, in general, Justice is determined by Law, the Law must be framed in accordance with Justice. Justice is directly and positively determined by Law; for a man's just Rights are those which the Law gives him. The Law must be framed in accordance with Justice; and must therefore reject all that is arbitrary and unequal, as soon as it is seen to be so. Hence the Law, in order that it may accord with Justice, may be changed from time to time, in proportion as different external facts are made objects of attention. For instance, if one State, (suppose Helos,) act with great violence and cruelty towards another; (suppose Sparta;) it may be just in Sparta, to punish Helos, by reducing its citizens to a condition of subjection, and depriving them of their property. But after several generations, when the transgression is fallen into oblivion, it would be unjust to make any Laws, on the ground of such transgression. When such a time has arrived, it may be just to make laws, in or-

der to render the condition of the Helots less subject; or in order to restore to them their territory.

490. On this imaginary case, we may make one or two further remarks. It may be objected to the above statement, that it cannot be just to punish a whole State for the offence of some of its citizens; still less to continue the punishment to succeeding unoffending generations. And this is true, so far as such a remark can be applied, consistently with the nature of Punishment, and of a State. But when one State is injured by another, it must deal with the offending State as a whole; and it cannot extend its regard to individuals, in such a manner as would render impossible the punishment of injuries done by the State. If individuals have offended against a foreign State; and if the State to which they belong, refuses to punish them, or to give them up; it makes itself a party to their wrong. And when, on this ground, a penal infliction takes place, this infliction must operate alike on the offenders and their fellow-citizens; alike on those citizens who were in being at the time of the wrong, and on succeeding generations. For the State, according to the conception of it, is a collective and perpetual body (470); its condition is communicated to contemporary and to successive members of it, by their being Members. In this, there is no injustice; any more than there is in the transmission of the Possessions, or of the Rank of a Family, to its Members, and to successive generations. Nations derive their prosperous or adverse condition from their history, and from their transactions with other nations; and individuals, more or less, share in the prosperous or adverse condition of the nation.

491. States have not, nor can have, any way of punishing Injuries, or of asserting their Rights against other States, except War. They have no common Superior Tribunal to which they can appeal

(214): and they can seek Justice in no other way. Also War would not answer its purpose, nor would it *be* War, if it did not produce some inconvenience to the vanquished State, and consequently to its citizens. Innocent citizens must be involved with the guilty, in the punishment; as the children of a guilty parent are necessarily involved in his punishment.

With regard to the seizure of the Property of the vanquished by the victorious State; it may further be remarked, that the citizens of the vanquished State derived Rights from their State; and that, therefore, they necessarily lose their Rights, when their State loses its power of maintaining Rights*.

It is not therefore necessarily unjust that there should take place, between States, acts of violence, which affect, through succeeding generations, the distribution of property and the relation of classes. The possibility of such events, is a necessary condition of the existence of States. The Actions of States, as of individuals, produce permanent consequences. If they did not do so, questions of justice and injustice respecting such actions would be of little importance.

492. But if such violent events have at some time taken place, must their consequences remain unchanged? If calamities have been inflicted by one nation upon another, even as a just punishment; does justice require these inflictions to be perpetuated without limit? If a nation have been enslaved and despoiled, even for their wrongs, may not the time come when they may be restored to freedom and property? We reply, in accordance with what has been said, that in proportion as the traces of the wrong are obliterated in men's minds, Justice will aim at obliterating them in their condition also. The privations and subjection of the subjugated class, so soon

* Such maxims may be much mitigated in practice by International Law, as we shall see hereafter.

as they cease to be looked upon as penal, appear as arbitrary, and therefore unjust. As soon as the inequality appears as an arbitrary one, Justice requires that it shall be removed.

But then, no present inequality can be quite arbitrary, because every actual inequality depends upon the Laws and Habits by which the present is derived from the past; and such Laws and Habits are requisite, in order that there may be, between the present and the past, that connexion which the continuity of the Life of States (475) requires. The Events of History have, at every step, led to present inequalities; to a difference of high and low, rich and poor. Justice does not require that we should abolish all such distinctions; for to do this, would be to abolish Rights, the necessary conditions of Justice. What then is the course which Justice prescribes?

493. We answer, that *Justice requires us to aim constantly to remedy the inequalities which History produces.*

We do not say that Justice requires us to *restore* any previous condition which has been unjustly changed, but to *remedy* the effects of the change. For, in fact, a previous State of things never can be restored; and when a change takes place, then, after a short time has elapsed, there have grown up, under the new State of things, new Rights, which it would be unjust to annul. What has once happened, can never cease to have happened. In the course of a nation's history, what has been done, cannot be undone. We may do something of an opposite tendency; and when what has been done was unjust, it is just to do something to remedy the injustice. If we are asked whether the consequences of events are to be perpetual; we may answer, that the consequences of events *are* perpetual; but that the consequence of a second event may counteract those of a former one. And we pronounce that such a second event ought to

take place, when there exist inequalities, originating in the injustice of a former event.

494. Such remedying of Injustice is a part of the general Duty of Moral Progress, which belongs to States as well as to individuals (475). We have already said, that the Law must perpetually and slowly tend to the Idea of Justice. We now see further the import of this assertion. The Law must tend *slowly* towards Justice, because the influence of the Facts of History upon existing Rights must always be great: and it is not just to disregard this influence. The influence itself is, however, weakened by the lapse of time, and the intervention of new events. It is the Duty of men to act justly, in these new events: it is the Duty of States, to make just Laws, in reference to the new aspect which those new events give to history. And Justice, thus, and History as regulated by Duty, constantly, but slowly, mould each other.

495. Again, the Law must tend *perpetually* towards Justice: that is, its progress in that direction can never be looked upon as terminated. For the influence of the past Facts of History upon Law, though constantly wearing out, can never be quite obliterated. Even if, in all present events, men did act justly and legislate justly, still there would remain traces of the ancient order of things. For instance, the distribution of landed property at present must always continue to depend upon the original and ancient migrations of mankind, by which each Nation became possessed of its present territory; and upon many succeeding events; some of which have been acts of Injustice. The administration of Law, and the progress of Legislation, can never obliterate the effect of these bygone arbitrary and unjust acts; while new arbitrary and unjust acts are constantly happening. Thus Law, who must constantly travel onwards towards Justice, must always have some part

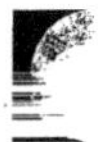

of her journey still to perform. Or to use another image: the pure waters of Justice are constantly poured into the mingled stream of the Law, in order to purify it; but we cannot hope to see the time when all the impurities which the latter has collected, in its passage through the realms of History, shall have disappeared; and the clear united current shall flow on indistinguishable.

And thus both the maxims which have been stated retain their truth and validity. *Right cannot be founded on Injustice:* such is the negative maxim which serves to define the Idea of Justice. *Justice assigns Rights according to existing Conditions:* such is the positive maxim which makes Justice applicable to Facts.

We have taken the exemplification of the conditions of Justice from imaginary relations between States, because in such a case there is not, as in all transactions between individuals there is, a mixture of the considerations of Law, with the question of Justice. But still Justice, as distinguished from Law, is to be considered in questions between individuals The term employed to designate Justice in this point of view, is *Equity*.

CHAPTER XXII.

EQUITY.

496. Equity derives its Name from *Equality;* and in the Conception, also, is understood to imply, in some way, equal advantages assigned to the parties contemplated. In this sense, attempts have been made, at various periods, to introduce the Conception of Equity, as explanatory of, or supplementary to, the Conception of Justice. It will be found that this mode

of conceiving Equity, has led to some maxims which are worthy of notice.

Aristotle* says that Inequality is one kind of Injustice; and that Injustice is to be remedied by Equality;—by Equality of Ratios, in Distributive Justice;—by Equality of Shares, in Corrective Justice. Thus Distributive Justice makes A's share be to B's share as A's right is to B's right: Corrective Justice takes from A, the wrong doer, and gives to B, who is wronged. But this view of the equality which constitutes Justice is partial and fanciful: it cannot be extended to cases in general. Still, there is a notion of Equality, as a kind of Justice. Cicero says†, "Jus constat ex his partibus, Natura, Lege, Consuetudine, Judicato, *Bono et Æquo*, Pacto." This expression *Bono et Æquo* was familiarly used in this sense by the Roman Lawyers. Thus Ulpian‡, "Jus est Ars Boni et Æqui." And this notion of equal justice has been carried into some detail. Thus Grotius makes Equality the Rule of Contracts§; they require equality of knowledge; equality of liberty; and, within certain limits, equality of advantage.

497. Justice and Equity, originally conceived as identical, in the course of time were separated; for Justice, in its administration, was necessarily fixed and limited by Laws and Rules; while Equity was conceived as not so limited. And as Laws and Rules, however much meant to be just, and however carefully constructed, will yet press upon individual cases in a way which seems hard; Equity was conceived as that kind of Justice which was not thus bound by Laws and Rules, and which was disposed to relieve such hardships. The Virtue which exists

* *Eth. Nich.* v. 2.

† *Ad Herenn.* II. 13. Jus consists of these portions; Natural Law, Positive Law, Custom, Decisions, Equity, Contract.

‡ *Dig.* I. i. 1. § *B. et P.* II. xii. 8.

in such a disposition, is termed by Aristotle*, Ἐπιείκεια; and he defines it to be, The Correction of the Law, where it is defective by reason of its universality. The Law, he says, is necessarily universal in its expressions: but some things cannot rightly be expressed universally. There is a defect, not in the Law, nor in the Lawgivers; but in the nature of things. And the ἐπιείκες, or *equitable*, is opposed to the ἀκριβοδικάιον, or *rigidly just*. The same opposition is repeatedly recognized in the Roman Law. Thus†, "Placuit in omnibus rebus præcipuam esse justitiæ æquitatisque, quam stricti juris rationem." And in another place‡, "Hæc Æquitas suggerit, etsi jure deficiamur." And the Prætor's judicial office was sometimes described as if its object were to administer Equity in this sense§: "Jus Prætorium est quod Prætores introduxerunt, adjuvandi, vel supplendi, vel corrigendi juris civilis gratiâ, propter utilitatem publicam." Similar functions have often been ascribed to the Jurisdiction of the Court of Chancery in England. Thus Bacon, on occasion of assuming the office of Chancellor, says||, "Chancery is ordained to supply the Law, not to subvert the Law:" and Chancellor Finch says, that the nature of Equity is to amplify, enlarge, and add to the letter of the Law. This has sometimes been stated by saying, that Equity decides¶ "de rebus quas Lex non exacté definit, sed arbitrio *boni viri* permittit."

* *Eth. Nich.* v. 10.

† *Codex.* III. 1. 8. It has been thought good that regard be had to Justice and Equity, rather than to strict Rights.

‡ *Dig.* xxx. iii. 2. 5. This is suggested by Equity, although Law fails us.

§ *Dig.* I. 1. 7. Prætors' Law is that which the Prætors have introduced, for the public good, for the sake of helping out, supplementing, and correcting the Civil Law.

|| Bacon's Works, IV. 488.

¶ Grot. *De Æquitate.* Concerning things which the Law does not exactly define, but leaves tot he discretion of a good man

498. But this description of Equity is too vague to be applicable; and has not been really accepted and acted upon in the administration of Justice, either in Rome or in England. For a Justice, administered, not according to Rules, but according to the immediate aspect of each case, would be deficient in the first requisite of Justice, that of being consistent with itself. We have already said (339), that Rules are necessary in Morality, to subdue the temptations of special cases; they are especially necessary as regards Justice, to correct the delusive aspect of particular cases. To leave the decision of cases to the conscience of the Judge, however wise and good, would lead to those arbitrary decisions which Justice especially abhors. In this view, Selden's condemnation of Equity is deserved*; "For Law we have a measure, and we know what to trust to. Equity is according to the Conscience of him who is Chancellor; and as that is larger or narrower, so is Equity. 'Tis all one as if they should make the standard for the measure the Chancellor's foot. What an uncertain measure would this be!" Since Morality is governed by fixed Rules, Equity, which is a part of Morality, must also have its fixed Rules. And as the Rules of Law are the foundations of Justice, the Rules of Equity cannot be in general inconsistent with those of Law.

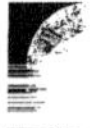

499. Accordingly, the Prætor's power did not extend to the overthrow or disregard of the written Law. When the law was applicable, the Prætor was to stand by it†; and we find such remarks as this‡: "Quod quidem perquam durum est; sed ita lex scripta est." Nor does a Court of Equity in England decide differently from a Court of Law, ex-

* *Table Talk.*

† Story. *Commentaries on Equity*, p. 6.

‡ *Dig.* xl. ix. 12. 1. This is very hard: but this is the written law.

cept in cases which involve circumstances to which a Court of Law cannot advert. Equity, as we have said, has its Maxims; and one of the first of these Maxims is*, *Æquitas sequitur Legem;* Equity follows the Law.

500. Nor does Jurisprudential Equity fill up the measure of the description of Moral Equity, that it *abates the rigour of the Law.* Blackstone has shown how far this is from being a description of the Equity of English Courts. No such power of abating the rigour of Law, he says, is contended for by the Court of Chancery†. The Law is rigorous, which declares that land which a man bequeaths to a legatee shall not, after his death, be liable to simple contract debts, even if the debt be for money employed in purchasing this very land. The Law is rigorous which commands that the father shall never immediately succeed as heir to the land of the son: yet in these cases, a Court of Equity can give no relief. Jurisprudential Equity, therefore, does not extend to Cases of legal hardship in general.

501. In a certain sense, however, and to a certain extent, Equity does supply defects in the Law. Equity, as a branch of Jurisprudence, must, like all branches of Jurisprudence, act by definite Processes, and according to fixed Rules. But the Processes and the Rules of Equity Jurisprudence, came into being, at first, as remedies to the defects of Law: and though, by being reduced to a fixed form and settled maxims, they can no longer be appealed to as remedies for all hardships and defects of Law, they have still a remedial and suppletory character.

This agrees with the account which the best authorities give of the origin of the Equitable Jurisdiction of the Court of Chancery in England. In the Common or traditional Law of England, the process of an action began by certain writs or documents of

* Story *Eq.* † *Comm.* III. 430.

prescribed form, which were issued from the King's Chancery, on application made there; and which brought the action into the Courts of Common Law. The Chancellor, therefore, (according to Lord Hardwicke,) when any petition for such a writ was referred to him, was the most proper judge, whether such a writ could be framed and issued, as might furnish an adequate relief to the party; and if he found the Common Law remedies deficient, he might proceed according to the extraordinary power committed to him by the reference*; "Ne Curia Regis deficeret in justitiâ exercendâ." Thus the exercise of an equitable jurisdiction by the Chancellor, arose from his being the Officer to whom applications were made, for writs on which to ground actions at the Common Law. Where that Law afforded no remedy, he was led to extend a discretionary remedy; and thus, the forum of Common Law and the forum of Equity were separated in England†.

502. It is not necessary to prosecute further our account of *Jurisprudential* Equity; since our business is rather with *Moral* Equity. And by tracing the course of the development of this Conception, as we have now stated it, we are able to give a connected account of this moral quality. We may accept, as a starting point, Aristotle's Definition: Equity is a Correction of Law where it is defective by reason of its universality. But Equity itself must proceed by fixed Laws, otherwise it would be defective in consistency. As the Rules of Equity thus become fixed, Equity ceases to be able to correct all the defects of Law; and becomes itself, as Law was at first, an imperfect expression of Justice; and thus we have, in the notion of Equity, a recognition of two Maxims to a certain extent opposite to each

* Lest the King's Court should be deficient in administering justice.

† Story. *Eq.* 44.

other; that *Fixed Rules are requisite for the expression of Justice:* and that *No Fixed Rules can so completely express Justice, but that the conception of Justice will, in some particular cases, seem to require exceptions to the Rules.*

503. The administration of Equity has led to the currency of many Maxims, which may be considered Maxims of Moral, as well as Jurisprudential Equity; since their acceptance in the Courts of Law has been due to their presumed agreement with Justice. We may notice some of these Maxims; not as being always universally true, or free from doubt and difficulty in their application; but as bringing forwards some of the points on which Equity must principally depend; and as showing, by examples, the kind of *Equality* in which it consists. Among such maxims are the following.

504. *Æquitas sequitur legem;* "Equity follows the Law." And this may be understood in two senses; either that Equity is based upon the Relations which the Law establishes; or that Equity follows the Analogy of the Law. We have already said, that Justice assumes the Definitions of Rights which Law gives. Hence Equity supposes *that* to be a man's Property, that to be a Marriage, that to be a Contract, which the Law makes such. Yet if there be merely some formal defect in a Contract, moral Equity will still hold it valid. Again, Equity follows the Analogy of Law; thus in England, where the Law gives the whole landed property to the eldest son, that would not be an equitable decision which should divide the property amongst the children equally.

505. *In equali jure melior est conditio possidentis;* "Where Rights are equal, Possession is a ground of preference." As if two persons have been equally innocent, and equally dilligent, the one in trying to recover a property lost by fraud; the other

in transacting a *bonâ fide* purchase of the property; he who is in possession is preferred.

But there are other maxims, which throw the task of judging of deficiencies in the property on one side especially: for instance, in matters which are apparent on due examination, the Rule is *Caveat emptor*, Let the buyer take care of himself (172).

506. *Qui sentit onus, sentire debet et commodum; qui sentit commodum, sentire debet et onus;* "He who bears the burthen ought to receive the profit; he who reaps the profit ought to bear the burthen." Thus, if a man, dying, leaves his wife pregnant, so that it is uncertain who will be heir to his lands; if the next presumptive heir, in the mean time, sow the land, it is equitable that the harvest also shall be his. And on the other hand, they who enjoy the benefit of any improvement of land arising from public works; as, for instance, from a general drainage; ought to contribute to the expense of the works.

507. There are other maxims which refer to the general responsibility of actions, as for instance, *Necessitas non habet legem;* "Necessity has no law;" which we have referred to in speaking of cases of necessity (418). And again: *Qui facit per alium facit per se;* "What a man does through the agency of others is his act." Others refer to the mode of interpreting Laws or Contracts, and administering Justice: as, *Expressio unius est exclusio alterius;* "The mention of one person is the exclusion of another." *Nemo debet esse judex in propriâ causâ;* "A man is not to be judge in his own cause." All these maxims may be looked upon as indications and fragments of a supposed Natural Law: which can never be expressed except by indications and fragments; since, as we have said, no Rules can express Equity, so as not to require exceptions.

508. Other Indications of the assumed existence of a Natural Law, the necessary result of Jus-

tice and Equity, may be traced in expressions, which are often used in moral and political discussions. Thus, we hear of the *Natural Rights* of man; and as examples of these, of the *Right to Subsistence*, the *Right to Freedom*, and the like. In speaking of these Rights as *Natural*, it is not meant that they are universally recognized by the Laws of States. In truth, Rights of the citizens to Subsistence and to Freedom, are so far limited and modified by the Laws of most States, that they can hardly be said to exist as *general* Rights. By speaking of such *Rights*, and describing them as the dictates of *Natural Justice*, as is often done, it is meant that the Laws *ought* to recognize and establish them. But something more than this seems to be meant, by speaking of the *Natural Right* to Subsistence, and the like; for to say that such a Right is what the Law *ought* to establish, is merely to class the recognition of this Right with all the other prudential improvements, of which the Laws of any State are susceptible. The Laws *ought* to aim at securing the Purity and Rationality, as well as the Subsistence, of the people. By speaking of the Claim of men to Subsistence as a *Right*, it appears to be meant that it is not only conformable to the Duty of States, in the general sense in which it is their Duty to make their laws constantly better; but that it is conformable to Justice in some more special sense, in which Justice is expressed by definite and universal Principles.

509. Yet the Principles of Justice which have been propounded as the basis of the Natural Rights of Men, are such as it is difficult to establish, in a definite and universal form. It has, for instance, been said, that *All men are born equal.* But it is evident that this is not true as a fact. For not only are children, for a long time after birth, necessarily in the power of parents and others; but the external conditions of the society in which a man is born, as

the laws of property and the like, determine his relation to other men, during life. If it be said that these are extraneous and accidental circumstances, not born with the man; we answer, that if we reject from our consideration, as extraneous and accidental, all such conditions, there remains nothing which we can call intrinsic and necessary, but the material conditions of man's existence; and if we were to adopt this view, the principle might more properly be stated, *All men are equally born.* The relations of Family, Property, and the like, are as essential to man's moral being, as Language, without which his mind cannot be unfolded to the apprehension of Rules, and the distinction of right and wrong. If therefore our assumed equality rejects the former circumstances, it must reject the latter.

510. But though in Fact men are not born equal, they are all born with a capacity for being moral agents: and this Idea is the basis of all Morality. And we may lay it down as a universal Principle, from which we may hereafter reason, that *All men are moral beings.*

This Principle may be perhaps considered as rather a Principle of Humanity, than a Principle of Justice. For this, and any other Principle from which we derive the claims of men to Subsistence, Freedom, &c., must involve a recognition of that Common Human Nature, by which all mankind are bound together. We shall therefore treat of such Rights in treating of the Conception of Humanity.

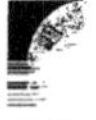

CHAPTER XXIII.

HUMANITY.

511. It has already been stated, that a universal Benevolence towards all men, as partakers of the

same Common Human Nature with ourselves, is a part of the Supreme Law of human being. But the lapse of time, the growth of institutions, and the development of man's moral nature, are requisite to bring this affection into its due prominence. The affections of men, in a rude condition, are confined within narrower limits; and have, for their main or sole objects, the persons who are bound to them by especial ties. The family affections which connect parent and child, husband and wife, brothers and sisters, have their force in every form of human society. The sympathies which bind together a kindred in a wider sense, the feelings of clanship, are powerful, in communities in which a more comprehensive kind of benevolence is unfelt. In rude and half-savage tribes, in which clansmen assist each other with unbounded zeal, the stranger is looked upon as naturally an object of enmity. The historians of Greece and Rome notice indications of this having been the early condition of man's feelings in those countries. But the progress of the culture of those nations led to a more moral state of the affections. The Greeks had a name for the Love of man as man. This affection they termed φιλανθρωπία, and reckoned it a virtue. Aristotle expresses this* by saying that all men have a feeling of kindred and good-will to all. And the Stoics called this tie of general good-will by a name borrowed from the word which Aristotle here uses (οἰκείωσις), as *kindness* is connected with the word *kin*. The Romans in like manner, though at first they had but one word to designate a stranger and an enemy (*hostis*), came to be sensible of the universal bond of good-will which unites man to man. They received with applause the verse of Terence:

> Homo sum: humani nihil a me alienum puto.
> A man am I, and feel for all mankind.

* *Anth. Eth. Nich.* VIII. 1. ὡς οἰκεῖον ἅπας ἄνθρωπος ἀνθρώπῳ καὶ φίλον.

And their philosophers followed the Greeks, in assuming the common social feeling of mankind as one of the foundations of their morality. Thus Cicero adopts, what he calls the *Formula* of the Stoics*: "Detrahere aliquid alicui, et hominem hominis incommodo suum augere commodum, magis est contra naturam quam mors, quam paupertas, quam cætera quæ possunt aut corpori accidere, aut rebus externis; nam principio tollit convictum humanum et societatem." In the same strain Seneca says†, "Societatem tolle, et unitatem generis humani quâ vita continetur, scindes."

512. The Roman conception, of a Law, identical with Natural Law, and yet the benefits of which were the peculiar privilege of Roman citizens, for a time impeded the application of such maxims; for men who had no right to justice, could have little claim to kindness. The current conception of a true marriage, as being limited to the union of Roman citizens, and of domestic slavery as being a part of the order of society, were circumstances unfavourable to the development of a benevolence equally embracing all men. But these circumstances gradually lost their hold on men's minds. The distinction of Roman and Provincial marriages faded away; and there grew up a feeling of horror towards the cruelty which slavery involved. We find a recognition of this view in the Roman Lawyers. Thus Ulpian says‡,

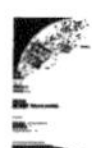

* *Off.* III. 5. For a man to abstract anything from another man, and to increase his own comfort by the discomfort of another, is more against Nature, than death, than poverty, than any other thing which can happen, either to his body or to his external havings. For in the first place it takes away human society and community of life.

† *De Benef.* IV. 18. Take away society, and you rend asunder the unity of the human race in which our life is bound up.

‡ *Dig.* I. i. 4. Manumission of Slaves had its origin not in natural but in positive Law. For by the Law of nature all are

"Manumissio a jure gentium originem sumsit, utpote quum jure naturali omnes liberi nascerentur, nec esset nota manumissio, quum servitus esset incognita. Sed posteaquam jure gentium servitus invasit, secutum est beneficium manumissionis; ut quum uno naturali nomine homines appellarentur, jure gentium tria genera esse cœperunt, liberi, et his contrarium servi, et tertium genus, liberti, id est, qui desierant esse servi." And with regard to marriage, the Roman lawyers sometimes appear to incline to extend the notion of it even to brute animals*. "Jus naturale est quod natura omnia animalia docuit: nam jus istud non humani generis proprium, sed omnium animalium quæ in terra, quæ in mari nascuntur, avium quoque, commune est. Hinc descendit maris et fœminæ conjunctio, quam nos matrimonium appellamus, hinc liberorum procreatio, hinc educatio: videmus enim cætera quoque animalia, feras etiam, istius juris peritiâ censeri." Attempts such as this, to extend the meaning of *Jus*, in any sense, to brute animals, can only perplex the subject. The word *Rights* has no meaning, as applied to animals, which cannot understand the word. Our Rights and our Obligations are necessarily limited by the limits of human nature. They all spring out of the recognition of our common Humanity. Our duties with

born free, and when there was no slavery there could be no manumission. But when by the positive Law of nations, slavery was introduced; the relief from this infliction by manumission was also introduced. And thus men, who by nature were all alike men, were divided into three kinds, freemen, slaves, and freed men, who had been slaves.

* *Dig.* I. i. 1. Natural Law is that which nature teaches all animals: such Law is not peculiar to the human race, but common also to beasts, fishes, and birds. Hence arises the union of male and female which we call marriage, hence the procreation and nurture of children; for we see that brutes, and even wild beasts, are acquainted with the Natural Law which regulates such matters.

regard to brute animals depend upon no mutual Rights; but upon the Duty of Self-culture; to which our treatment of them, like our other actions, must be made subservient. Animals offer to us images of some of the lower parts of our nature; but except so far as these elements are directed and governed by the higher elements, they are not subjects of moral consideration. As far as the limits of humanity extend, however, there are mutual ties of Duty which bind together all men; and as the basis of all others, a Duty of Mutual Kindness; which, as we see, is acknowledged by the Jurists, as well as by the Moralists, of Rome, in spite of the originally narrow basis of their Jurisprudence.

513. The progress of the Conception of *Humanity*, as a universal bond which knits together the whole human race, and makes kindness to every member of it a Duty, was immeasurably promoted by the teaching and influence of Christianity. In the course of time, domestic slavery was abolished; and marriage received the sanction of the Church, and was alike honourable in all. The antipathies of nations, the jealousies of classes, the selfishness, fierceness, and coldness of men's hearts; the narrowness and dimness of their understandings, have prevented their receiving cordially and fully, the comprehensive precepts of benevolence which Christianity delivers; but as these obstacles have been more and more overcome, the doctrine has been more and more assented to, and felt to be true, by all persons of moral culture; that there is a Duty of Universal Benevolence which we are to bear to all men *as men;* and which we are to fulfil, by dealing with them as men; as beings having the like affections and reason, rights and claims, which we ourselves have.

514. This conception of Humanity, as a Principle within us, requiring us to recognize in others the same Rights which we claim for ourselves, may be

further illustrated. Such a principle of Humanity, requiring us to recognize men as men, requires us more especially to recognize them as such, in their capacity of moral agents. They have not only like desires and affections with ourselves; but also, like faculties of Reason and Self-guidance; by which they discern the difference of right and wrong, and feel the duty of doing the right, and abstaining from the wrong. This view of their condition as Moral Agents, is that by which we must entirely sympathize with them; as it is the view of our own condition in which we are fully conscious of ourselves. Humanity requires that we should feel satisfaction in the desires and means of enjoyment of our fellow-men; but Humanity requires, still more clearly, that we should feel a satisfaction in their having the desires and the means of doing their Duty. Now the fundamental Rights of which we have so often spoken, the Rights of the Person, of Property, and the like, are means, and necessary conditions, of Duty. It is necessary to moral action, that the agent should be free, not liable to unlimited and unregluated constraint and violence; that is, that he should have Rights of the Person. It is necessary to moral action, that the agent should have some command over external things; for this is implied in action; that is, it is necessary that he should have Rights of Property. And in like manner, in order that any class of persons may exist permanently in a community, as moral agents, it is requisite that they should possess the Right of Marriage; for without that Right, some of the strongest of man's desires cannot be under moral control; nor can the sentiment of Rights be transmitted from one generation to another. The Right of Contract is a necessary accompaniment of the Right of Property; for if the person can possess, he may buy and sell. And thus, these Rights are means, and necessary conditions, of men's being moral agents; and the Hu

manity which makes us desire that all men should be able to regulate themselves by a Love of Duty, requires that *all should be invested with these Rights*.

515. These Rights, which Humanity requires that all men should possess, may be called *Natural Rights;* and in this sense, we may say that Man has Natural Rights of Personal Security from Violence, of Sustenance and Property so far as is implied in moral agency, and of Marriage. But we must distinguish these *Natural Rights*, which men *ought* to have, from the Rights of which we have hitherto spoken, which men really *have* in Civil Society, and which may be called *Civil Rights*.

516. As the Natural Rights, of which we speak, are those which are implied in Moral Agency; so, on the other hand, they imply Moral Agency, and consequently imply Duties, or Moral Obligations. As there is a Natural Right of Security against violence, there is a Natural Obligation to abstain from violence. As there is a Natural Right of Property for every man, to some extent or other; so there is a Natural Obligation to abstain from the Property of others, and to fulfil our Contracts. As there is a Natural Right of Marriage, so there is a Natural Obligation of Forethought, which directs men to make provision for the Sustenance of a Family, before they add to the existing numbers of the Community.

517. Humanity requires us to insist upon these Rights, and upon the corresponding Obligations, with equal force. We may declare such Rights to be natural, universal, necessary; but we must declare the Obligations to be equally natural, universal, necessary. Humanity requires that men should have the means of doing their Duty; she requires also no less that they should do it. She is solicitous about their welfare; in the first place, about their welfare in the subordinate sense, the means of enjoyment and of action; in the next place, about their

welfare in the superior sense, the pursuit of right ends by right means. To insist upon man's Natural Rights, and to lose sight of the corresponding Obligations, is not the tendency of the Humanity of a moral man.

518. Such Natural Rights as we have mentioned, are sometimes spoken of as *indefeasible* and *inalienable*. When, by such expressions, it is meant that no act, either of a man's own or of other men, can make it cease to be an object of Humanity that he should possess such Rights, the expressions are just. No constraint and violence, actually exercised upon men, can prevent the humane man from desiring that they should have Rights which may protect them from such inflictions; and even if a man, for himself, renounce the Rights which are requisite to his being a moral agent, the humane man must still desire that they should be restored to him. If these Rights are taken away, or given away, it is right that they should be given back to every man; and in this sense, they are indefeasible and inalienable.

But if it be meant, that when the Law takes away, or the act of the individual gives away, these Rights, the Law and the Act are not to be regarded, this application of the words is not admissible. The Laws of every State have their validity; and if these Laws are contrary to Humanity or to Justice, such vices of the Laws are to be remedied, not by the Moralist declaring such Laws null and void of themselves; but by the Legislator annulling them, or substituting better Laws in their room. And although it may be humane and right, that the Laws should not sanction Contracts by which a citizen renounces the fundamental Rights of man; yet if such a Contract is made according to Law, the Law enforces it, and the Moralist, as before, may say that the Law ought to be changed; but he may not say that, till changed, it ought not to be executed.

519. Thus, those which we have called the *Natural* Rights of man, may be, for a time at least, superseded by their not being *Civil* Rights. They may be Rights in the eye of Humanity ; that is, such as *ought to be* the Rights of all members of every community ; but not Rights in the eye of Law, that is, such as *are* the Rights of all members of a given community. Natural Rights are the Ideal conditions of moral society ; they may be suspended in Fact ; the Idea being imperfectly realized. When this is so, it is the business of all good men constantly to make the Fact approach to the Idea : to make Law agree with Humanity : to make Civil Rights coincide with Natural Rights.

In many communities, this task may at the present, or at any given time, be imperfectly fulfilled ; and in such cases, there exist Classes of the Society which possess, in an imperfect degree, or in no degree, the Natural Rights of Man. It will be proper to examine more particularly some of these States of Society, with their characteristic Classes : and to consider the manner in which they exemplify the doctrine which we have been propounding.

CHAPTER XXIV.

SLAVERY.

520. In ancient nations, we find the existence of Slaves everywhere familiar. Bondmen and Bondwomen, and the buying and selling of men, occur frequently in the Books of Moses. In Homer, and the Greek tragedians, domestic slavery is contemplated as the general lot of those conquered in war, their wives and children. The slaves, thus obtained,

were employed, both in the business of the house, in the labours of agriculture, and as workmen in various handicrafts. They were so universally thus employed, that they were considered as a necessary portion of society. A State, says Aristotle*, consists of Families; a Family, of Freemen and Slaves. And in like manner, the Roman Law lays this down as the primary division of persons†, "Omnes homines aut liberi sunt aut servi." Slavery, thus derived from the ancient world, was, in the course of time, nearly extinguished in Christian States. But in modern times, a new form of slavery has grown up; the slavery of the Negroes, who are carried from Africa to America; and employed there, they and their descendants, as domestic servants and agricultural labourers.

521. The character of complete Slavery is, that the Slave has no Rights. And this complete kind of Slavery has been recognized and ordained by the Laws of many nations. Gaius, the Roman Jurist, says‡, "In potestate sunt servi dominorum. Quæ quidem potestas juris gentium est; nam apud omnes peræque gentes animadvertere possumus dominis in servos vitæ necisque potestatem fuisse, et quodcunque per servum acquiritur id domino acquiri." Thus the Slave had neither the Right of protection from extreme violence and death, inflicted by his master, nor the Right of property in anything which he might happen to produce or acquire. The Slave is the property of the Master, in the same manner as a horse or a cart is. And these maxims are promulgated in modern Laws. "A Slave," says the Lou-

* *Polit.* I. 2. † *Inst.* I. 3.

‡ *Dig.* I. 6. 1. Among the "things in our power" are the slaves of which we are masters. And this "power" is a general institution of nations; for we may observe that in all nations alike the master has the power of life and death over the slave; and whatever is acquired by the slave, is acquired for the master.

isiana Code*, "is in the power of the Master to whom he belongs. The Master may sell him, dispose of his person, his industry, his labour; he can do nothing, possess nothing, nor acquire anything but which must belong to his master." The Laws of South Carolina say, "Slaves shall be deemed, taken, reported and adjudged, to be chattels personal in the hands of their Masters, and possessions to all intents and purposes whatsoever." Accordingly, it is held in America that the cohabitation of Slaves, being limited by the pleasure of the master, cannot be marriage; and that a slave cannot bo guilty of *theft;* just as dogs and horses cannot marry and cannot steal. It is true, that in some countries, in which the most complete slavery prevails, the master is not allowed by the Laws to put his slave to death; and some punishment is inflicted if he does so. But such a Law does not invest the slave with any Rights. It is only a Law against what is shocking to the general feeling, like the English Laws against cruelty to animals. It is now penal in this country to torture a horse or a dog; but a horse or a dog are still only objects of possession, without any Rights or any acknowledged moral nature.

522. Slavery is contrary to the Fundamental Principles of Morality. It neglects the great primary distinction of Persons and Things (45); converting a Person into a Thing, an object merely passive, without any recognized attributes of Human nature. A slave is, in the eye of the State which stamps him with that character, not acknowledged as a man. His pleasures and pains, his wishes and desires, his needs and springs of action, his thoughts and feelings, are of no value whatever in the eye of the community. He is reduced to the level of the brutes. Even his Crimes, as we have said, are not acknowledged as Wrongs; lest it should be supposed that, as he may

* Channing's Works, Vol. II. p. 17.

do a Wrong, he may suffer one. And as there are for him no Wrongs, because there are no Rights; so there is for him nothing morally right; that is, as we have seen, nothing conformable to the Supreme Rule of Human Nature; for the Supreme Rule of his condition is the will of his master. He is thus divested of his moral nature, which is contrary to the great Principle we have already laid down; that all men are moral beings;—a Principle which, we have seen (510, 514), is one of the universal Truths of Morality, whether it be taken as a Principle of Justice or of Humanity. It is a Principle of Justice, depending upon the participation of all in a common Humanity: it is a Principle of Humanity as authoritative and cogent as the fundamental Idea of Justice.

523. All men are moral beings, and cannot be treated as mere brutes and things, without an extreme violation of the Duties of Humanity. In some communities, the Conception of Humanity may be dimly and vaguely developed; and the guilt of this violation of Duty, in this as in other cases, may be modified by this circumstance. The offence of the defender and promoter of Slavery, may not be that of acting against Conscience, but of not enlightening his Conscience; of not raising his standard of morality. And this offence, again, may be modified by the circumstances in which a person is placed. In the ancient world, especially in the earlier periods, when the friendly intercourse of nations was rare, the feeling of Humanity very imperfectly unfolded, and the thoughts by which such feelings are fostered and supported not yet familiar among men; the opportunity of enlightening the conscience and raising the moral standard were wanting; and if, in such cases, virtuous men practised slavery without doubt or misgiving; and with the natural mercy, in their treatment of slaves, which benevolence cultivated in the other relations of life would usually produce in this; we

may pronounce them to have been excusable, on the ground of the defects of their national standard of morality (453): though upon such men, and upon all men, there was a duty incumbent, of raising the national standard of Morality. But now, after morality and religion have so far raised the standard of morality in Christian nations, that among them the Slavery which they inherited from the ancient world has been extinguished; Nations, which do not adopt the Standard of Morality thus elevated, are chargeable with a voluntary preference of inhumanity and injustice to humanity and justice (455).

524. A very little progress in humanity, is sufficient to lead men to see the cruelty and immorality of making slaves, of men *of our own race*. Plato* notices it as a necessary result of an improved morality, that Greeks should not make slaves of Greeks. This injunction had already been given to the Jews†: *If thy brother* (which in this place and others means thy fellow-countrymen) *be sold unto thee, thou shalt not make him serve as a bondman.* No man can think it conformable to Justice and Humanity that he, or his Family, should be thrown into a state of slavery; and in considering his fellow-countrymen, he can readily sympathize with them, and identify his case with theirs; and thus, he acknowledges that to make *them* slaves, is inhuman and unjust. The Romans, as we have seen, extended this feeling to all the world; and their Jurists declared, that no man was a slave by nature. It is indeed plain that our Humanity, in order to be consistent, must extend to all men. To conceive slavery a cruel and unjust lot for our countrymen, but a reasonable and tolerable fate for foreigners, can arise only from dulness and narrowness of mind, and benevolence scantily cultivated. In the eye of Morality, all men are Brothers; and the crime of maintaining Slavery,

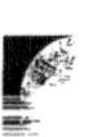

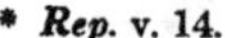
* *Rep.* v. 14.

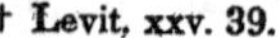
† Levit, xxv. 39.

is the crime of making or keeping a Brother a Slave.

525. There is one defence of negro slavery, which represents the negro as a being inferior to the white man in his faculties. He is asserted to approach in his nature to the inferior animals; and hence it is inferred that he may be possessed as a Thing, like the animals. But this defence is manifestly quite baseless. The same faculties of mind have appeared in the negro, as in the white, so far as the condition of negro nations and negro classes has afforded opportunities for their development. The negroes do not appear to be duller, ruder or coarser, in mind or habits, than many savage white nations; or than nations, now highly cultured, were, in their early condition. The negro has a moral nature, and is therefore included in the consequences which follow from the Principle, that all men have a common nature. The negro has the same affections and springs of action as we ourselves. He loves his wife, his children, his home, and any security and stability which is granted him. He can buy and sell, promise and perform. He has, as much as any race of men, moral sentiments. He can admire and love what is good; he can condemn and hate what is bad. He has the Sentiment of Rights and Wrongs also. Though the Law allows him no Rights, he can feel bitterly the monstrous Wrong of the Law. His Reason is the Universal Reason of men. He understands the general and abstract Forms in which Language presents the objects and rules, with which Reason deals. He recognizes, as we do, a Supreme Rule of Human action and Human being; for, like us, he can direct his thoughts and acts to what is absolutely right. In short, there is no phrase which can be used, describing the moral and rational nature of man, which may not be used of the negro, as of the white. The assertion that there is, between the

white and the black race, any difference on which the one can found a Right to make slaves of the other, is utterly false.

526. If it be said, that the negro approaches in his external form to some kinds of monkeys; and if it be asked how we draw the line between man and such inferior animals; we reply, that all beings are men, who have a moral and rational nature, such as we have described: but if some plain and simple criterion of the difference between man and brutes be required; we can point at such a character at once, in the use of *Language*. A being who can understand and apply the general terms of which language consists, can apprehend Rules of action, Means and Ends, and hence, the Supreme Rule. He is a rational, and consequently a moral being. He is our brother.

527. It is difficult to believe that those who, in defence of their own practice of slavery, allege the inferiority of the negro race, do really think their assertion true. To such persons, negro women are objects of sexual desire. Upon their asserted view, they are thus guilty of an offence which men have everywhere looked upon as bestial and horrible. Moreover, the Laws of Nature contradict their assertion; for the offspring of such mixtures are marked with the physical and moral characters of both parents, as in other human unions. And when the slave-owner treats his own child, thus produced, as a slave; and works him, tortures him, or sells him, as he would a brute animal; (which it is said slave-owners do;) he tears out of his heart those affections which are the roots of all Morality, and the absence of which makes lust entirely brutal.

528. Again, in States where negro Slaves are numerous, to teach them to write or to read is forbidden by Law, under the severest penalties. Such Laws suppose the capacity of negroes for intellectual

culture; and are an implicit confession that it is necessary to degrade their minds, in order to keep their bodies in slavery. When such practices and such Laws prevail, to defend negro slavery by asserting the inferiority of the negro race, can hardly be free from the guilt of wilful blindness of conscience, persisted in, in order to uphold conscious wrong.

529. The Moralist, then, must pronounce Slavery to be utterly inconsistent with Humanity; and with Principles, which, being derived from the universal nature of man, may be deemed fundamental Principles of Justice. Slavery is utterly abhorrent to the essence of Morality, and cannot be looked upon as a tolerable condition of Society, nor acquiesced in as what may allowably be. Whenever Slavery exists, its Abolition must be one of the great objects of every good man.

530. It will, of course, be understood, from what has already been said, that this Abolition is to be sought by legal and constitutional means only. When Slavery exists, its annihilation is an end which must be constantly kept in view; but to which we must sometimes be content to approach by degrees. It is an Idea to which we must endeavour to make the Fact conform; but the conformity may not be immediately brought to pass. The Laws of the State are to be observed, even when they enact Slavery; for the Moralist cannot authorize the citizen to choose what Laws he will obey, and what he will not. Natural Rights must yield to Civil Rights, in the hope that Civil Rights will be more and more made to harmonize with Natural Rights. Slavery is never to be acquiesced in, always to be condemned; but we may, and must, tolerate a gradual transition from Slavery to Emancipation, such as the conditions of Legislation and even the benefit of the slave, render inevitable. Still, on the other hand, we are to recollect, that delay is to be tolerated, only so far as it is inevitable

and that to quicken the course of Emancipation is no less humane and just, than it is to give Legislation this direction, and to prepare both slaves and masters for the change.

531. It may be hoped, by the Moralist, that the emancipation of the negro race will go on with accelerated rapidity; for every State in which free negroes live, as moral and rational beings, is a refutation of the solitary argument in defence of negro slavery, drawn from the asserted unfitness of the negro for freedom. When the free negro population of cultured communities have, by the manifestation of their moral and rational nature, made themselves recognized as brethren by their white fellow-citizens, it cannot be that *their* black brethren will long be kept in slavery in neighbouring States professing a like reverence for freedom.

532. Slavery nowhere exists in Europe in a form so repugnant to Humanity as is negro slavery. But there are, in some parts, many vestiges of slavery, and classes intermediate between slaves and freemen. The *Serfs*, who have existed and still exist in different countries, may be considered as holding such an intermediate place; and in different countries in different degrees. In Russia, serfage is hardly distinguishable from slavery. The labourers are bound to the soil by the Law: they are *prædial* serfs (128). By the general custom of the country, they are bound to work on the demesnes of the landowner three days in the week; and have land allotted to them from which they extract their own subsistence. But the peasant is, with all his family and descendants, at the disposal of the lord. In some parts, the Serfs have been allowed the privilege of acquiring and transmitting personal property; and in some, they may even purchase or inherit land. In other parts of Europe, Serfage has assumed a less slavish character. In some parts of Germany, the peasant is no

longer attached by the law to the soil: and his labour which he owes to his landlord is definite in kind and amount. Such peasants are called *Leibeigener*. In other parts this labour-rent is commuted for a corn-rent or a money-rent, though the tenant is still liable for some trifling services. Such tenants are called *Meyer**.

533. The social structure of England has gone through these several forms. For two centuries after the Norman Conquest, a large proportion of the body of cultivators was in the situation of the Russian serf; they were termed *Villeins*. During the next three hundred years the unlimited labour-rents paid by the Villeins were gradually commuted for definite services, still payable in kind; and they had a legal Right to their lands which they occupied, which legal Right was called *Copyhold*. It is only about two hundred years, since the personal bondage of the Villeins ceased to exist in England.

534. The contemplation of the change which has taken place in this country, and which appears to be taking place elsewhere, from a condition in which men are little better than Slaves, to one in which they are Freemen; and of the manifest and immense advance in moral and intellectual culture, which such a change has brought with it; must strongly stimulate the Moralist to recommend and promote the progress of social freedom and the removal of every law and custom that contains any trace of Slavery.

535. We distinguish *social* from *political* freedom; the former depending upon the domestic or prædial relation of Servant and Master (128); the latter, upon the relation of Subject or Citizen, and Government. If men have Rights of the Person, of Property, and the like; they may be *socially* Freemen; however despotic the established government

* Jones *On Rent*.

be. They are *politically* free, when each Class has such a share in the Government, as enables it to assert and secure its Rights. But Social Freedom can hardly exist, without Political Freedom: the Lowest Class can hardly have and retain Rights, without possessing some political power of maintaining them. In countries where Serfage prevails, the Serfs have no political power. The landlords form an Aristocracy; and the Sovereign and they, possess, between them, the powers of the State. When Serfage gives place to Social Freedom, there must be, in the Constitution, an *Estate* of the People, or some other Political Authority, representing and protecting the general body of free citizens.

But the subject of Political Freedom must be considered hereafter.

CHAPTER XXV.

PLEASURE, INTEREST, HAPPINESS, UTILITY, EXPEDIENCY.

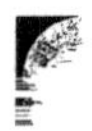

536. We may follow the subject of Humanity or Benevolence somewhat further. Humanity is, as we have said, a Principle, in virtue of which we represent to ourselves other men as of the same nature with ourselves, and enter into their feelings, hopes, and prospects, as if they were our own. We desire the good of others as we desire our own good.

But the *Good* which we desire for ourselves is contemplated under various aspects. We may have, as the Object of our desires in a general form, *Pleasure*, Enjoyment, or Gratification; we may have *Interest*, or Advantage; we may have *Happiness*. And as our desires point to one or other of these general Objects for ourselves, they may also aim at the like Objects for others. Our Benevolence may urge us to give pleasure to others, or to promote their interest, or to make them happy.

In order to see how these views affect the Duties of Benevolence, we may examine further the Conceptions of Pleasure, Interest, and Happiness.

537. Pleasure arises from our attaining the objects of our Desires. It is what we feel, when our Desires are satisfied, or in some measure gratified. All actions which are not directed by the Reason, may be conceived as performed in order to obtain Pleasure, or to avoid its opposite, Pain. Actions directed by Reason, may also be directed to Pleasure. They may be directed to the objects of Mental Desires, which Reason presents to us under general abstract forms; as Wealth, Power, and the like: and to obtain such objects, may give us Pleasure. But Pleasure is more especially considered as the object of less abstract and reflective Desires, as Bodily Pleasure, and the like. Pleasure is sought simply and *for itself;* not as a means to an end, nor in obedience to a Rule. If we seek Wealth or Power *as means* to an end, we do not seek them merely *as pleasure.*

538. Since Pleasure is sought, not in obedience to a Rule, but simply for itself, to make Pleasure our object, is not consistent with the Supreme Rule of Human Action. To make Pleasure the object of human action, is to reject the supposition of a Supreme Rule, and a Supreme Object. For if Pleasure be the Highest Object, it is also the Lowest. If Pleasure be the Highest Object of Human Action, nothing can be absolutely *right;* nor can be right in any other sense, than as the right road to Pleasure. If Pleasure be the object of human action, we must reject Duty as the guide of Human Actions. The good man makes Pleasure his object, only so far as it is con-

sistent with the Supreme Rule of Duty. He does not desert Duty for Pleasure, but he finds his Pleasure in Duty.

539. Since we cannot rightly desire for ourselves Pleasure, as our ultimate object, we cannot rightly desire it for others, whom we love in some degree as ourselves. Merely to give Pleasure to men, without regarding whether the pleasures be right or wrong, is not a moral kind of Humanity.

But though we may not make it our business to promote the Pleasures of those around us, as an ultimate object, for them and for us; we may rightly make the promotion of their Pleasures, so far as they are not wrong Pleasures, one of our main objects; both as a manifestation of Benevolence, and as a means of cultivating that affection. The sympathy with other men, which Morality requires of us, is best fostered and strengthened, by an habitual participation in their efforts to obtain those objects which give them pleasure.

540. Though Pleasures are sought, as independent and ultimate objects of desire, they often involve references and consequences, and trains of feeling and thought, which connect them with higher objects, and with Moral Rules. The Desires of the Body point simply to Selfish Pleasures; but the Pleasures of the Affections imply a Sympathy with other persons, which is a kind of benevolence; and therefore, of the nature of virtue. The Pleasures to which the Love of Knowledge leads, involve a culture of the mind, which gives activity to the Reason; and which, thus, may aid the moral culture. And when the moral culture is so far advanced, that Conscience is heard clearly, and Virtue is beloved; the approval of Conscience, and the conscious activity of Virtue, may be sought, as the greatest Pleasures of which man's nature is susceptible.

But in general, *Pleasure*, as an object of action, is

distinguished from, and opposed to, *Duty ;* and so far as this is done, although we may aim at promoting the Pleasures of others, as a step in our moral culture, a due regard for the moral culture of others will not allow us to make their Pleasure a supreme and ultimate object.

541. Another general form under which the object of action presents itself to us, is *Interest.* We seek our own Interest: and hence we are bound, by the Duties of Benevolence, to seek the Interest of others also. Interest is conceived as an object of affection or desire, approved of, to some extent, by Reason. A prudent man seeks his own Interest. When Interest and Pleasure come in competition, Reason directs us to follow our Interest, and to resist the temptation of Pleasure. We may estimate our Interest according to various Standards; but in speaking of Interest, we suppose *Some Standard.* We say that one thing is *more* for our Interest than another: for example, we may say that it is more for our Interest to be honest than to be cunning. In stating such a maxim, we take, for our standard of Interest, the acquisition of wealth, or the establishment of our good name. The Standard of Interest is not an absolute, but an assumed Standard; just as the ends aimed at by Prudence are not absolute, but assumed ends (258). But we sometimes suppose an absolute and supreme Standard of Interest; we speak of our *true* Interest, our *highest* Interest. We say that our true and highest Interest is, the elevation and purification of our moral being. Also, the Affection which we feel towards a person, or for a mental object, is spoken of, as an Interest which we take or feel: that is, the person or object is conceived as of considerable amount, according to our Standard of Interest. But we may estimate another man's Interest differently from his own feeling respecting it. We may say, it was such a one's *Interest* to improve his estate,

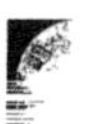

but he *took no Interest* in it. Again; different classes of objects of action imply different Standards of Interest. A man's affections are employed on one set of objects, his thoughts on another. Hence we have the Interests of the Heart, and the Interests of the Intellect. The Interest of the Individual may point one way; the Interest of the State, another.

542. Of course, Benevolence directs us to promote the true and highest Interest of other men, as it directs us to seek our own. We may also seek to promote the Interest of others, in a lower and narrower sense; as we may seek to promote their Pleasures: and such a course may be a part of morality, either as a manifestation, or as a discipline, of Benevolence. But to promote any Interest of men, which is not the highest; or any seeming Interest, which is not a true one; cannot rightly be made our ultimate object.

543. It has sometimes been said, that men, in all their actions, necessarily *seek their Interest*, or what appears to them their Interest. The notion involved in this assertion appears to be, that every action may be considered as a tendency to some object, which may be included in the term *Interest*. The brave man, when he rushes into battle, seeks victory, or glory, which, for the time, he thinks are his Interest. The timid man, when he runs away from the enemy, seeks safety, which seems to him his Interest. But the assertion thus made, involves a confusion of thought and language, such as not only would prevent our being able to state any distinct doctrines of Morality, but such as even common usage may teach us to correct. The brave man is not impelled to seek victory or glory, nor the timid man, to seek safety, by any view of Interest, such as that with which the prudent man thoughtfully seeks his Interest. The springs of action in these cases are Courage, and Fear: not any seeking of an Abstract Object, which Interest is; still less, any seeking of an Abstract Object involving

a Standard of value by which all things are compared, which Interest also is. If we say that the brave man rushes into the battle, and the timid man rushes out of it, each seeking his Interest, we must also say, that the bull-dog attacks his antagonist, and the frightened horse runs away from his master, seeking his Interest; which it would be reckoned absurd to say. The proposition, that all actions are prompted by the prospect of our own Interest, is, not asserted, in general, as anything more than an identical proposition. But to make it true, even in that character, the common usage of language must be violated.

544. *Happiness* is the object of human action in its most general form; as including all other objects, and approved by the Reason. As Pleasure is the aim of mere Desire, and Interest the aim of Prudence; so Happiness is the aim of Wisdom. Happiness is conceived as necessarily an *ultimate* object of action. To be happy, includes or supersedes all other gratifications. If we are happy, we do not miss that which we have not; if we are not happy, we want something more, whatever we have. The Desire of Happiness is the Supreme Desire. All other Desires, of Pleasure, Wealth, Power, Fame, are included in this, and are subordinate to it. We may make other objects our ultimate objects; but we can do so, only by identifying them with this. Happiness is our being's end and aim.

545. Since Happiness is necessarily the Supreme Object of our Desires, and Duty the Supreme Rule of our actions, there can be no harmony in our being, except our Happiness coincide with our Duty. That which we contemplate as the Ultimate and Universal Object of Desire, must be identical with that which we contemplate as the Ultimate and Supreme Guide of our Intentions. As moral beings, our Happiness must be found in our Moral Prog

ress, and in the consequences of our Moral Progress: we must be happy by being virtuous.

546. How this is to be, Religion alone can fully instruct us: but by the nature of our faculties, this must be. And as this is the nature of the Happiness which we are to seek for ourselves, so is it the nature of the Happiness which we are to endeavour to bestow upon others. We are directed by Benevolence, to seek to make them happy, by making them virtuous; to promote their Happiness, by promoting their moral Progress; to make them feel their Happiness to be coincident with their Duty.

The identification of Happiness with Duty on merely philosophical grounds, is a question of great difficulty. It is difficult, even for the philosopher, to keep this Identity steadily fixed in his mind, as an Operative Principle; and it does not appear to be possible to make such an identity evident and effective in the minds of men in general. But Religion presents to us this Truth, of the identity of Happiness and Duty, in connexion with other Truths, by means of which it may be made fully evident and convincing, to minds of every degree of intellectual culture: and the minds of men, for the most part, receive the conviction of the Truth from their Religious Education.

547. We may also, as an exercise and discipline of Benevolence, seek to make them happy, in a more partial view; namely, by placing them in a condition in which they have no wants unsupplied; for, as we have said, this is part of the conception of happiness. If we make this our object, we shall have to supply those wants which are universal, and do not depend upon special mental culture; and we shall have to impart such mental culture, as may make them feel no wants which cannot be supplied. We shall have to minister to their human needs; and to moderate their wishes: in short, to make them content. *Content* is a necessary part of Happiness; and

men may be rendered content, by gratifying their desires in part, and limiting them in part, till none remain unsatisfied. That men's desires should be moderate and limited, is a condition very requisite to Content; and therefore, to Happiness; for except some moderating influence be exercised, the Desires, both bodily and mental, grow with indulgence Hence, we promote the Happiness of men by moderating their Desires; and any influence of this kind, which we can exert upon them; as for instance, by teaching and discipline, may be a work of Benevolence. But on the other hand, we must recollect that the objects to which many of our Desires tend, are means of moral action; and that it is necessary to the moral activity and moral culture of a man, that he should desire and obtain such objects. We ought not to wish to reduce a man to a state of Content, by taking away the desire of the fundamental Rights of man. We ought not to wish the Slave to be contented in his Slavery; living like a brute animal in dependence upon his master, and looking to no law, higher than his Master's Will. On the contrary, we ought to wish that he should both desire and have Liberty, in order that he may enter upon that course of moral agency and moral progress, which is the only proper occupation of his human faculties. In order to promote the Happiness of mankind, we must endeavour to promote their Liberty; both the Social Liberty, which invests them with the Fundamental Rights of man; and the Political Liberty, which is the guardian of such Rights, and the most favourable condition for moral and intellectual progress. We shall pursue this subject hereafter.

548. In some Systems of Morality, the Desire of our own *Happiness*, and of that of mankind, has been made to occupy a larger space than we assign to it. This Desire has, indeed, been made the basis of the whole of Morality, and the ground and measure

of all our Duties. It has been said, that our Principle of action, so far as we ourselves are concerned, must be to attain, as much as possible, our own Happiness; and that the Rule which is to guide us in actions which affect others, is to increase as much as possible their Happiness. This view of the subject has been so much insisted on, that we may make a few remarks upon it.

We may remark, that according to the explanation which we have given above, of the Conception of Happiness, it is quite true, that we ought to act so as to increase as much as possible our own Happiness and the Happiness of others; but we must add, that this Truth cannot enable us to frame Rules of Duty, or to decide Questions of Morality. It is an *identical* Truth. Since Happiness is the ultimate object of our aims, and includes all other objects; whatever else we aim at, we identify with Happiness. Whatever other end we seek, we seek that as the *far* end. And with regard to other persons; Benevolence urges us to promote their Happiness; for in that, all good is included, and we wish to do them good. But these Maxims, though true, are, of themselves, altogether barren. The Questions still occur, *What* are the things which will increase our own Happiness? What will increase the Happiness of others? Of what elements does Happiness consist? According to our account of it, Happiness does not imply any special elements; but only a general conception of an *ultimate* and *sufficing* Object. How are we to measure Happiness, and thus to proceed to ascertain, by what acts it may be increased? If we can do this, then, indeed, we may extract Rules and Results, from the Maxim that we are to increase our own and others' Happiness: but without this step, we can draw no consequences from the Maxim. If we take the Conception in its just aspect, how little does it help us in such questions as occur to us! I wish to

know whether I may seek sensual pleasure; whether I may tell a flattering lie. I ask, Will it increase or diminish the Sum of Human Happiness to do so? This mode of putting the question cannot help me. How can I know whether these acts will increase or diminish the Sum of Human Happiness? The immediate pleasures of gratified sense, or of gratified vanity, I may, perhaps, in some degree, estimate; but how am I to estimate the indirect and remote effects of the acts, on myself and others; and how am I to measure the total effect thus produced, on Human Happiness? By a sensual act, or by a lie, I weaken, it may be said, the habit of temperance and of truth in my own mind; and by my example, I produce a like effect on the minds of others. Suppose, then, that I regard this consequence, and see that the act thus leads to something of unhappiness; still, this effect is perhaps slight and precarious; how am I to balance this result, against those direct gratifications which are produced by the acts now spoken of? It does not appear that, under this form, the question admits of an answer.

549. The mode in which Moralists have been able to apply this Principle, of aiming at the greatest amount of Human Happiness, to the establishment of Moral Rules; has been, by assuming that man must act according to *Rules*. I say *assuming;* for it does not appear, that we can *prove* that the Principle of increasing as much as possible the Happiness of man requires us to act by general Rules. The man who is tempted to sensual pleasure, or mendacious flattery, may say, I do not intend that what I do now should be a Rule for myself, or for others. At present I seek to promote Human Happiness, by making an exception to Rules: in general I shall conform to the Rules. To this, the Moralist replies, that to speak and think thus, is to reject Rules altogether: that Rules are not recognized, except they be applied in

all cases, and relied upon as the antagonists of the temptations which particular cases offer. In short, he says, that man, by his nature, must act by Rules; and that he, the Moralist, who has to decide respecting the character of human action, has to establish Rules of human action. Thus he assumes, in addition to his Principle of the Greatest Amount of Human Happiness, another Principle, of the Universality of Rule; and it is this latter Principle, which really gives a Moral character to his results. If we are to have Rules of action, we must have Rules, that men are to be temperate and truthful; though special violations of temperance or of truth may seem to offer an increase of human happiness. Such Rules as, that we may lie to please a friend, or may seek bodily pleasure where we can find it, are inconsistent with man's nature. But that they are so, is shown, by reasoning from the necessary conditions of Rules of action, not by considering the notion of Happiness; for the pursuit of Happiness does, really, often lead men to follow such immoral Rules as have just been mentioned. The Rules, *to be temperate* and *to be truthful*, are not established by showing that they lead to the greatest amount of Human Happiness; for we have no means of estimating the amount of Human Happiness which results from any given hypothesis. These Rules may, indeed, be said to be proved by a consideration of the intolerable unhappiness which would result from the absence of such Rules. We have already (65) used this consideration in establishing Moral Rules in general. But this line of reasoning is quite a different course from employing the Conception of Happiness, as a means of comparing one particular Rule of Duty with another; an employment of the notion of Happiness for which it is, as I have said, quite unfit.

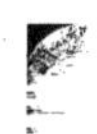

550. The Principle of aiming at the greatest amount of Human Happiness, has been strangely

dealt with by the Moralists who have principally employed it. As we have already said, in order to deduce Moral Rules from it, it seems to be necessary to find some measure of Happiness; or to resolve it into some more definite elements; and then, to estimate the moral value of actions, by means of this measure, or those elements. But this course has not been followed by such Moralists. Dr. Paley, who rests Moral Rules upon their tendency to promote Human Happiness, has, indeed, begun by giving some account of his view of Happiness. It does not, he says, consist in the pleasures of sense; nor in exemption from pain, labour, and care; nor in greatness and elevated station; it consists in the exercise of the social affections; in the exercise of the faculties of body or mind in the pursuit of some engaging end; in the prudent constitution of the habits; and in health: and, as he suggests in a note, perhaps in a certain condition of the nerves. Having given this analysis of Happiness, we naturally look to see how he next brings the word into use in his reasonings. We find the word occupying a very prominent place in the first sentence of his next chapter; in which he tells us, that "Virtue is the doing good to mankind for the sake of everlasting Happiness." But it is plain that, in this use of the word, there is no reference to the analysis of Happiness contained in the preceding chapter; and we are therefore, so far as reasoning is concerned, here thrown back upon the general notion which the word *Happiness*, without any special explanation, suggests.

551. When Paley proceeds, a little further on, to establish Moral Doctrines, for instance the Right of Property, he rests the propriety of this Institution of Property upon its advantages;—that it increases the produce of the earth; preserves this produce to maturity; prevents contests; and increases the conveniency of living. Doubtless all these results may

be understood, as *additions* to the Sum of Human Happiness; but there is no attempt made to show that these additions counterbalance the *subtraction* from Human Happiness arising from the wants of some persons, the superfluity of others, the contests and crimes of many, which Property produces. The Principle of the Greatest Human Happiness, thus loosely applied, leaves the Right of Property to stand upon a general apprehension of its advantages. The same is the case with the other Fundamental Rights of Man, and the Fundamental Rules of Morality. They are not proved, in Paley's work, by showing, in any distinct manner, that they increase the Sum of Human Happiness; for no way is offered of measuring this sum, or its Increase. But the Fundamental Rights and Fundamental Rules are asserted; and the student is told that they are necessary to Human Happiness. This all can readily assent to; for the end for which Rights and Rules exist, whatever other name it bear, may be considered as included in the term *Happiness*. And thus, Fundamental Rights and Rules, and the vague general notion of Human Happiness as their ultimate end, stand side by side in such systems of Morality, but have not really any logical connexion.

552. There is, however, one character of such Systems which is implied in this mode of employing the term *Happiness*. They seek to deduce the Rules of Action from a Supreme *Object of Desire;* whereas we have deduced them from a Supreme *Rule of Action*. They direct men to aim at Happiness; we direct them to aim at Acting Rightly. We deduce our Rules from the Constitution of man's nature; they, from the Objects of his desires. As expressing this difference, the Terms and Reasonings employed in such systems may be worthy our consideration.

553. There is an expression often used by Moralists of this class, which may be noticed in this

point of view. They often declare *Utility* to be the Ground and Measure of the Morality of actions. Now Utility cannot be in itself an Ultimate End. That is *useful,* which is subservient to some further end. A wheel is useful as a portion of a carriage; a carriage is useful in order to take a journey; a journey is useful, in order to visit a friend; to see and talk with a friend is useful, if it makes us happy. All things which have a value for their utility, have a reference to some ulterior end; and if we assume some Ultimate End, such as Happiness is conceived to be, all things may be estimated by their Utility. Thus the estimate of actions by their Utility may be conceived as identical with the estimate of them as contributing to Human Happiness; and accordingly, the two phrases have been principally used by the same school of Moralists.

554. The judgment which we have to pronounce upon Utility, as a ground of estimating the character of actions, is implied in what has been already said. We cannot estimate the value of anything, as being useful to an End, except by assuming the value of the End. If a Coach be a thing of no value, a Coach-wheel must be a thing of no value. If travelling be of no use, a travelling carriage is of no use. The measure of the value of actions by their Utility, is liable to all the inconvenience and indefiniteness of the determination of the End for which they are useful; and besides, to the difficulty of determining how far they are useful to the end. A system in which actions are estimated by their Utility in promoting Human Happiness, will be liable to the objections already stated against the Principle of the Greatest Human Happiness; and will also require a just mode of measuring the value of Actions as Means, the End being given. We have all along been applying a very different method, in order to judge of actions. We ask, What is *right?*

not, What is *useful?* acknowledging, as we have said, a supreme Rule, and not being content with seeking Means which derive their value from the assumed value of their Ends.

555. Another Term which has been much used by Moralists of this School is *Expediency*. "Whatever is expedient," says Paley, "is right*." Now we have to observe here, as before, that the main significance of such assertions is in the rejection, which they imply, of any independent and fundamental meaning in the term *right*. Those who make such assertions, intend to say, that Actions are right because they promote some object; Human Happiness, for instance; and that those who speak of acts, as absolutely right, are in error. In the common use of language, we speak of actions as *expedient*, when they promote some end which we have selected, and which we do not intend to have questioned. If we are prepared to put forwards the end of our actions as the Proper End of action, we call them, not *expedient*, but *right*. It may be expedient for a man to lie, in order to free himself from captivity. He may stay in captivity, because he will not tell a lie; but in this case, we say, he does what is right, and rejects what is expedient. *Expedient* implies, according to its etymology, a way out of difficulties. But Morality places before us a higher object than merely to escape from difficulties. She teaches us to aim at what is right. What is expedient, may be expedient as a means to what is right. It may be expedient to tell the truth, in order to rescue an innocent person from death. But we do not describe such an action properly by calling it *expedient*. It is much more than expedient, it is right: it is recommended, not by Expediency, but by Duty. In such cases, we can speak approvingly, not only of the action, as a right means, but of the end, as a right end. Truth

* Paley, B. I. c. 6.

is not properly commended, when it is described as a good way of getting out of a difficulty, or of gaining our ends.

Those who use this term, *Expediency*, to describe the proper end of human action, are prompted to do so by a wish to reject Terms which imply a Supreme Rule of action; they wish to recognize none but subordinate Rules determined by the Objects at which men aim. And it is true, in this sense, that whatever is expedient with a view to an end, is the right way to the end: but this does not justify the Moralist in confounding what is *relatively expedient* with what is *absolutely right:* nor in speaking of things as expedient *absolutely*, without pointing out *the purpose* which they are expedient *for*.

CHAPTER XXVI.

MORAL EDUCATION.

556. The Laws of each Community lay down certain Rules of Action, commands or prohibitions, for the members of the Community. But they do more: they direct that certain *Punishments* shall be inflicted on those who transgress the Law; as Fine, Imprisonment, Bodily Pain, Mutilation, Infamy, Exile, Death. And the Community, by its officers, inflicts these Punishments. It is in this manner, that the Laws become real Rules of action; and that in the minds of all men, Law-keeping and Law-breaking become objects which are sought and avoided, with the same earnestness and care as the other objects of the most powerful desires and aversions of men. The Punishment which thus gives reality to the Law, is the *Sanction* of the Law.

557. The Laws command what is in the community deemed right, and hence, Punishments are inflicted upon actions which are deemed wrong: although all wrong actions are not necessarily punished by Law. We have already explained (457, 458) the relation between the National Law and the National Morality. The National Law expresses certain fixed and fundamental portions of the National Morality: but not the whole. Law deals with external and visible acts, such as affect men's Rights; Morality deals, besides, with acts which are right or wrong, though they do not directly affect Rights; and with internal springs of action. The Law must always be just; but there may be many things which are just, and which yet cannot be enforced by Law. The Law must prohibit only what is wrong, though it may not prohibit all that is morally wrong.

558. Since the Law must always be just, Punishments must be inflicted only on what is morally wrong. It is sometimes said that the sole object of Punishment is the prevention of harm to the members of the community; but this is not the conception of Punishment. Punishment implies moral transgression. Crimes are violations of Law; but Crimes are universally understood to be offences against Morality also. If, in enforcing any law, of which the sole object were the prevention of harm to the community, some individuals were subjected to pain, these individuals being morally blameless, the pain would not be conceived as Punishment; if the infliction were to take the character of Punishment, the proceeding would be considered as intolerable. When persons, afflicted with or suspected of contagious disorders, are put in constraint for the good of the community (as in quarantine), this constraint is not called Punishment. A Law that such persons should be put to death, even though the health of the community might be so best secured, would be rejected by all men as

monstrous. An object of Punishment is the prevention of Crime; but it is the prevention of Crime *as Crime*, and not merely as Harm.

559. Thus the Laws, with their Sanctions, express in some measure the moral judgment of the Community; and by expressing it, they impress it upon the minds of individual members of the Community. That which the Law condemns and punishes, is understood by all to be wrong; and thus, each person who lives under the Law has a number of fixed points, which direct his mind in the determination of right and wrong. The Laws, with their Sanctions, are a part of the *Moral Education* of each citizen's mind.

560. As we have said, there is a National Morality, which is of wider extent, and more deeply seated in men's minds, than the written Law. The expressions of moral judgments respecting actions and characters, which are put forth in speeches upon public occasions, in the poetry and literature of the nation, and the like, take for granted a general agreement of men on points of Morality: and such expressions of moral judgments also produce their impression on individuals; they diffuse and perpetuate the judgment which they express; and form a part of the Moral Education of the citizens.

This Moral Education of the members of a community, must be such as tends to bring the moral judgments of individuals into harmony with those of the community. In order that the business of any community may be carried on, the citizens must have their moral judgments, in a great measure at least, in harmony with the Laws, and with the general jural and moral maxims which prevail, and have prevailed, in the community. If Judges and Litigants, Governors and Subjects, Magistrates and Legislators, all believed the Laws, and the usual procedures of the State, to be unjust and wrong; they would no longer go on executing and obeying them. They would no longer speak of them with respect: and magistrates who should speak disrespectfully of the Law, would not themselves be respected. The Laws being disregarded, the State would tend to dissolution. Thus, without some harmony between the moral judgments of the Community, as expressed in its Laws and Customs, and those of individuals, the continued and coherent existence of the State is impossible.

561. But though the Laws, with their Sanctions, and the public currency of moral sentiments and opinions in harmony with the Laws, form an important part of the moral education of the citizens, the moral judgments of each person are, for the most part, formed, in a still greater degree, by the influence of Parents, and other Friends, among whom childhood and youth are spent. This Domestic Teaching is the most effective portion of every one's moral education. The moral judgments respecting actions, characters, virtues, vices, objects and rules of action, which prevail in the domestic sphere, are so mingled with the moral conceptions, in every stage of their development, that they cannot be separated and dissevered by any subsequent operations; and thus, such moral judgments are imparted to each person in his earliest years, and transmitted from generation to generation.

562. In general, this Domestic Moral Education must be in harmony with the National Morality, and the National Law; for otherwise, as we have said, men would not perform their business as citizens in such a manner as to keep up the life of the State. But yet domestic education may often be something much more varied and peculiar, than it would be, if it were the mere echo of the Law, or the repetition of public formularies of morality, with explanations and commentaries. The Morality of different nations is very different in its Rules; and still more, in the

doctrines and beliefs which form the foundation of the Rules. These doctrines and beliefs are transmitted to successive generations, mainly by domestic teaching. But it may happen that a Family, belonging to one nation, dwells, even for several generations, in the country of another State: as the Jews dwell in the various States of Europe, and Christian merchants in China. In such cases, the domestic teaching may not agree with the morality of the nation among which the Family resides; but will rather be derived from the belief of the nation to which the Family belongs. Such a Family will commonly teach to its children obedience to the laws of the State of their abode; but it will instil such moral sentiments and opinions as are usual in the Nation of its origin. For such persons, the belief belonging to the scattered Nation, supersedes the doctrines locally prevalent in the State. In this case, the moral education of each person fits him, it may be, to be a peaceable resident in one nation; but it fits him to be a faithful member of a distant community.

563. But further: though each person's moral judgments are much influenced by the moral judgments of the community to which he belongs, and still more, by those of the family of which he is a child, they are not entirely derived from those sources. Each person has, also, Something Individual in his moral sentiments and opinions. A person may accept the Standard of morality which is established among his neighbours; but each person may for himself improve and elevate this Standard. A person may accept the Doctrines and the Belief which prevail among his neighbours, but he may also employ his own thoughts in determining what is the true doctrine, and what he must believe as being true. Indeed, in a certain degree, a man is bound, as a moral and rational being, to do this. He is bound, as a moral being, continually to elevate his Standard of Morality (366). If he acquiesce passively in a National Standard, his moral progress must be small. Again: he is bound, as a rational being, to accept, as Truth, only what he sees as Truth. It may be, that he believes what his nation believes, with regard to the foundations of morality; but this his belief is an act of his own Reason; and if it be not so, it is not belief. Now each man's own Reason presents to him the Truth under various aspects, depending upon his personal intellectual culture. The Truth, as he sees it, may not agree with what he has been taught by others. He obtains, by his own efforts, a more perfect view of the Truth, than the national formularies convey to him. He elevates his Standard of Truth above the National Standard; as he elevates his Standard of Morality above the National Standard. To do this, is Self-education; and this Education operates, in addition to the National Education, and Domestic Education, in forming a man's moral character.

564. The Self-education by which a man arrives at his own view of Virtue and Truth, must be, finally and specially, his own act; but the mental processes and habits by which he is led on, from step to step, in his progress towards such views, may be determined or aided by the influence of other persons, especially by such influence exerted in his youth. Masters and Teachers, of various kinds, may discipline and instruct the mind, so that it shall be more or less ready and apt to seek a knowledge of Virtue and Truth; and to recognize them, in proportion as they present themselves. And the teaching which thus unfolds the Faculties of the pupil, as well as that which communicates to him Opinions and Beliefs, is Education. This Education is highly important to our moral being. For it especially fits us for that perpetual progress which is our highest moral duty, and which includes all our other Duties (345).

565. A knowledge of Truth is requisite, as the

foundation of Morality. And although the aspect of the Truths which are the foundations of Morality may vary, according to the various intellectual culture which those who contemplate them have received, there is one general Truth which must always form a part of those foundations: namely, the Truth that Duty is the way to Happiness. But as we have already said (546), the identification of Happiness with Duty, on merely philosophical grounds, is a line of thought and reasoning, full of difficulty; and this difficulty is effectually removed only by Religious Education.

We are thus led to Religion, as the next step of our progress; and to that we now proceed.

END OF VOLUME THE FIRST.

www.ingramcontent.com/pod-product-compliance
Lightning Source LLC
LaVergne TN
LVHW020115110826
845151LV00001B/160
* 9 7 8 1 4 2 5 5 4 2 7 7 1 *